Peter Laurie was born in Reigate in 1937 and was educated at Lancing. After reading mathematics and law at Queen's College, Cambridge, he worked as a writer and photographer for *Vogue*, did f... ... ... Mail and the *Sunday ... ... Times Magazine* sho... ... to 1978 he contribute... ... *New Scientist*. He is n... ... *Computing*. Peter Lau...

Also by Peter Laurie

Teenage Revolution
Drugs, Medical, Psychological and Social Facts
Scotland Yard
Meet Your Friendly Social System

Peter Laurie

Beneath the City Streets

A Private Inquiry into Government Preparations
for National Emergency

A PANTHER BOOK

GRANADA
London Toronto Sydney New York

Revised and expanded edition published by
Granada Publishing Limited in 1979
Reprinted 1980 (twice)

ISBN 0 586 05055 8

First published in Great Britain by
Allen Lane, The Penguin Press 1970
Revised edition published by Penguin Books Ltd 1972
Copyright © Peter Laurie 1970, 1972, 1979

Granada Publishing Limited
Frogmore, St. Albans, Herts AL2 2NF
and
3 Upper James Street, London W1R 4BP
866 United Nations Plaza, New York, NY 10017, USA
117 York Street, Sydney, NSW 2000, Australia
100 Skyway Avenue, Rexdale, Ontario, M9W 3A6, Canada
PO Box 84165, Greenside, 2034 Johannesburg, South Africa
61 Beach Road, Auckland, New Zealand

Printed and bound in Great Britain by
Cox & Wyman Ltd, Reading
Filmset in Linotype Times

Granada ®
Granada Publishing ®

Acknowledgment

If this edition of *Beneath the City Streets*, which was first published nearly ten years ago, is any better than the other two, it must largely be due to the many people who have sent me information, help, advice and encouragement in the meantime. I had originally intended to publish a list of names by way of thanks, but in the light of the Secrets Trial of 1978 this might turn out to be an invidious distinction. You know who you are, and I have not forgotten: I am grateful none the less.

One name that must be recorded here is Duncan Campbell's. His determined resistance to the charge brought against him under Section 1 of the Official Secrets Act (see Appendix A) did me – by making it possible to republish this book – and the whole of British journalism, an inestimable service. I am proud to be able to thank him as a friend and a collaborator.

My thanks to Leonora Box who did the drawings – again.

P.L.

Contents

Introduction

This book is an attempt to understand the defences of the modern state against violent threats. It extends my earlier *Beneath the City Streets* and incorporates the work of many people who were stimulated by it to make their own researches into this interesting question. Although the viewpoint has changed a little, so that we now talk about defences against revolution as well as nuclear war, the basic structure and material remains much the same. I hope, however, that those who found the first *Beneath the City Streets* interesting will still find enough new here to make reading it worth their while.

The central argument is simple. There are two threats to a modern western state: external attack, almost certainly with nuclear weapons, and internal revolution. Any government must plan, somehow, to survive these dangers, and these plans, normally kept secret, or at least not openly avowed or publicized, should be of great interest to the conscious citizen, because they show him, as no other evidence could, what is at the reality of government. In the concrete of the bunkers, in the radio towers, the food stores, the dispersed centres of government, he can read the paranoia of power. This evidence is written on the face of England: if I quote extensively from, as it were, contemporary political archaeology here, it is only because it is under my hand; the same arguments, the same evidence can no doubt be drawn from any civilized country.

It might be argued that these things are kept secret, and rightly so, and that this book should not have been published. On the practical level, the answer to that is fourfold. First, no government can rely on secrecy alone for its strength. Some of these installations are decades old, some centuries; it may be as long again before they are called on for use. By that time one must assume that any possible enemy knows all about them. Second, if we are to have a revolution here, as some people suggest may be necessary, I am concerned, as one who might be unwillingly involved, either that it should be a good one, or that it should not be attempted at all. It seems that those who most advocate revolution have least idea of the formidable practical difficulties involved in bringing it to a happy conclusion. The British people have achieved their reputation for being politically stable partly because of the British government's (and by that one means the civil service's) great ability to detect and defuse revolutionary threats against it. Part of the reason for that ability is the complete range of preparations to protect itself from – not to put too fine a point on it – *us*, which are described here.

It might be objected that these preparations enable a government to put itself out of the reach of its people. It can take any action it likes under cover of them without fear of violent repercussions. In time, a more repressive government than any we have seen so far may take advantage of this armour, and that would be regrettable. But on the other hand it would be naïve, I think, to argue that this armour should be dismantled. In the conditions of the modern world, where nations can do instant violence to each other, it may well be the saving of us all that our government can resist the threat of attack in a tense showdown. If an enemy cannot destroy our government, it has hardly any reason to attack us.

Recently, a third good reason for publication emerged. The 'ABC' case, as it became known to the press, in which two journalists and an ex-soldier were charged with offences against the Official Secrets Act, rumbled through 1977 and most of 1978, coming to a trial in the autumn of that year. One of the original contentions of the Crown was that a journalist who – like myself – collects openly published information and from it deduces matters which the government thinks should be secret, thereby commits an offence against Section 1 of the Act. Happily, charges relating to this activity on the part of one of the defendants (Duncan Campbell) were dropped by the Crown halfway through the trial. But the fact that a prosecution could be brought at all shows that it is necessary to defend the right to observe, to think, to deduce. The best way to defend a right is to exercise it. And that is what this book does. (A brief account of the trial and the difficulties this book went through on account of it will be found in Appendix A.)

The ABC trial was stopped after ten days because it had emerged that three members of the jury had signed the Official Secrets Act and could therefore hardly be expected to be unbiased towards the question in issue. When it resumed on 3 October, the Crown offered no evidence against Campbell on the Section 1 charge, relating to the collection of information. The *Guardian* reported:[1]

> Mr John Leonard [the QC leading for the Crown] said he had taken the decision during the course of the first trial which was abruptly stopped after 10 days. 'When I opened the case originally, I told the jury that much of the information was no doubt culled from published sources.
>
> 'It was the Crown's contention, nevertheless, that Campbell had committed an offence because much of the information was added to and interpreted with his observations as a skilled scientist, and was built up so as to be likely to be of value to an enemy.'
>
> But in cross-examination, Mr Leonard said that Lord Hutchinson, Mr Campbell's counsel, had produced a great deal of published material that matched much of the information in Mr Campbell's possession.
>
> This included semi-official and official publications which were unknown to him. 'Information from such sources is obviously of greater value to a potential enemy than any journalistic writings, however distinguished they may be,' he said.

This sensible decision made it possible to go ahead and publish this book. However, the question posed at the end of the *New Scientist* article (see Appendix A) remained unanswered. After the collection charge against Campbell had been dropped, I again wrote to the Minister of Defence (see Appendix B), telling him that I proposed to publish, but that I was still willing to consider proposals to minimize the risk to security which my book might present. But – answer came there none.

Fourth, there is a practical reason. For two decades now, civil defence has been a joke in Britain. In one way it was right that it should be: as we shall see later on when we glance at nuclear strategy, there was no advantage to an attacker in starting a nuclear war, since he could not hope to destroy the other side's missile silos and submarines. And if there is no advantage in being the attacker, there is little advantage in having a war at all. Unfortunately this situation looks like changing. Great increases in the accuracies of nuclear missiles; the development of the terrain-following cruise missile which promises to be accurate enough to attack a silo with a high-explosive warhead alone; and the tremendous efforts being made by all parties to develop techniques for locating missile submarines at sea, mean that it may soon be possible to mount an attack that effectively cripples the other side's nuclear weapons.* As soon as this is possible the balance of war and peace rests on a razor, and a war could well start without either side really wanting it. In this situation the considerable protection which relatively simple civil defence can give might be very comforting. It is significant that very energetic civil defence programmes are under way in all the Warsaw Pact countries. In Europe only Switzerland and Sweden have persevered, but the completeness of their preparations is astounding. In Switzerland, for instance, every household is obliged to build and maintain a shelter. In public places there are shelters for thousands of people, stored for a stay of two months. There are 600 underground hospitals lavishly furnished and

---

* It is hoped that the deployment of beam weapons in space will make nuclear missiles obsolete. However, at the time this book went to press (Spring 1979), these devices had yet to prove their military utility, and were many years away from active use. And it may turn out that they are even more fearsome weapons of mass destruction than the H-bomb.

equipped. The Swiss think it even money that there will be a nuclear war in Europe before the end of the century, and they do not propose to come out of it the worst.[2]

America still spends $71 million a year on civil defence, while recently the Russians have increased their spending to $1000 million a year.[3]

If this book serves to reawaken some interest in this sensible kind of life insurance, then it may be worthwhile.

NOTES

1. The *Guardian*, 4 October 1978.
2. Peter Laurie, *Sunday Times Magazine*, 28 March 1976.
3. *Aviation Week and Space Technology*, 14 June 1976, p. 17.

1 *Civil defence: pre-nuclear history*

The story behind the impact of the H-bomb on the British government goes back at least to the beginning of the First World War. The protection of society against disruption caused by bombing is called civil defence. One perhaps thinks of it in terms of sand buckets, stirrup pumps and whitewashed windows. But these aspects, though important, are only fragments of the whole. Properly, civil defence should be concerned with everything that is necessary to preserve society against forcible dissolution. This may be due to enemy action, but it can also be caused by revolution, terrorist attacks, internal turmoil. A relevant Home Office Circular says, 'Aims of home defence: (a) to secure the UK against any internal threat . . .' Natural disasters also come within its purview – fire, flood, earthquake, oil spills, explosion of chemical plants or nuclear reactors. There is a growing worldwide movement among civil defenders to redefine their role in terms of all these catastrophes, using common procedures and standards so that international cooperation at an operational level can be swift and effective. But the fundamental function of civil defence, on which all its other functions, if any, must be built, is the preservation of government. This in turn reduces to the preservation of decision-makers, the means of getting information to them about the state of the country, and ways for them to transmit what they decide. Government can be menaced by other dangers than nuclear war, and the present British civil defence system has grown out of responses to different types of threats arising over the last two centuries.

Our present system began in recognizable form in 1914. It seemed likely that Germany would try to invade Britain and, as part of the defensive preparations, a committee was formed to consider what should be done about the civilian population. In forming its opinion it came to much the same conclusions as its predecessors had in planning to deal with Napoleon's threatened invasion of 1803–4 (planners then had looked back to the arrangements made to deal with the Spanish Armada of 1588). The problem was to secure the continuity of government in parts of the country cut off by invasion forces from London, or wherever the government had gone. The solution was to give lords-lieutenant and mayors emergency powers, allowing them to make most decisions that would otherwise be made centrally.

In the event, there was no German invasion. But another form of enemy action showed the need for more stringent civilian control than the local organs of government were capable of. In June 1915 a single Zeppelin raided Hull, dropped bombs that killed 24 people, injured 40 and destroyed as many shops and homes. This was a new moment in the British people's experience of war. For the first time the civilian was in the front line, exposed to the enemy's fire. He could no longer shelter behind the navy or the expeditionary army. The extraordinary moment pro-voked an extraordinary reaction. The shock to the populace was so severe that – notwithstanding British sang-froid – rioting broke out. Shops with suspected German connec-tions were sacked and order had to be restored by troops. In the summer of 1917 there were two daylight raids on London by Gotha bombers which caused 832 casualties (216 deaths) at the rate of 121 casualties per ton. These were followed by a series of night raids on the Midlands which, says the official history of civil defence, 'caused a degree of public nervous-ness out of all proportion to the total material damage inflicted'.[1]

All told, the Germans dropped 300 tons of bombs on Britain during the First World War. They killed 1413 people, and injured 3407, at an average rate of 11·4 casualties per ton.

The British government were reluctantly impressed with aerial bombardment as a weapon against civilians. It had caused the British an enormous amount of bother, panic and

wasted war production through sheltering, and in general
had a most demoralizing effect on the population.

Another facet of the problems of large populations in the
twentieth century was revealed in 1917 when Russia collapsed into the arms of – as it seemed from Whitehall – the
rabble. It is difficult now to realize how imminent the British
revolution seemed in the troubled years at the end of and
immediately after the First World War. Thomas Jones,
secretary to successive prime ministers from 1916 to 1930,
reports a Cabinet conference held in February 1920, on the
pressing question of industrial unrest:[2]

LLOYD GEORGE (*PM*): You won't get sabotage at the beginning of the strike.

ROBERTS (*Food Controller*): You will have to take sabotage
at the beginning of the strike into account. There are large
groups preparing for Soviet government.

GEDDES (*Minister of Transport*): You have got to reckon on
the electric power stations being put out of order.

LLOYD GEORGE: 10 000 troops would be of little use. How
long will it take the well-disposed to range themselves on
the side of law?

LONG: The peaceable manpower of this country is without
arms. I have not a pistol less than 200 years old. A Bill is
needed for licensing persons to bear arms. This has been
useful in Ireland because the authorities know who were
possessed of arms.

SHORTT (*Home Secretary*): The Home Office had a Bill
ready, but in the past there have always been objections.

BONAR LAW: All weapons ought to be available for distribution to friends of the government.

We can now see that the revolution was more imaginary
than latent. But it was true the war was both preceded and
followed by periods of extreme unrest. In 1911, for instance,
well within living memory, troops had had to open fire on
mobs at Liverpool and Llanelli; in each place they killed two
people. Even before the end of the war the government was
faced with a series of strikes, of which the first, and perhaps
the most alarming, was that of the Metropolitan Police in

August 1918. Police wages had fallen so low that many officers' families were literally destitute. Lloyd George bought off the strikers with a massive rise and afterwards said that the country had never been so close to Bolshevism as on that day.[3] In 1919 a smaller proportion of the police struck again, this time for the right to have a union. In Liverpool the citizens ran hog-wild: troops and warships had to be sent in. Order was restored by volleys over the heads of the crowd and bayonet charges.[4] People began to talk about a general strike, then the ultimate weapon of Bolshevism, which would bring the government to its knees – and the government began to make preparations against it.

Foreseeing that the major problem would be the distribution of food, wide emergency powers were given to the Food Controller – an official left over from wartime emergency planning – who had sixteen district commissioners under him. He was soon in business. A rail strike was declared on 26 September 1919.[5] Motor transport was requisitioned by the Food Controller and his organization and volunteer 'Citizen Guards' raised. The strike ended on 6 October, and the Controller scheme lapsed.

Proposed British intervention in the Russian Civil War of 1920 elicited hostile reactions from the TUC, and in the autumn the miners went on strike. An attempt was made to bring the supply and general workers out too, and in reaction the government rushed an emergency powers Bill through Parliament. This Emergency Powers Act 1920 still remains in force. It provides that the government may declare a state of emergency by proclamation if action has been taken or threatened 'which is calculated to deprive the community, or any substantial portion of it, of the essentials of life by interfering with the supply and distribution of food, water, fuel or light, or with the means of locomotion'. If Parliament is not sitting it has to be summoned within five days, and any regulations made under the emergency powers must be approved by both Houses within seven days or they lapse. Such regulations may confer powers on the government to preserve the peace and to secure the necessities of life, but they must stop short of military or industrial conscription, and may not make it an offence to take part in a strike. Courts of summary jurisdiction may be set up, but Habeas Corpus may not be suspended, and no right can be created under the Act to imprison or fine without trial.

The miners struck again in April 1921 and the government duly proclaimed a state of emergency to contain a threatened general strike. The emergency organization was revived, but after a fortnight the threat of a general strike faded away. Lloyd George never took the revolution seriously, but Baldwin's government of 1923 overhauled the emergency plans, which took on the shape that they still retain. The functions of the organization were to be broadened from supply and transport to embrace the whole authority of government. Circular 636 of the Ministry of Health informed local government about the new divisional organization for the first time in November 1925. This established the principle that: 'Commissioners were empowered, if necessary, to give decisions on behalf of the Government', and named as their headquarters, Newcastle, Leeds, Nottingham, Cambridge, London, Reading, Bristol, Cardiff, Birmingham and Liverpool. In Scotland the organization was slightly different, as it is today. Headquarters were at Edinburgh, Dundee, Aberdeen, Inverness and Glasgow.

Towards the end of April 1926 it became apparent that a general strike was inevitable. On 30 April the government proclaimed a state of emergency and issued regulations under the Emergency Powers Act. Its plans were as efficient as those of the strikers were confused. Hyde Park became, almost overnight, an enormous hutted headquarters camp, with perimeter fencing, its own heating and electricity plant, a telephone exchange and a big lorry park.[6]

A private army – the Organization for the Maintenance of Supplies – was raised by the government, and told before the strike that it might have to hit hard, and even hit to kill.[7] This notice was published in the *British Gazette*:[8]

All ranks of the Armed Forces of the Crown are hereby notified that any action which they may find it necessary to take in an honest endeavour to aid the Civil Power will receive the . . . full support of HMG.

But the strikers took it easy, the expected revolution failed to catch alight, and so the civil commissioners did not have to use their powers in earnest. A slight demonstration of how roughly the government was prepared to play was given in the way it broke the strike at the London docks. Squads of Cambridge undergraduates were taken into London by lorry and brought down river in barges under tarpaulins, so that they could unload flour from ships in the docks. This was moved out under the machine-guns of the Guards. The *New York World* reported:[9]

> The sullen mass of strikers who gathered after dawn were awed by the military and permitted most of the moving on to be done by the mounted police, unarmed as always, but backed this time by enough artillery to kill every living thing in every street in the neighbourhood of the mills.

O'Brien, summing up the strike in his history of civil defence:[10]

> The political issues of this strike are of less importance . . . than the machinery set up and the relationships established between the Government and the public under such unusual conditions. As one example of the latter factor, it will be recalled that on the second day of the strike the only newspapers procurable were the news sheets of the Government and the Trade Unions . . . The Government, in addition, made effective use of a broadcasting system which was just emerging from its experimental stage into the state of adolescence represented by some two million receiving licences. The system was used to inform the public of the daily course of events, and as a vehicle for the broadcast of instant messages by the Prime Minister, Mr Baldwin, in person.

From one point of view the opposition between the TUC and the government resolved itself into a conflict of technologies. The strikers controlled coal and steam, which meant they could influence the public by depriving them of heat, transport, food, newspapers. The government controlled internal combustion engines, which meant that they could bring food by road, and broadcasting so that they could speak directly to the people. It was significant that one of the first official acts was to send a dozen Scotland Yard detectives armed with pistols to guard the then solitary BBC transmitter at Daventry.[11]

All this time, while civil commotion exercised the government, the potential effects of bombing achieved in 1915 and 1917 were being multiplied by the rapidly increasing size of aircraft and European air forces. In 1923 Trenchard told a sub-committee of the Committee of Imperial Defence: 'In a democratic country like ours, power rests ultimately with the people and war cannot be continued unless the bulk of the people support it. If the people are subjected to sufficient bombing they will compel the Government to sue for peace.'[12] That is, they will be forced to revolt. By 1924 the Air Staff predicted, they thought conservatively, that an air war would produce the following casualties in London:

Table 1: Air Staff casualty predictions (1924)

	Killed	Wounded	Total
First 24 hours	1700	3300	5000
Second 24 hours	1275	2475	3750
Each subsequent 24 hours	850	1650	2500

'These calculations presented the ARP [Air Raid Precautions] Committee with a formidable problem. To plan adequate precautions against attacks on this scale seemed quite impossible.'[13] Quite apart from the killed and injured, it seemed likely that total chaos and panic in the community would result from enemy action on this scale. The experts foretold a mass outbreak of hysterical neurosis among the civilian population under the strain of air raids. 'People would regress to an earlier level of needs and desires. They would behave like frightened and unsatisfied children, and they would demand, with the all-or-nothing vehemence of infants, the security, food and warmth which the mother used to give in the past.'[14] It was estimated that the Metropolis represented about a third of the belligerent strength of the nation – a force that must not be allowed to be disrupted. So in 1933 an Air Raids Commandant (Designate) was appointed. O'Brien writes: 'This addition to the machinery had a significance apart from its practical contribution over the next two years. He demonstrated the planners' continued belief that their problem was in a large measure military, or at least quasi-military. London would become a battlefield, and special forms of discipline and control would be essential.'[15]

At one stage it was proposed to augment the Metropolitan Police by an extra 120 000 men who would form a physical cordon[16] round London to drive civilians, fleeing from the raids, back to their duties. One is used to generals preparing to fight the last war but one, and here one finds an attitude of mind among civil servants also that would have been more appropriate to a commander sending his khaki sheep into Passchendaele. In some respects developments in Germany were anticipated: a Ministry of Food memorandum of the same period proposed herding these refugees into 'concentration camps',[17] handing them iron rations for two days and then forcibly returning them to their homes in the capital.

An Army Council directive to Commanders-in-Chief said, 'The public should be aware that there are available formed and disciplined bodies of troops ready to assist in minimizing the effect of air raids.'[18]

The 'effect' was of course panic and flight, the 'minimising' was to be done with the bayonet.

Happily the officer[19] who became Air Raids Commandant (Designate) realized that though the problems might be military, the solutions must be civilian. The problem was basically one of morale. He minuted, '. . . in organizing the whole civilian population to protect themselves they must be organized on a civilian basis in a civilian organization . . . The ARP service must create and maintain its own honourable status and prestige and not lean upon some other service.'[20]

The scheme of control that emerged to deal with air raids centred again round the regional commissioner, although he had originally been appointed to deal with revolution. Essentially the idea was to anticipate the chaos of war by secretly re-dividing the state into a dozen little ones. The scheme anticipated a collapse of central government, either by the destruction of London, national panic and hysteria, or by invasion and the physical separation of most of Britain from the capital.

Regional commissioners were created who would, in the ordinary emergency, merely act as the chairmen of a committee of civil servants entrusted with the powers of their ministries and sent into the regions. In dire emergency the commissioners would be able to assume, in person, all the powers of the state. In fact no commissioner ever assumed executive authority, because things never got nearly as bad as government had expected. Throughout the war the commissioners, who were people like Admiral Sir E. Evans, Sir Ernest Gowers (of *Plain Words*), Lord Harlech, Lord Portal and lesser figures, made themselves useful by settling quarrels among officialdom in the provinces, liaising between the forces and local authorities – borrowing soldiers to get the crops in – persuading the police and the fire service to work sensibly together, and debunking pessimistic astrologers. The one operational episode in their career was during the bombing of Southampton. The attack was so severe that people were 'trekking' out of the city every evening to sleep in the fields. In fact this was an eminently sensible thing to do, and analysis afterwards showed that no war production was lost,[21] but to officialdom at the time it seemed that this was the beginning of the predicted mass collapse of morale. So the commissioner set up an office in the centre of the city, co-ordinating rescue and welfare services until things got better.

The headquarters of the regional commissioners were London, Tunbridge Wells, Bristol, Cardiff, Reading, Birmingham, Cambridge, Nottingham, Manchester, Leeds, Newcastle, Edinburgh – much as they had been in 1926.

But we are less concerned with what actually happened

than with what was expected, because on this was built what
became the civil-defence organization after the war. As aircraft continued to gain in speed and size during the pre-war
years, so the expected scale of attack rose alarmingly. By
1938 the Air Staff expected that Germany could deliver 600
tons of bombs a day in spite of active defences. Multiplying
this by the casualties per bomb of the First World War, they
expected 70 000 casualties a week.

It is fair to say that by the outbreak of the Second World
War, any intelligent person in touch with the trend of official
expectations was anticipating a quarter of a million
casualties in London in the first three weeks, 3 to 4 million
psychiatric casualties, 3 million refugees and half the
buildings in the capital destroyed. So, apart from the time
scale, people were thinking *then* of devastation essentially
nuclear in character. One of the first overt air-raid preparations made by central government was the distribution of a
million burial forms to local authorities by the Ministry of
Health in 1939.[22] At Scotland Yard, for instance, it was
being debated whether the bodies of dead Londoners should
be dumped wholesale into the gravel pits to the west of what
is now London Airport, or whether it would be better to
throw them into the Thames at high water, to be taken by the
tide.

Of course, as it turned out, the reports of our deaths were
grossly exaggerated. Far from reproducing the best results
of the First World War, at 121 casualties per ton, 71 270 tons
of German bombs, rockets and shells (on Dover) during the
whole of the Second World War killed 60 595 and seriously
injured 86 182: a rate of just over 2 casualties per ton.[23] In
effect, enemy action added a year's natural deaths to those
that occurred anyway during the six years of war. The
expected panic, the catastrophic loss of morale, did not
happen. If anything, rates of incidence of mental illness and
crime dropped during the war years. A more reliable indi-
cator of morale was the way people continued to turn up for
work – they might be shaken or miserable but, it was argued,
there could be little fundamentally wrong with them. It was
found that the only thing that made people stay away was

damaged houses, and even that had surprisingly little effect: on the average, complete destruction of someone's home caused six days' absence from work.

The very much reduced rate of attack presented the ARP and particularly the rescue service with a problem it could almost always deal with. It became a matter of honour to rescue, as a veteran of the Blitz told me, 'every last finger joint from the rubble'. In the three quietish years after the hectic months of the Blitz there was time to elaborate procedures. By the end of the war the ARP service had a fine and not altogether unjustifiable opinion of itself. It was disbanded in 1946, and rapidly reformed in 1948 as the Civil Defence Corps when the future of the wartime alliances became apparent, and it became obvious that the West would have no long monopoly of atomic and nuclear weapons. These promised that, if war came again, civilians would be exposed to destruction on a considerably more vigorous scale than anything that had been achieved during the last war.

So, as far as fears and anticipations go, the tools of modern intercontinental war date from the early years of the Second World War. The idea of the atom bomb first appeared in newspaper stories* in 1939; it was first properly described by the refugee scientists, Frisch and Peierls at Birmingham University in the spring of 1940.[24] The ballistic missile, as everyone knows, was under development by von Braun from the mid 1930s, and brought to a practical device in the V2 of 1944. But distorted rumours of this weapon had been filtering into British Intelligence from the beginning of 1943. It seemed then that the rocket might be driven by cordite, weigh 80 tons, with a warhead of as much as ten tons.[25] An unexplained German weapon, code-named *Big Ben*, fleetingly appears in the Cabinet papers: this may be it. In any case, only the Army war-room under Montagu House (probably on the site of the new MoD building in Whitehall) was strong enough to withstand it. Even if this warhead were only high explosive the effect would be

* *The Times*, 1 February 1939; *Deutsche Allgemeine Zeitung*, 15 August 1939, cited by David Irving, The Virus House, London, 1967.

frightful, but if it carried an atomic bomb – and there was no positive assurance that the Germans had not developed one – the effect would be to realize the worst anticipations of 1938–9. So, for civil defence, the nuclear age began a good many years earlier than for the rest of us.

NOTES

1. T. H. O'Brien, *Civil Defence* (*History of the Second World War, United Kingdom Civil Series*), London, 1955, p. 11.

2. Thomas Jones, *Whitehall Diary*, vol. 1, Oxford, 1969, p. 100.

3. Gerald W. Reynolds and Anthony Judge, *The Night the Police Went on Strike*, London, 1968, p. 5.

4. *The Times*, 3 and 4 August 1919.

5. For the general outlines of government civil-defence planning between the wars, I have leant heavily on Nicholas Walter's pamphlet, *The RSGs, 1919–63*, published by Solidarity, 1963.

6. Julian Symons, *The General Strike*, London, 1957.

7. Max Nicholson, *The System*, London, 1967, p. 225.

8. *The British Gazette*, 8 May 1925.

9. Cited by Symons.

10. O'Brien, pp. 29, 30.

11. Asa Briggs, *History of Broadcasting in the United Kingdom*, vol. 1: *The Birth of Broadcasting*, Oxford, 1961, p. 367.

12. Andrew Boyle, *Trenchard*, London, 1962, p. 468.

13. O'Brien, p. 16.

14. R. M. Titmuss, *Problems of Social Policy* (*History of the Second World War, United Kingdom Civil Series*), London, 1950, p. 338. (A book which, had the Treasury had its way, would never have been published.)

15. O'Brien, p. 43.

16. Titmuss, p. 18n.

17. R. J. Hammond, *Food II* (*History of the Second World War, United Kingdom Civil Series*), London, 1956, p. 285.

18. Titmuss, p. 19.

19. Major General H. L. Pritchard, RE.

20. Cited by O'Brien, p. 45.

21. Titmuss, p. 341.

22. Titmuss, p. 21.

23. O'Brien, pp. 678, 680.

24. Margaret Gowing, *Britain and Atomic Energy 1939–1945*, London, 1964, Appendix 1.

25. David Irving, *The Mare's Nest*, London, 1964.

2 What the H-bomb does to people, houses and other things

The overriding threat to modern government is the H-bomb. If you can protect yourself against that, then you are in a fair way to being invulnerable to many other threats as well. So we will begin our examination of government's carapace by looking at what the bomb does when it goes off.

Explosion

When, in the jargon American phrase, a 1-megaton (MT)* nuclear weapon is initiated, it turns itself within two-thousandths of a second into a small, hot ball of vapour.[1] It immediately begins to expand, heating the air around it by compression. This rise in temperature makes the air transparent to the ultraviolet radiation which is produced copiously by the nuclear reaction, carries most of the bomb's energy, and can therefore escape. Expansion also produces a spherical acoustic shock-front in the undisturbed air around the fireball. After another two-thousandths of a second the fireball expansion is slower than the progress of the shock-front. Although it is so violent that it heats the air to incandescence, it nevertheless masks the main fireball, whose apparent temperature is then some 2000°C, although inside it may be 300 000°C. Once the shock-front has passed

* The yield of H-bombs likely to be used in war ranges from about 0·3 MT to 10 MT. Throughout this chapter we use 1 MT as an example.

The important parameter for predicting blast damage is the peak overpressure P, and the scaling law for a weapon of yield W at range R is:

$$P = k\frac{W^{\frac{1}{3}}}{R}$$

The cube root implies that in terms of damage per pound weight, large weapons are much less effective than small ones.

over the observer, the fireball, now unmasked, radiates strongly again. Its apparent temperature rises again to 8000°C, and in the next ten seconds a third of the bomb's total energy is radiated as heat, light, ultraviolet and X-rays.

The fireball continues to swell until it reaches a diameter of about a mile. At the edge, the blast overpressure (maximum air pressure caused by the blast wave) is about 60 pounds to the square inch (p.s.i.) (4·2 kg/sq cm). The hot gases have rushed so violently away from the centre of the fireball that they have left almost a vacuum behind. The average density of the fireball has fallen below that of the surrounding air, so the ball begins to float upwards. As it does so, the drag of the surrounding air on its sides makes it spin inwards, and within five seconds it is a smoke ring. It leaves a trail as it rises, and has become the well-known nuclear mushroom cloud. The spinning ring of the doughnut contains the bomb debris and whatever radioactive isotopes have been formed from the fission of the uranium trigger.

The blast wave, which causes most of the damage done by the bomb, and carries half the energy released, continues to expand in two spheres: around the point of initiation, and its reflection in the ground or sea. At 11 seconds the thermal radiation is finished, the blast wave is 3·2 miles (5·1 km) from ground zero where it produces an overpressure of 6 p.s.i. (0·42 kg/sq cm) and a wind speed of 180 m.p.h. (290 k.p.h.). By 37 seconds the blast front is 9½ miles (15·2 km) away, where the overpressure is 1 p.s.i. (0·07 kg/sq cm), the wind speed 40 m.p.h. (64 k.p.h.). The cloud is 7 miles (11·2 km) high and the bomb's destructive effects are finished. The passage of the positive pressure wave is followed by a negative pressure and gentler winds towards the point of initiation as the atmosphere tries to fill up the hole left by the bomb's expansion.

Within 10 minutes the bottom of the cloud is at a height of 15 miles (24 km) but, apart from the rapidly thinning vapour, there is no other atmospheric evidence to show that a nuclear weapon has exploded.

The total cost for a weapon is not high: in 1966 the United States Atomic Energy Commission quoted $570 000 for supplying and detonating a 1-MT device for approved commercial purposes.[2] In fact a megaton weapon is the cheapest source of power known. Its energy costs about 4 per cent of the cost of generating the same energy as electricity and 0·03 per cent as TNT.

Ground-burst
If the point of initiation is less than a tenth of the final fireball diameter from the ground, the explosion uses much of its energy in scouring out a crater. In dry earth a 1-MT burst makes a hole 1300 feet (400 m) across and 140 feet (43 m) deep. A ground-burst gives reduced blast: the same over-pressures are reached at about 75 per cent of the range for air-burst weapons. An earthquake effect is propagated through the ground but its effect is negligible within three crater radii – in this case ¾ mile (1·2 km).

Radiation
As the weapon explodes, radiation of all sorts is emitted from the fireball, including a good deal of harmful gamma rays. But since for the sort of large weapon relevant to attacks against cities, blast and instantaneous gamma effects are equally lethal at the same distances, this 'prompt' radiation poses no extra problems. And as the cloud rises, and newly formed isotopes with short half-lives[3] decay, so prompt radiation at ground level falls to negligible proportions. But also, as the cloud rises, so it cools, and the stable isotopes that are formed after complicated chains of fission from uranium-235 begin to condense out. If the weapon is air-burst there will be no solid nuclei present for these vapours to condense on. The isotopes therefore form spheres of ten microns or less in diameter – about the size of large bacteria. They are strongly radioactive, but too small to fall quickly to earth. Rain may bring them down, causing some local fall-out, but otherwise they will drift in the upper atmosphere for months, contributing to worldwide fall-out.

If the bomb is ground-burst, then the scoured-out lumps of soil offer nuclei for condensation of the isotopes, and most of the radioactive produce will fall back to earth within twenty-four hours. However, the presence of dangerous isotopes in this fall-out depends on the construction of the device. A 'normal' H-bomb consists of a uranium-235 atom bomb as a trigger, surrounded by hydrogen, inside a jacket of uranium-235. When the atom bomb explodes, the very high temperature it generates makes hydrogen atoms fuse together into helium. Large numbers of neutrons are produced; they are used to further the explosion by causing fission in the outer uranium jacket. This outer explosion presumably helps to contain the hydrogen–helium reaction. This sort of bomb is called a fission–fusion–fission bomb. While some types yield 50 per cent of their energy in fission products which can cause fall-out, it is possible to reduce this. President Eisenhower claimed in 1957 that America had a bomb which was '90 per cent clean', i.e., only 10 per cent of its energy ended in fission products, and the Russians exploded a 60-MT device in 1961 which dispensed with the outer coat of uranium, and gave only 2 per cent fission products. It is also apparently possible to make bombs whose fission chains end largely in harmless radio-isotopes. The possibility is also in sight of initiating fusion reactions, and therefore hydrogen explosions, by lasers.[4] The only radioactive residue from this sort of device would be a heavy isotope of hydrogen, which is weakly radioactive, has a half-life of twelve years and is soon absorbed in the oceans.[5]

So, although fall-out is generally thought to be an inevitable accompaniment to nuclear bombardment, it can only occur if the bomb is designed to be 'dirty', and if it is exploded a short distance from the ground. It is equally possible to go the other way, to produce a weapon that is either extremely dirty or produces large amounts of prompt radiation. The first possibility is often ascribed to states which possess nuclear power plants but not the equipment or know-how to make proper atom bombs. It would be simple to irradiate various materials in a reactor and then to disperse them as radioactive dust from some sort of high-explosive bomb. Given the right weather conditions and a compact target, one could make oneself extremely unpleasant at little cost in this manner.

The second possibility was realized by the United States in 1977 in the neutron bomb. The idea is to produce such high dose rates that soldiers in the open, and even crews protected by the armour of tanks, will be instantly incapacitated over large areas, without much damage being done to vehicles and buildings. An example quoted in the press* is the detonation of a 1-kT enhanced radiation weapon 500 m above the target. The circle of blast destruction would reach to 500 m from ground zero; people within the 1-km (0·625 miles) circle would be instantly incapacitated; people within a 2-km (1·25 miles) circle would suffer severe radiation sickness and death within a month. Assuming uniform spreads of people and objects in the target area, the neutron bomb damages one quarter of the property; but kills and injures 120 times as many people as a conventional nuclear weapon. It is an admirably capitalist device. The neutron bomb is said to be necessary to counter Russia's overwhelming superiority in armour on the central European front.

Damage

Although the explosion of an ordinary nuclear device involves many complicated processes, the end results in terms of damage are fairly predictable and easy to measure. There are four main effects: blast, wind drag, thermal radiation, fall-out. For practical purposes blast follows a simple scale law: the distance at which a particular overpressure is experienced is proportional to the cube root of the yield of the bomb. By using a simple calculator (see Figure 1) one can instantly work out overpressures at all distances for all sizes of bomb.

Solid objects, like bunkers or steam locomotives, that have no openings and cannot be blown over, are damaged mainly by static overpressure. For objects such as houses, crushing is not the only effect: as the pressure wave passes, the windows blow in and the house fills up with high-pressure air. When the blast wave has passed over and has been

* Frank Barnaby, *New Scientist*, 19 January 1978, p. 151.

succeeded by the low-pressure wave, the pressure difference between the inside and the outside may be several pounds per square inch (see Figure 1). This is a predicament houses are particularly unsuited to withstand. They have some resistance to pressure inwards because they have to stand up to wind, but they have no strength at all to resist expansion. As a result they tend to explode.

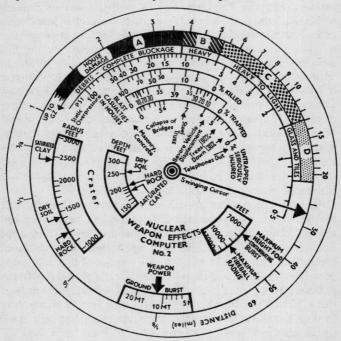

Fig. 1 Civil-defence officials are issued with weapons-effect calculators like this. Once the size of the weapon is set – here for 12-MT ground-burst, or 5-MT air-burst – a great deal of information about the damage it causes at different ranges can be read off. (WITH ACKNOWLEDGMENT TO BRL LTD).

Structures with some crushing resistance but large surface are more vulnerable to wind drag. This is dependent on distance, but rather more so on weapon size, and increases rapidly in importance with weapons in the megaton range. Typical objects which are damaged more by wind than blast are: aircraft, cars, trees and radio-transmitting towers. Reinforced concrete factory chimneys are resistant to nuclear blast because they are almost impossible to crush and are designed to resist high winds. Bridges also are strong: the pressure wave bearing down on the top surface is balanced by a reflected wave from the water or ground beneath. These two kinds of structure were almost the only ones that survived intact at Hiroshima and Nagasaki.

Injuries to people

Human beings, since they are mainly soft and incompressible, are fairly blast-resistant. With high explosives, whose pressure wave lasts only a fraction of a second, an overpressure of 200 p.s.i. (14 kg/sq cm) is needed to cause death. But megaton weapons produce a wave that lasts several seconds and appears to be a good deal more lethal. No definite figures are available, but probably 50 p.s.i. (3·5 kg/sq cm)[6] is the mid-lethal overpressure, i.e., one that would kill half the people exposed to it.

But since this overpressure is only attained just outside the fireball, or farther away only if caused by freak reflection effects, the question is rather academic. A far more serious blast hazard is that posed by flying fragments, mainly of glass. Three-quarters of London's casualties in the Blitz were from this cause (blast is blast, and flying glass is flying glass whatever sets it in motion – a 500-pound bomb next door, or a 1-MT bomb in the next county) and it is expected that this will be a very real danger out to about 3 p.s.i. (0·21 kg/sq cm), i.e., 4¾ miles (7·6 km) from a 1-MT explosion.

A person standing up in the open would be blown over by the blast wind out to 2·3 p.s.i. (0·6 kg/sq cm), i.e., 7½ miles (12 km). If he lay flat on the ground at right angles to the direction of the blast, he would be moved bodily as far out as 5·5 p.s.i. (0·39 kg/sq cm), i.e., 3¼ miles (5·2 km). But since most people will, if the early-warning service works, be indoors if not in shelter, the effects on people in the open are not likely to be significant in arriving at an overall picture of bomb casualties.

In common with other death-dealing agencies nuclear weapons have very much greater effects on the very young and the very old than on those in the prime of life. So, at Hiroshima, a 30-year-old man closer than 3200 feet (970 m) to ground zero had a third the chance of being killed of someone in the same position aged 0 or 60. One might expect this effect to make a drastic change in the proportions of the ages of the survivors of a nuclear attack, but, as with all other weapon effects, the number of people who are not exposed so outweighs those who are, that, even after the heaviest conceivable attack, the national impact is likely to be negligible.[7]

Injuries to houses

As we have noticed, houses are peculiarly susceptible to blast damage. Most British city houses are terraced or semi-detached and consist essentially of parallel, massive brick walls running from front to back, with brick screens in front and behind which are pierced for doors and windows. These front and back walls also support the joists for floors and roofs. As the blast overpressure is increased, these elements are damaged in the reverse order. First, between 0·75 and 1·5 p.s.i. (0·05 and 0·1 kg/sq cm), i.e., 12½ and 7½ miles (20 and 12 km), glass is blown out of the windows and tiles off the roofs. These houses can be made habitable again with resources that are likely to be available after an attack. Then, between 1·5 and 3 p.s.i. (0·1 and 0·2 kg/sq cm), i.e., 7½ and 4¾ miles (12 and 7·6 km), window frames and doors are blown in, and roofs are bared of tiles. From 3 to 6 p.s.i. (0·2 to 0·4 kg/sq cm), i.e., 4¾ to 3 miles (7·6 to 4·8 km), ceiling plaster comes down, roof timbers are completely stripped, and front and back walls are either demolished or extensively cracked. From 6 to 11 p.s.i. (0·4 to 0·8 kg/sq cm), the front and back walls are demolished. The floors and roof, having no support, necessarily fall, leaving the side walls more or less intact. From 11 p.s.i. (0·8 kg/sq cm), i.e., 2·2 miles (3·5 km) in, these too are demolished, leaving a low heap of rubble and timber.[8]

Houses as shelters
The chances of survival of people in such relatively fragile structures would seem to be small, but Second World War experience shows that they are better than one thinks. The main danger to people inside houses is collapse; but although the weapon that demolishes a house may vary enormously in size and range, the weight of a house remains the same, and in most cases the staircase is strong enough to support the debris that will fall on it. So people who shelter under the stairs – idiotic as this may sound for a precaution against nuclear weapons – will also be protected against heat flash and flying glass and have a good chance of surviving the almost complete destruction of their homes. Even at the 11 p.s.i. (0·8 kg/sq cm) line there should be no more than 11 per cent of people actually killed. During the Blitz many people were dug out of houses in the state shown in Figure 2(a). In Düsseldorf in 1943, 30 per cent of the houses were destroyed, but only 0·01 per cent of people were killed or injured. Of course digging out is unlikely after a nuclear strike, but the possibilities for survival are there.

The risks for people sheltering in houses from a 1-MT air-burst are summarized in Figure 3, which shows the probabilities of being killed, trapped and injured at different distances, together with a curve that shows the total risk of being incapacitated. It is not easy to translate these risks into the numbers of people who would be incapacitated in any particular attack. We may have fair confidence in our knowledge of bombs' effects, but we have little definite idea where they will explode. Even if we knew the enemy's aiming points, we do not know in a manageable form where all the houses are in relation to them, and even if we did, we wouldn't know with certainty where all the people would be. They might be in bed, evacuated to the country, standing in the street gazing at the sky, hiding under the stairs. Each situation would make an enormous difference to the casualty roll.

Fig. 2a The appearance houses would have at the 11-p.s.i. (0·77 kg/sq cm) ring (2·25 miles, 3·6 km, from a 1-MT air-burst). These are classified as being in damage category A – irreparable.

Fig. 2b Houses at the 6-p.s.i. (0·42 kg/sq cm) line (3·1 miles, 5 km). B damage.

Fig. 2c The outer limit of C damage – so severe that repairs are not possible under war conditions. This is the 1·5-p.s.i. (0·7 kg/sq cm) line, at 7·5 miles, 12 km.

Fig. 2d The outer limit of D damage at 0·75 p.s.i. (0·05 kg/sq cm) (12·5 miles, 20 km). From here into the beginning of C damage, houses would be repairable.

These photographs were taken during the Second World War in British cities. They are reproduced from Home Office Civil Defence Data Sheet 4, TARGET RESPONSE TO AIR BLAST *(HMSO), with the kind permission of the Controller of Her Majesty's Stationery Office.* CROWN COPYRIGHT.

Still, in order to clarify our ideas, we imagine a circular, uniform city of ordinary British brick houses with ground zero at the centre. The population density is the UK big city average of 12 000 per square mile (4600 per sq km) – see Table 3, p. 46. Integrating the total casualty curve in Figure 3 over circles of increasing radius, we find that 95 per cent of the people within 1½ miles (2·4 km) of ground zero of a 1-MT explosion are killed, trapped or seriously injured, but less than 50 per cent of those within 4 miles (6·4 km) are so affected. By 6·8 miles (11 km) the bomb has done its worst and kills no more. It is perhaps surprising that the total casualty figure for this imaginary city (rather larger than Birmingham, which would fit into a circle 5 miles in radius, but much smaller than London, which would fill a circle of 14 miles radius) is only 17 per cent, or 310 000 people. The other 83 per cent, or 1½ million, will be shaken but on their feet.

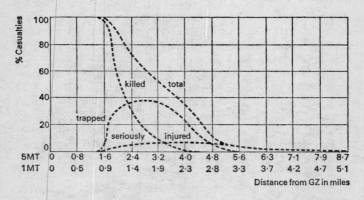

Fig. 3　These curves (adapted from Home Office material) show the chances of people sheltering in houses being killed, trapped and injured, and also the total chance of being disabled, at various ranges from 1 to 5-MT air-bursts.

Damage to other targets

Information of weapons' effects on other interesting targets is less neatly graded. *Effects of Nuclear Weapons* gives tables from which one can abstract distance from ground zero for four classes of damage, which correspond to the four photographs in Figure 2. Since it is interesting to consider the prospects for national survival after a nuclear attack, we can forget about all damage categories except D (see Figure 2), which means that objects can be made usable with little or no repair. Again, simply to clear the mind, we can calculate the number of survivors of 1- and 5-MT air-bursts over the centre of an idealized London, 15 miles in radius.[9] If we assume that the objects we are considering are scattered randomly across the city, then, for instance, 75 per cent of brick houses and 97·2 per cent of railway locomotives survive the 1-MT burst.

These survival figures are surprisingly high, and may bear little relationship to intuitive ideas of H-bomb damage when so many people seem eager to take total destruction for granted. If this is so, it is due to the normal presentation of bomb effects in terms of ranges which mean little by themselves, instead of in areas. One's overall appreciation of the harm done is dominated by the extreme damage near ground zero, and one forgets that this represents a very small part of a city.

We can think of these results either as showing the proportions of survivors, or as showing the chance of survival that any object would have if it were placed at random in the city. Thus a person has 96·5 per cent chance of surviving a 1-MT burst, a bridge 95·3 per cent. Broadly speaking, when one is thinking of an accumulation of resources and people[10] on the scale of a city like London, the damage inflicted by a 1-MT bomb is negligible and that by a 5-MT slight on everything except housing – which, as I have stressed before, is peculiarly vulnerable.

Thermal radiation

Damage done by heat radiated from the fireball is less easy to quantify. As we have seen, there are two heat pulses: one, very short at initiation, carries 1 per cent of the total thermal energy and is relatively harmless; the other, some two seconds later, lasts for ten seconds and carries the rest of the thermal energy. Altogether, they carry a third of the bomb's total energy.

Generally speaking, an extensive second-degree burn is incapacitating and we can take the range at which it occurs as being the effective thermal injury distance for people. For a 1-MT weapon it is 8·7 miles (14 km) in very clear weather; for 5-MT 16 miles (26 km).

Detailed experiments have been done on the distances from ground zero at which different materials are set on fire. It seems that in general only cloth and paper are set alight outside ranges at which blast damage is significant. Solid wooden objects – tables, chairs, etc – are charred, and may flame briefly, but 'persistent ignition is improbable under the conditions of a nuclear explosion'.[11] It is possible that the thermal ranges quoted here may considerably exaggerate. An American scientist who took part in the mid 1950s series of megaton tests in the Pacific writes:[12] 'Reliance on the *Effects of Nuclear Weapons* for valid conclusions has its shortcomings. For example . . . I was on deck . . . some twenty miles from the shot point of a detonation with a yield near ten megatons. The thermal flash did not produce the predicted second degree burn on the back of my neck, or indeed any discomfort at all.'

And even if these ranges are true of the clear skies of the Nevada desert or of the Pacific, they are almost sure to be drastically reduced by overcast British skies. In average weather the limit of the serious fire zone is expected to be about 9 miles (14 km) for a 5-MT burst.

It is often supposed that nuclear weapons will start firestorms in British cities, as conventional bombing did in Dresden and Tokyo during the Second World War (there was no firestorm at either Nagasaki or Hiroshima). Although Second World War experience may seem to have little relevance to the nuclear age, it is in fact to the point. To cause a firestorm in a German city, the RAF found it had to drop 200 tons of bombs per square mile (80 tonnes/ sq km). The composition of these bombs was important since raising a firestorm was very difficult. All in all the RAF failed almost as many times as they succeeded. It was necessary to begin with a good deal of high explosive to get the defenders down into their cellars, and to open buildings up. This had to be followed by a large number of four-pound thermite bombs, and then by more high explosive for at least half an hour to suppress the fire-fighting services and to keep householders from running upstairs to put the incendiaries out. Each incendiary burnt for five to ten minutes at a temperature up to 6000°C – about the same as the fireball's surface, but actually in the room. Yet it was found that five out of six incendiaries failed to set anything alight. Often an incendiary would burn its way from floor to floor, leaving a small charred hole in the boards. And then a firestorm wouldn't develop unless every third house was set alight over more than a square mile (2·5 sq km), and houses were close enough together for flames to jump between them.

When one relates these facts to a nuclear weapon, it does not seem overwhelmingly more likely to start a firestorm. The initial high-explosive bombardment is lacking since the heat pulse comes *before* the blast wave. Also, the heat enters houses only through those windows that happen to be facing the fireball. It would be difficult to do a thorough survey, but my own typical three-storey terraced house in Paddington will illustrate the problem. In the horizontal plane objects in all the rooms can 'see' – or be seen from – about a third of the horizon. Things on the ground floor are shielded by neighbouring houses from all bursts except those so close that blast would make the fire question academic. Things in the first-floor rooms can see sky from 20° to 40° above the horizontal. Bursts lower or higher than this are shielded, either by neighbouring roofs, or by the overhang of the window. Objects in the top floor rooms can see from 15° to 40°.

From this crude model, we may conclude that the fireball will shine through at least one window of every third house out to eight miles (13 km) or so. The inner limit of a possible firestorm is set by the outer limit of complete demolition of 4·5 miles (7·2 km). But since 99·99 per cent of people will be on their feet in this area after a 1-MT burst, and 57·8 per cent after a 5-MT burst, it is not impossible that many of these fires could be put out before they got a hold. Failing fire-fighting – and the efficacy of personal effort was often crucial during the continuous bombardment of Second World War raids – it is still unlikely that firestorms will develop, because even in the centres of British cities buildings are not close enough together.[13]

Fig. 4 This diagram shows schematically how city houses shield each other from the heat radiation of an air-burst H-bomb.

Surveys by the Home Office[14] show that the necessary building density of 30 per cent over at least a square mile is seldom achieved.

Fall-out
So much for prompt effects. After blast and heat the other major hazard caused by nuclear weapons is fall-out.

When the uranium-235 atoms of an atomic bomb, or of the trigger and fission components of a hydrogen bomb, absorb a neutron each, become unstable and split into two, the process ultimately produces a complex mixture of 200 isotopes of 35 different elements. Those that are radioactive have half-lives ranging from a fraction of a second to centuries, but the total mix obeys a simple law. Radiation decays in proportion to $T^{1.2}$ where T is time. From this it follows that when the time increases by a factor of seven, radioactivity decreases to a tenth of what it was. It is difficult to visualize just what this means, but if one adds up the total radiation emitted by a statistically typical particle over its whole life, half is emitted in the first hour, and nearly three-quarters within the first twelve hours. So if the environment remains the same, radiation soon ceases to be a significant hazard.

The important quantity when thinking about survival is the total dose received in the first two weeks, for on that depends whether one lives or dies. It can be argued that the slow radiation dose which kills 50 per cent of the people exposed to it is 900 REM.[15] It is possible to calculate the probability of death at any dose. This produces a curve rather like that in Figure 3, which showed the chance of being killed by prompt effects, but is rather more difficult to translate into casualty figures. In Figure 3 we knew where the effects were with reference to ground zero, but we were uncertain about the positions of people, houses and other things; this time we don't even know for certain where the fall-out will land.

The pattern of fall-out after a ground-burst has two components: a roughly circular region around ground zero, of relatively small area, which consists of the fall-back of debris dragged into the stem of the mushroom, and a much larger elliptical area which is the fall-out from the remains of the fireball. The size, shape and alignment of this second area are difficult to predict because the fall-out consists of particles of widely differing sizes that have fallen through different wind layers – emitting radioactivity as they fall – over periods that vary from one hour to two days. This 'plume' may in practice be an irregularly shaped cabbage around ground zero, or a thin, hot trail over miles of country. But for planning purposes it is generally assumed that the average European wind of 15 m.p.h. (24 k.p.h.) is blowing at all heights, and that fall-out is deposited first in circles that move slightly down-wind from ground zero, and then in ellipses.

Ideal dose-rate contour

To translate this into casualty figures one has to make several assumptions. Since fall-out plumes are likely to stretch for hundreds of miles across Britain, over field and village, town and city, it seems appropriate to take the national density of 550 people a square mile (210 per sq km) to represent the population affected by the elliptical pattern. We calculate casualties on the assumption of average protection factors (PF) of 3, 10, 40.[16] These correspond to the least protection one could get by sheltering in the flimsiest caravan prefab, or by carrying on with life as normal by staying on the ground floor of an average house without any preparation, or in a room adapted as a fall-out shelter in accordance with Handbook No. 10.[17] These three assumptions represent Britain taking no precautions at all, Britain staying put indoors, but without any other civil defence, and Britain with all practicable protection against fall-out. The results can be summarized in Table 2, which shows the deaths caused by fall-out from 1 and 5-MT weapons ground-burst in open country.

Table 2: Casualties due to fall-out, assuming country targets and 550 people per sq mile (210 per sq km)

Yield (MT)	Casualties PF3	PF10	PF40
1	118 000	43 000	15 000
5	478 000	176 000	62 000

The chances of death in the fall-out plume from a 1-MT ground-burst are indicated in Figure 5, which assumes, in map (a), that the PF everywhere is 3 and in (b) that it is 40. The advantage of civil defence is striking.[18]

Ground-bursts in cities present a more difficult problem. We have to allow for the varying sizes and densities of British cities, and also for the fact that much of the circular fall-out pattern covers areas that have already been devastated by blast. A precise treatment would in any case be tendentious, so I have repeated the calculations using probabilities that allow for death by fall-out as well as blast. The result is interesting. Naturally the death totals vary with the protection factor available. But at PF3 the reduced blast of a ground-burst is only slightly more than compensated for by

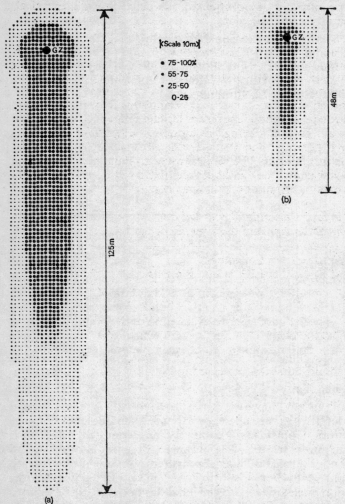

Fig. 5 *These maps, adapted from a computer print-out, show the chances in different places (indicated by the size of dot) of being killed by the fall-out from a 1-MT ground-burst H-bomb if, in map (a), one took no precautions at all; and if, in map (b), one protected one's home in accordance with CD advice.*

deaths due to fall-out, while at PFs 10 and 40 the ground-burst kills fewer.

To arrive at a reasonable comparison of casualties due to ground- and air-bursts we have to add urban and country totals together. Naturally the results will vary considerably with the size of the town attacked. As an illustration, we take a city the size of Birmingham:

Table 3: Casualties due to 1-MT air- and ground-burst bombs on Birmingham

| Air-burst | Ground-burst | | |
	PF3	PF10	PF40
310 000	434 000	201 000	161 000

The two attacks are more or less evenly balanced at PF3, and perhaps surprisingly, the air-burst attack is twice as effective at PF40.[19] Together with other considerations which we examine later, this lack of a clear advantage for ground-burst weapons in attacking large city populations might well persuade an attacker not to use them.

These figures ignore evacuation of the plume areas, and also the cleansing effect of rain which, by washing fall-out into underground sewers, may very largely abate the nuisance.

Civil-defence possibilities

In this section we are concerned only with simple, practical defences against nuclear weapons. As civil defence becomes more sophisticated, expensive and comprehensive, so it acquires strategic significance. Preparations which fall under this head, like deep shelters, are discussed later (see page 146). Perhaps surprisingly, in view of the vast destruction nuclear weapons can inflict, a good deal can be done to mitigate their effects by taking relatively simple precautions.

A specific example will illustrate the point. If everyone whitewashed their windows before an attack, the amount of heat entering each house by radiation from the fireball would be reduced by 80 per cent. This would reduce the range at which houses caught fire by a factor of 0·45, and the number of houses that catch fire to 20 per cent of those that would have burnt otherwise. In fact whitewashed windows or shut venetian blinds would eliminate the fire problem, for, at 20 per cent of the ordinary fire range, blast entirely predominates. Yet it sounds so absurd to defend oneself against an H-bomb by painting the window panes that no other civil-defence proposal has been so ridiculed.

BEFORE

AFTER

Fig. 6 The advantages of whitewash. These three wooden huts were built in the Nevada Desert for an H-bomb test. The two black ones burnt; the white one survived.

Fundamentally the civil-defence problem is a sort of fatalistic egocentricity: everyone imagines that the bomb will fall directly on him, and that therefore no practicable civil defence is worth bothering about. But we do not reflect that if the bomb falls on *me*, there are then millions of people it does not fall on; and since there is no particular reason why it should land on me rather than on one of them, I might as well multiply what chance of immunity I have.

Paradoxically the more damaging an effect, that is the farther out its lethality stretches, the more can be done about it: in the last fall of its power it covers vast areas, where small mitigations will save very large numbers of people. For simplicity we briefly consider what can be done to counter each effect, in the order they were described earlier.

Blast precautions

The major danger to people is caused by flying debris caught up in the blast wave. Most casualties are caused by flying glass, others by being caught in collapsed buildings. I have mentioned the protection afforded by the staircase of an ordinary house. In modern reinforced concrete offices, hotel buildings and flats the best protection which could be reached in the available time would be in and around the central concrete service column. If no real refuge from glass is possible, then it is best to lie down under the window itself, face to the wall, so that the pane blows overhead, or to get under some solid piece of furniture. In the open it would be best to lie face down at the corner of a solid wall, or in the gutter.

Wind drag is likely to blow vehicles over. The best people in them can do is to get out and lie down, as should people standing up in the open.

All these steps can considerably increase the individual's chance of survival, or the total number that will survive any particular attack. They all need warning to be effective. This may well be supplied by the Royal Observer Corps system[20] (see page 122), but even without this, a large bomb acts as its own herald over large areas. This is because the blast wave arrives up to half a minute after the heat and light flash of the actual explosion.

This is evidently increasingly useful to larger and larger numbers towards the outer limits of blast damage.

Heat precautions

Heat flash is too, to a certain extent, its own warning, because the bright flash as a megaton weapon explodes precedes the dangerous heat pulse by two seconds or so – a time that would give the lucky, agile and quickwitted an opportunity to throw themselves into shadow. Otherwise, given a few minutes' warning, the same precautions that one would take against blast almost automatically protect against heat flash too. The sort of clothes one is likely to be wearing in the open air in Britain will give substantial protection against flash at most ranges; which will be made more complete if people cover their faces and hands with a coat as they lie down. As we have seen, there are likely to be people left unhurt by blast and flash indoors over large areas who will be able, if they are prepared, to put out fires in buildings that would be amenable in their early stages, but which, if left untouched, would soon develop into dangerous conflagration.

Fall-out precautions

Protection against fall-out is mainly concerned with the gamma rays given off by decaying isotopes. Alpha rays cannot penetrate the skin, beta rays are only harmful if radioactive dust is left on the skin or if they are eaten on vegetables. But protection against gamma rays almost automatically defends against the others. Having taken care to avoid physical contact with fall-out dust, substantial protection against gamma rays is only given by removing oneself to another part of the country, keeping the fall-out physically at a distance, or interposing a considerable mass of gamma-ray-absorbing material between oneself and it.

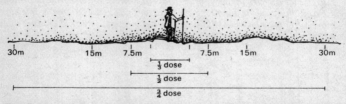

Fig. 7 *Most of the radiation received by a man standing on level ground covered by fall-out comes from the area immediately around him. If he could sweep the dust away for 100 feet (30 m) all around, he would reduce his dose-rate by a factor of four.*

Since fall-out can take up to twenty-four hours to arrive in large quantities, flight is evidently a perfectly practicable defence, given an efficient system for predicting where the plumes are going. The system in operation in Britain is described on page 151. If one can't fly, then a house gives considerable protection in the second sense because it provides a hollow space into which the fall-out can't get. Fall-out lies on the ground, and on the roof, so simply standing in

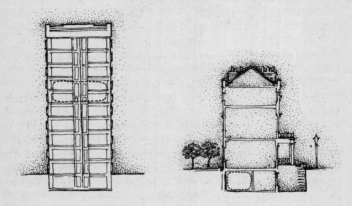

Fig. 8 Fall-out lies mainly on the roofs of houses and the ground around them. In this case the best place to be is at the back of the basement. In a high block of flats or an office building, the best place to be is rather more than half-way between ground and roof.

Fig. 9 A boat or yacht makes a good fall-out shelter. Dust settles to the sea bottom and is shielded by water; or can easily be washed off the decks.

the middle of the house that affords protection by absorb-
ing no gamma rays is a considerable help.

*Fig. 10 Since gamma radiation goes with difficulty through soil, a trench
gives good protection. Russian civil defence doctrine advises a roof of
brushwood covered with earth.*

Similarly the middle of a tall office block is good. And,
because gamma rays shoot up from and along the surface of
the ground, but only a small distance through it, a trench is
not bad, and it is better still if it has a roof of earth. Russian
civil defence teaches people to support earth cover on
fascines of brushwood; the British Army uses tents of wire
mesh-toughened plastic which are erected on steel hoops in
excavations to support back-filled earth cover.

Fall-out drops from the sky and lies on flat surfaces: it is
likely to be washed away by rain and caught in sewers underground where its radiations are much absorbed. Fall-out
after an experimental shot in the Marshall Islands was much
reduced by a rainstorm, but there is little sound evidence to
show how effective this could be. It might do a lot.

American Civil Defense proposes to take advantage of
the USA's huge pleasure-boat fleet by advising people to
shelter in them. Fall-out would sink through the surface of
the water, lie on the bottom of the sea or river and be
shielded by the water; a small amount would settle on deck,
but could easily be washed overboard.

NOTES

1. This account of an H-bomb explosion is condensed from *The Effects of Nuclear Weapons*, US Government Printing Office.

2. Carl R. Gerber, *Journal of the British Nuclear Society*, vol. 6, no. 1, January 1967, p. 24.

3. The time taken for the activity of a radio-isotope to decay to half its original value.

4. Ronald Brown, *New Scientist*, 6 February 1969, p. 294.

5. Neville Brown, *New Scientist*, 6 February 1969, p. 295.

6. Ira S. Lowry, *The Post-Attack Population of the United States*, Rand Corporation, Santa Monica, 1966.

7. Lowry, p. 77.

8. Lowry, p. 77.

9. Ranges are taken from *Effects of Nuclear Weapons*.

10. 4 per cent – 320 000 – casualties in London represents two years' natural deaths.

11. *Effects of Nuclear Weapons*, p. 303.

12. Carl F. Miller, *Scientist and Citizen*, February–March 1966, p. 17.

13. Perhaps because of centuries of actual and threatened siege, Continental cities are generally far denser than British ones. People typically live in flats rather than houses, and the front and back gardens that are normal in British cities are almost unknown.

14. Personal communication, 1967.

15. The REM (Radiation Equivalent, Man) measures the lethal intensity of radiation at a point. Its definition is far from simple. The *instantaneous* mid-lethal dose is probably 500 REM (cf. D. E. Barnes and Denis Taylor, *Radiation Hazards and Protection*, London, 1963, p. 25) but over an exposure period of a fortnight, the body has a chance to repair itself and can therefore tolerate a higher dose.

16. The protection factor measures the reduction of radiation inside a building. Thus, if a building has a PF of 40, the radiation inside it is a fortieth of that outside.

17. *Advising the Householder on Preparations against Nuclear Attack*, HMSO, 1963.

18. The basis for these maps was a computer print-out. The program was written by Dr C. A. Atkinson from information given in *Effects of Nuclear Weapons*.

19. I understand that Home Office studies have shown the same balance between air- and ground-burst attacks on big cities at plausible protection factors.

20. Fylingdales radar, one of three Ballistic Missile Early Warning System (BMEWS) stations, is said to give fifteen minutes' warning of missiles fired against Britain (*Reader's Digest Atlas*). But depressed trajectory, FOBS or SLEMS could cut this to seconds.

3 *The Third World War*

So far we have been thinking of individuals and how the H-bomb affects them. But the bomb is not a random thing like a lightning bolt. It will be used with a purpose, and before we can think usefully about it, we have to have some idea of what that purpose might be. In effect, we have to consider a scenario – however vague – for a Third World War. It will not be just a spasm exchange of nuclear weapons. Tactics and strategy will play just as important a role in it as in any other war.

First, how will it be fought? One can see that there are at least four possibilities:

  (i) a nuclear exchange between America and Russia;
 (ii) a land and tactical air battle with conventional and nuclear weapons in Europe;
(iii) a naval war aimed at destroying submarines, or at preventing America reinforcing and re-supplying troops in Europe by sea; and
(iv) a battle in space to destroy reconnaissance, navigation and communications satellites.

There may also be a land war somewhere else – presumably the flashpoint for the whole sorry affair.

One could easily write a whole book about the preparations for the Third World War, but here we can take only a hasty look at what the possible conflicts imply for the citizen.

In strategic nuclear war, doctrine is shifting, certainly on the American side, from the idea of an attack on the Russian *will* to win by striking at her cities – an idea which was influenced by the inaccuracy of early missiles – in favour of an attack on the Russian *means* to win by striking at her hardened point targets. These are missile silos, warhead dumps and communications centres.

In order to get some grasp of the arguments one has to understand how accuracy affects missile performance – and indeed the performance of any weapon. A weapon consists of two parts: a delivery system and a striking system. In a gun, the delivery system is the gun itself, its sights, observation system and the ability of the bullet to travel far and straight. The striking system is the impact of the bullet or the explosive in it. The more accurately the bullet can be guided to its target, the less explosive it has to carry in order to make up for near misses, the smaller it can be, the more the gun can fire, and the more certain the target is to be destroyed.

A handy way of measuring accuracy is to specify the radius of a circle into which half the rounds fired will land. If the gunner is doing his job, the centre of the circle will be the target. Some of the rounds – which might be pistol bullets, ICBMs, bombs dropped from aeroplanes, or depth charges fired from a ship – will not work at all and so will fail to arrive anywhere near the circle. Some will get near it but not near enough, owing to inaccuracies in guidance, propellant, aiming intelligence. But by definition, since the radius of this circle is the Circular Error Probability (CEP), half will land within it.

The mathematics are more complicated and statistical, but this is the meat of the argument: suppose we have a rocket which is 60 per cent reliable, has a destructive radius of 0·05 miles (0·08 km) against the target we want to attack – say a missile silo – and a CEP of 0·15 miles (0·24 km). Now the area over which the warhead is effective is a circle with a radius of 0·05 miles – an area of 0·078 square miles (0·2 sq km). The 50 per cent, CEP circle has an area of 0·07 square miles (0·18 sq km). Assuming that the rockets that land within it land randomly, there is a 4·5 per cent chance of one destroying the target. And since only 60 per cent of the rockets work properly (this sounds bad, but if you have a million parts, each of which is a million-to-one reliable, the chance of everything working on the day is evens), the actual chance of each rocket fired destroying the target is reduced to 3·3 per cent, or, its chance of missing is 96·7 per cent. The war plan will probably call for enough rockets to be fired to give, say, only a 5 per cent probability of the target's survival. If we fire two of these wretched things the chance of missing is reduced to 96·7×96·7 = 93·5 per cent. If we fire three, the chance is 96·7×96·7×96·7 = 90·4 per cent and so on. To reduce the chance of missing to less than 5 per cent, we have to fire 122. Under such conditions, your rockets are best left in their silos where they will destroy 122 of the enemy, rather than fired when they will account for only 1/122 of an enemy rocket each. Happily for the peace-loving civilian, under these conditions, the outbreak of war may be expected to be long delayed.

Of course the military are not happy to leave things in such a convenient posture. They have worked hard at improving accuracies, and in defence at reducing damage radii by hardening the missile silos. If d is damage radius, c is error radius, R the reliability and n the number fired, then we have for a 95 per cent chance of destroying the enemy target:

$$n = \frac{\log 0·05}{\log\left(1 - R.\frac{d^2}{c^2}\right)}$$

If you can get c down to about d, then the chance of missing is the chance of the rocket not working: $1-R$. Which means that even if you can hit the target, you have to fire three missiles that are 60 per cent reliable, or two if they're 80 per cent.

If the accuracy and yield of attacking warheads is enough, they can each knock out one of the other side's missiles. At this point things become serious. In the earlier phase, which is now just ending in the US–USSR strategic balance, the side which started the war lost it. Therefore, the longer the delay before the war the better. Now the side that starts wins, so the sooner the war the better because it prevents him doing it to you first. If you think he will attack you on Sunday, you had better go for him on Wednesday – and in fact why wait till then, what about this afternoon? and on second thoughts – *Now!*

Military situations in which the attacker has a disadvantage are good for peace; those where early action gets results are bad for it. One theory of the outbreak of the First World War attributes it to the Russian and Austrian systems for mobilization and manning the frontiers. The complicated railway systems took three days to get the men into position: the side that started even half an hour earlier had half an hour at the end in which the opposition was not quite ready. Thus the outbreak of war was made certain when the system was drawn up.

So there is nothing new about this instability in the capability of missiles for mutual destruction.

In the early 1960s, CEPs of intercontinental rockets were a mile (0·625 km), which meant that they could only attack city targets, or big troop camps, aerodromes, etc. By 1969 accuracies of around half a mile were being mentioned at a hearing of the Foreign Relations Committee of the American Senate. In 1977 the theoretical limit of inertial guidance seemed to be within reach of the Americans, at a quarter of a mile, while experiments are being done with active homing in the terminal area by radio navigation, on-board radar, terrain recognition, etc., which are said to produce a CEP of 100 feet (30 m) or so (see page 58).

It is also necessary to know how likely these extremely complicated weapons are to work on the day. The highest figure mentioned in public is 80 per cent, the lowest, 40 per cent. Here we take 60 per cent.

By way of illustrating how these factors interact, the following table presents an attack with Minuteman 111 0·17-MT warheads on a silo that can withstand an overpressure of 1000 p.s.i. (70 kg/sq cm) (planned American technology. The Russians are going for 3000 p.s.i.). CEPs are taken to be 0·5 miles (0·8 km), 0·25 miles (0·4 km) and 0·125 miles (0·2 km). The kill range is 0·12 miles (0·19 km) for 1000 p.s.i.[1]

One solution to this unhappy inability of intercontinental missiles to knock each other out, one for one, is to make each one carry several independent warheads (MIRVs). These can be separately targeted. A recent review[2] of the missile balance looked ahead to the time (not far in the future) when America has installed cold-launch missiles in its silos. These are ejected by compressed air, making the present shielding against exhaust plumes unnecessary, and so allowing a heavier rocket. The missiles would carry ten MIRVs with a yield of 0·34-MT each and a guidance accuracy of 0·115 miles (0·18 km). In defence the Russians harden their silos to 3000 p.s.i. (210 kg/sq cm). The outcome of a first strike by America with missiles 60 per cent reliable would be 1381 Russian silos destroyed, 27 surviving.

Table 4: 1000 p.s.i. silo, kill range 0·12 miles

CEP	Chance of individual success	Number of rockets 60 per cent reliable for 95 per cent certainty
0·5 miles	3·4 per cent	85 approx.
0·25 miles	13·8 per cent	20
0·125 miles	60 per cent	4

ICBM warheads can in principle be shot down by ABM (Anti-Ballistic Missile) rockets – and the same sort of accuracy and reliability calculations apply to them too. They in turn can be misled by decoy warheads, and real but agile warheads that can jink away from attack.

An alternative to the ICBM is the cruise missile – in essence the pilotless V1 of the Second World War, but with longer range and accurate guidance derived from continuous measurement of ground contours beneath the flight path of the missile. This contour is matched with a stored map by a small on-board computer: accuracies of tens of feet are claimed which make it possible to attack even the hardest silos with high-explosive warheads. Hailed at first as the ultimate first strike weapon, the cruise missile actually has several weaknesses. It is difficult to shoot down because it is small and returns a weak radar echo, but because it is small it has a short range and must be launched from an aircraft or submarine off the enemy coast – which in turn becomes vulnerable to attack. And, though hard to shoot down by ground-based weapons, it would not be an impossible target for large radar-equipped aircraft such as AWACs with snapdown air-to-air missiles. To counter threats from cruise missiles and low-flying bombers, the Russians are said to be building a chain of radars on high towers along their northern coasts. And, of course, OTH (Over-The-Horizon) radar (see page 126) performs well against these targets.

An article on cruise missiles[3] claimed that the Tomahawk missile with terrain-matching guidance and a 200-kT warhead can achieve a 90 per cent probability of kill against 'hundreds of targets in the USSR with a hardness of 200 p.s.i.'. This yield, ground-burst, produces 200 p.s.i. (14 kg/sq cm) at about 0·6 miles (0·96 km), so one must assume that Tomahawk is reliability limited against these targets. Minuteman 111 with the NS-20 guidance system and a 350-kT warhead in the Mk 12A re-entry vehicle attains a 76 per cent (fire two) kill probability, and Poseidon with less accurate guidance and smaller warhead weighs in at 71 per cent (fire three). Against a 1000 p.s.i. (70 kg/sq cm) target, Tomahawk's kill probability is 85 per cent. Kill range is then 0·03 miles (0·048 km), suggesting that the CEP is something like 0·06 miles (0·096 km), or about 100 yards.

A new warhead under development for the Pershing tactical missile, with a range of several hundred miles, has terminal guidance using a circularly scanning radar in the missile nose cone. The radar produces a picture of the land below which is compared with an image secured earlier from aircraft or satellites. The two main images are correlated (at the moment using analogue means, but in the future probably by digital techniques) so that the warhead can be steered to its target with a CEP of 100 feet (30 m). It is claimed[4] that jamming will be ineffective, since the jammer can obliterate only a small part of the ground image, while correlation relies on a large number of data points.

The practical argument about the relative effectiveness of defence and attack also revolves around the effect of the Strategic Arms Limitations Treaty. It is in the interests of the USAF to show that the Russians are gaining ground, in order to prise more funds out of the American taxpayer (see page 273), but setting aside their bias, one can believe that things are not as stable as they were. This graph[5] shows how the advantage in terms of silo-based ICBM striking power will rest with the aggressor in 1990.

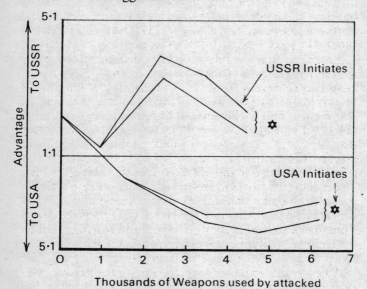

Fig. 11 This graph shows the stability of the new generation of ICBMs. As the total number of missiles rises, so the advantage swings in favour of the Russians.

Of course, all this assumes that the defender sits still – or rather his missiles do – to be shot at. There is really no need for this foolish course of conduct, and we who are interested in peace should applaud recent plans to make America's ICBM fleet mobile. Several schemes have been considered: to carry Minutemen in 747 transport aircraft for dropping

out of the tail and firing in mid-air; to mount them on lorries
or railway wagons that are constantly on the move – along
with dummy transporters to confuse Russian satellites; to
conceal missiles in buildings in out-of-the-way places; to
moor them in canisters in shallow water and to mount them
on railway trucks moving randomly along a shallow covered
tunnel up to 20 miles (32 km) long. For firing, the missile in
its canister is raised through the tunnel roof.

*Fig. 12 One proposal for protecting American missiles from a Russian
counter-force strike is to move them randomly through shallow tunnels. On
the command to fire the missile is jacked through the earth cover into a vertical
position.*

The same principle is behind the Polaris submarine, which
is able to hide in the depths of the ocean up to 2800 miles
(4480 km) from its target. If one – optimistically – allows
ten miles (16 km) as an extreme sonar detection range,
and assumes that only half the area of the circle 2800 miles
in radius round the target is sea, then the defender has a
1:40 000 chance of finding a missile submarine with a single
sonar.

In practice the chance is increased by a number of
measures. Enormous sea bed microphone systems have
been installed along the Atlantic and Pacific coasts of
America, across the Greenland–Iceland–Norway entrance
to the Atlantic, off Cape of Good Hope to detect submarines
and surface ships, and identify them by their acoustic
signatures. There are also said to be huge low-frequency
sonars mounted in the Faroes, the Azores, New Zealand
and so on that will scan a whole ocean basin. But neither of
these methods can give a precise enough position to an

enemy submarine for a successful first strike even in perfect conditions. If the enemy takes advantage of saline gradients and temperature differences, or hides in remote shallows, he is very unlikely to be found.[6] Which is a good thing.

There is a whole new class of weapons using intense electromagnetic beams, protons, alpha particles, radio waves, heavy ions, which may revolutionize strategic war and the deterrent balance over the next ten years. These weapons strike with the speed of light: if mounted in space they may be able to knock down ballistic missiles as they rise out of the atmosphere; if mounted on the ground, they may destroy missiles in the terminal phase of their flight. For energetic publicity in favour of these techniques, see *Aviation Week and Space Technology* (Autumn 1978). However, at the time of writing (October 1978) these weapons were hardly more than budget proposals, and the only positive demonstration had been the destruction of an anti-tank missile in flight by a laser at a range of about 1 km.

As long as the aggressor with nuclear intercontinental missiles gets no advantage, then war is very unlikely to break out, and the other possible theatres will continue undisturbed. However, military planners must suppose that things are not that simple, and must prepare for other forms of war as well. So, in Europe, we find large tank armies on both sides supported by fleets of anti-tank helicopters, troop-carrying helicopters, ground attack fighters, tactical bombers and air superiority fighters. There is an elaborate network of airfields, radars, command and communication bunkers and a chain of cable and tropospheric scatter radio links between them from Turkey to Northern Norway.

The best country for tank warfare is the plains of northern Germany where most of the British Army is deployed. Farther south the going gets hilly and the passes are full of nuclear mines. The Baltic is shallow and good for small ships and amphibious warfare. The Soviet thrust west will be split by the strong neutrality of Sweden, and the mountains of Norway, so an air attack on Britain would be first across

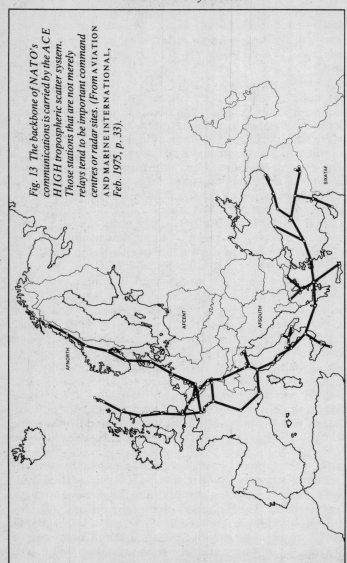

Fig. 13 The backbone of NATO's communications is carried by the ACE HIGH tropospheric scatter system. Those stations that are not merely relays tend to be important command centres or radar sites. (From AVIATION AND MARINE INTERNATIONAL, Feb. 1975, p. 33).

SIKATAF

AFNORTH

AFCENT

AFSOUTH

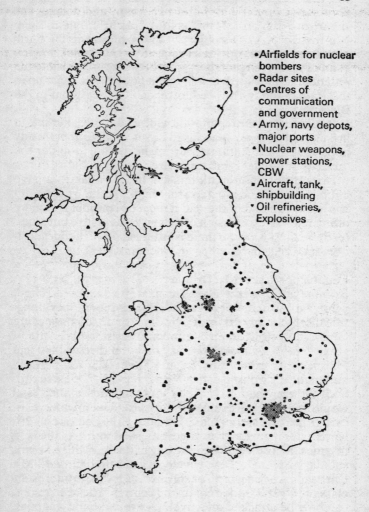

- Airfields for nuclear bombers
- Radar sites
- Centres of communication and government
- Army, navy depots, major ports
- Nuclear weapons, power stations, CBW
- Aircraft, tank, shipbuilding
- Oil refineries, Explosives

Fig. 14 Counter-force targets in Britain.

Denmark from airfields in East Germany and Poland, and then round North Cape southwards from fields near Murmansk. NATO's object in the naval war in the north would be to bottle up Soviet ships from Murmansk and the White Sea and prevent them from breaking through into the Atlantic; in the North Sea it would be to bottle them up in the Baltic; and in the Mediterranean to keep them in the Black Sea.

In all theatres the temptation will be for the weaker side to use tactical nuclear weapons to offset enemy strength: any hope that a conventional war might be fought under the 'nuclear umbrella' is rather absurd.

Britain's position in all this will be, as usual, as a large aircraft carrier and moated arms depot. As long as NATO has any command of the sea, it must be considerably more difficult to take possession of these islands than of our allies' territory in Europe. So there is an unusually high concentration of targets in this green and pleasant land.

Counter-force strike on Britain

Britain has no rocket silos. The nearest comparable target would be one of our or America's Polaris submarines alongside the depot ship in Holy Loch. Since these submarines are immensely strong to enable them to resist the pressure of great depths – some reports say they can dive to 1400 feet (420 m), and certainly more than 900 feet (270 m) – they will automatically withstand 450–750 p.s.i. (31·5–52·5 kg/sq cm). So if the crew had had time to shut the hatches, the vessel would seem invulnerable to air blast. Underwater blast carries farther than air blast, but since Holy Loch is only 200 yards (180 m) wide it is almost as hard to hit as the submarines themselves. The best way of dealing with a Polaris submarine seems to be to envelop it in the fireball; two 5-MT warheads are necessary, or six of 1-MT. A more interesting class of target is buried command centres. These, like silos, can only be attacked effectively by ground-burst weapons, but the lethal radius will be reduced according to their depth. Crushing stresses extend downwards about one-and-a-third times the crater radius:

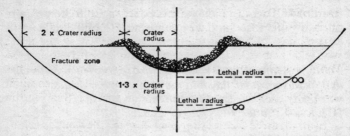

Fig. 15 A ground-burst nuclear weapon produces a crater partly filled with pulverized material that has fallen back from the stem of the cloud, and surrounded by a fracture zone which extends a distance of two crater radii on each side and about 1·3 radii downwards. Buried installations such as silos, shelter tunnels in the fracture zone will be damaged; the lethal radius of the weapon against them therefore depends largely on their depth.

The depth of the crater is considerably smaller, owing to fall-back of pulverized material. If one assumes then that the lethal zone is part of a sphere that cuts the ground surface in a circle two crater radii around ground zero, and passes 1·3 radii beneath it, one can calculate the lethal radii for structures at different depths.

As we shall see below, a nuclear attack on Britain would probably involve two phases: first a missile strike against our nuclear bombers to blunt a retaliatory blow, and against our air-defence organization in order to open our air space, followed by a more leisurely attack using bombers and stand-off air-to-ground weapons which would strike at our military-economic base, and in particular at the seats of government and high command, and our stores of unused nuclear weapons.

Since Russia's 5- and 25-MT warheads are carried by ICBMs, which are likely to have more targets than they can cope with in America, it seems unlikely that many warheads of this size will be delivered to Britain in the first missile strike. In general, it seems reasonable to expect attack by 1-MT warheads, carried by intermediate- and medium-range ballistic missiles, and missiles launched from submarines. Since the range of these missiles would be about a third of ICBMs', we may expect accuracies to be proportionately increased and we assume a CEP of 0·3 mile (0·48 km).

Table 5: Lethal radii for point structures buried at different depths in saturated clay and number of ground-burst warheads necessary to attack them (CEP = 0·3 miles, 0·48 km)

Yield MT	Lethal radius (metres)				Number of warheads			
Depth	100 ft (30 m)	200 ft (61 m)	300 ft (91 m)	600 ft (183 m)	100 ft (30 m)	200 ft (61 m)	300 ft (91 m)	600 ft (183 m)
25	6231	6099	6054	5890	2	2	2	2
5	3696	3509	3456	3271	2	2	3	3
1	2108	2030	1995	1766	5	6	6	7

If we quite arbitrarily say that Russia would not devote more than one per cent of her IRBM forces to any one target, then it appears that not even 600 feet (183 m) of clay offers any worthwhile shelter, while on the other hand 100 feet (30 m) of rock or more confers almost absolute protection against 1-MT weapons and a good deal against 5-MT.

In the second strike, by manned bombers or cruise missiles, one must expect the largest nuclear weapons[7] to be delivered with complete accuracy. Protection then can only be given by sheer thickness of rock. At first glance disused mines seem the answer, but coal lies under sedimentary rocks that give little protection and are themselves unstable and apt to subside. The headroom in deep British coal mines often shrinks from twelve to four feet (3·7–1·2 m) overnight, in spite of the strongest roof supports. It seems likely that protection of this sort would have to be specially excavated in the hardest rock available, which in Britain would be granite or other igneous rocks.

A 100-MT ground-burst excavates a crater of 2500 feet (750 m) radius in rock, so 5000 feet (1500 m) cover is required horizontally, and 3300 feet (1000 m) vertically.

There is no particular problem in digging a vertical tunnel of this depth, but the necessary pit-head gear in an area which must necessarily be devoid of coal mines would perhaps excite comment. It seems more practical to bore horizontally into a mountain, as the Americans have done at Colorado Springs to protect their air-defence headquarters. But even this expensive installation, with 1000 feet (305 m) of rock cover, is now vulnerable to Russia's largest weapons, and might just as well be housed in buildings on the surface – as Britain's equivalent ostensibly is.

Other attractive point targets might be blast-resistant surface buildings, oil storage tanks, radio and TV masts, GPO microwave towers, parked strike aircraft. These present little difficulty. The number of air-burst 1-MT weapons with a CEP of 0·3 miles (0·48 km) needed is set only by their reliability.

Polaris submarine at sea

The case of attack by missile on a Polaris submarine on patrol is worth attention. Let us assume by way of illustration that by some means the defender can find the submarine's position, but not its course or speed, aim a missile and fire it instantly. (Minuteman can be fired at a pre-chosen target in just over 30 seconds and re-targeted in 36 minutes.) Lethal ranges for underwater bursts and ordinary ships are given in *Effects*.[8] The result of such a burst is (a) to subject hull plates to a heavy overpressure which can distort or fracture them; (b) to subject the whole vessel to very rapid vertical and horizontal movement. This can severely damage internal components, particularly the supports of boilers and engines which can collapse. Steam lines, shafting and the brickwork of boilers are especially vulnerable. The sinking overpressure is thought to be 3–4000 p.s.i. (210–280 kg/sq cm), but some may sink at 2000 p.s.i. (140 kg/sq cm), and those which survive will be useless. These figures were obtained from the Bikini Baker tests, and the target ships were not built, as Polaris submarines presumably are, to resist these stresses. We can assume that a nuclear sub would be a good deal stronger, but to be on the safe side, we take 2000 p.s.i. (140 kg/sq cm) as the incapacitating over-pressure. Two 1-MT weapons assure destruction.

But if we assume that it may be moving in an unknown direction at 30 knots, at a distance away that is equivalent to the range of the missiles it carries, this considerably complicates the problem.

The early Polaris A-1 missile has a range of 1500 miles (2400 km) which it covers in roughly 14 minutes on a minimum energy trajectory.[9] A missile fired in return will take the same time. In that period the submarine can move 14 miles (22 km). Similarly a boat armed with Polaris A-3 or Poseidon, which have a range of 2500 miles (4000 km), can travel 18 miles (29 km). On our assumption these distances can be in any direction, and so in effect have to be added to the missile's inherent error. They are so large that there is no point firing at the position where the submarine was. It would be necessary to fire a salvo in some sort of pattern. Allowing for inaccuracy and unreliability some 40 1-MT missiles would have to be aimed and fired practically instantaneously to catch the A-1 Polaris; 70 to deal with the A-3 version. This unpromising procedure makes some unlikely assumptions, but the example does illustrate the magnitude of the problems involved in fighting a war even with 'ultimate' weapons.

Why war?

We have been talking about some features of a war that might break out between the heavily armed troops which lie on each side of the arc from North Cape to the eastern border of Turkey. This sort of war might happen there because, for historical reasons, much of the world's weaponry is concentrated along it. Just *why* either side would want to start a war on the borders of Europe is far less clear. In fact, I find it hard to imagine a credible scenario for such a conflict. It was not so in the 1950s and it may not be so again, but at this moment it is difficult to see what use Russia might have for a devastated Europe which presented no military threat to begin with, nor why any sane western leader would think it worth launching an attack on Russia. This is not to say there are no reasons for military strength on either side.

Consequently whatever small profit either party might, in a moment of aberration, see being won from a European war, can easily be offset by a small deterrent force. Which exists many times over. Consequently there is no real likelihood of a nuclear attack on Britain, and no reason for the expense and disruption which an effective civilian civil defence scheme would cost. It is worth the relatively small sums which are spent on protecting controls against fall-out so that (a) the government is immune to nuclear blackmail – perhaps by some small power, and (b) so that it can deal effectively with accidents, whether technical or political.

Static defence is extremely expensive if it has to be realized in a hurry; almost negligibly cheap if it can be incorporated in routine rebuilding. Thus the Swiss claim to spend only 1 per cent of their GNP on civil defence, and for that they have the best system in the world. The corollary to this approach is that one cannot be too selective about the threats one is defending oneself against. If the time scale of your preparations must be measured in decades, then you cannot afford to pay too much attention to current politics or technology. For instance, Russia seems much less of an enemy now than she did in the 1950s; massive nuclear attacks on city populations seem less likely than they did at the beginning of the 1960s. Yet one would not expect these changes – which may change back again – to be instantly reflected in the level of British civil defence. If the weapons are there and you are here, it is as well to make such preparations as you think worthwhile, even if the politicians tell you there is no likely chance of the weapons being used.

Two kinds of nuclear war, and their drawbacks

Before we can begin to talk sensibly about the civil results of a nuclear attack on Britain – or anywhere else – we have to inquire into a possible attacker's intentions, and then ask how nearly he possesses weapons in the numbers and quality needed to realize them. But before going any further, it may be useful to try to relate the general scale of nuclear war with more conventional forms of warfare.

One often thinks nuclear war is different in kind from other struggles. It is remarked, for instance, that there is enough nuclear explosive in the world to kill every man, woman and child a dozen times over. (It is difficult to see how such a calculation could be done; but there it is, many people believe it and it may be true.) However, this state of affairs is nothing new. As Schelling pertinently remarks,[10] the American Army could have bought enough ice-picks to kill everyone in the world long before the invention of the atom bomb. Doubtless the ammunition used in the trench bombardments of the First World War would have performed the same office if it could have been distributed. In classical times nations that rebelled against Rome were not infrequently extirpated to the last infant, their barns and harvests and homes burnt, their cattle driven off. The effect, though achieved piecemeal and by hand, was no different from the results close to ground zero of nuclear explosions. Nuclear weapons have not much increased the *scale* of damage that man is able or willing to do to himself, given time and opportunity, but they have significantly increased the *rate* at which he can work.

Our inbuilt ways of thinking about war are partly the traditional accumulation of centuries of experience during which wars often did very little harm. At the most civilized stage, during Marlborough's campaigns in the early 1700s, the maximum loss of life to Britain, during a major land war in Europe, was 5000 men a year,[11] and the damage done to the countryside in which the armies manoeuvred and battles were fought was almost negligible. Even the most destructive war of recent times, that between Russia and Germany,[12] accounted for only 0·008 per cent of Russia's real wealth in every hour, or 27 per cent in four years.

In the past both sides could embark on the gamble of conflict without having to steel themselves in advance to losses of any significance at all. War could be a game of chance at which the stakes were, in national terms, pennies. To be sure, over years of play, nations could get into quite serious embarrassment, but although many spent proportions of their patrimonies, few failed altogether and next time the school assembled, the familiar faces were still present.

In the same way admirals, generals and more recently air marshals, could not, however much they wanted, inflict more than pennyworths of damage on the other side. Death had to be brought to the enemy by the lorryload and painfully delivered, while he did the same in return. In order to harm civilians, the opposing army or air force had to be broken through and destroyed; and this was rarely achieved. Even in the last war, when the German and Japanese air forces had been practically suppressed, the bombing of enemy cities was ineffective as a means of killing civilians. Hamburg, one of the worst-hit, lost 47 per cent of its houses, but 3 per cent of its people; Frankfurt lost 33 per cent of houses and 1 per cent of people; Kobe, in Japan, lost 50 per cent of houses and 1 per cent of people.[13] The net effect of city bombing, once evacuation is taken into account, was that wartime death rates were everywhere *less* than they had been in peacetime.

But nuclear weapons offer a much increased rate of inflicting damage, and are also more or less invulnerable to active defence, so they bypass the enemy armed forces, and enable war to be made directly on his population.

The third important difference between nuclear and conventional war is the ease with which the weapons can destroy each other. This time the comparison is not to the advantage of the new. We are used to machines which can easily wreck each other, and go on to do more damage. A rifleman is able to shoot another rifleman and another and another. A tank can destroy another tank and be fit for further action, and the same with an aircraft carrier or a submarine. But paradoxically, as we have seen, the enormously more powerful nuclear missiles cannot yet do this.

The idea of the deterrent

In earlier times, or in conventional war now, the reasonable foreseeable social cost of any particular military enterprise could often be so small that it was easy to see the enterprise showing a profit – in whatever terms one cares to measure that elusive quantity. Now any all-out war between two well-equipped nuclear powers is likely to do so much damage that no conceivable profit can be made. The prize does not exist that would be worth the sacrifice. And this disproportion extends even to modestly equipped nuclear powers. The possession of a small number of protected nuclear weapons promises enough damage to neutralize any war profit. Thus even one of Britain's three Polaris submarines, which can fire 16 missiles each with a warhead of nearly 1-MT and are accurate enough to hit a Russian city, can offer enough damage, although negligible in terms of what Russia could do in return, to raise the ante above the level of sensible play.

The disadvantage of nuclear deterrent is that it only works over a limited, high range of aggressions. As the Americans have found out, the mere possession of unimaginable fire-power does not deter more mundane insults even by non-nuclear states, because the least possible nuclear response is so disproportionately great that it becomes itself an unjusti-fiable aggression. But at least the mutual possession of nuclear weapons sets an upper limit to play at the gaming table of war, and perhaps, through the uncertainty of reaction by any of the nuclear powers, reduces it. Though, on the other hand, many students foresee a renewal of conventional wars under the 'nuclear umbrella', in which the nuclear forces hold each other stalemated, and the rest proceeds as before. But if the losses in this 'privileged' sort of conventional conflict become too high, then one or the other power is likely to resort to nuclear revenge, and we are back where we were. But this does not much concern us, interested as we are in an all-out nuclear attack, its effects and likelihood.

We can now ask: supposing one wanted to fight an all-out nuclear war, what would be the best way to set about it? Although it is possible to refine to great lengths the per-mutations of nuclear possibilities – and some American writers have discovered arguments as subtle as those of the medieval schoolmen – there are basically three likely ways of using nuclear weapons. They are: (a) a suicidal response, where a country with a small store of weapons threatens to inflict as much damage as possible on an enemy if attacked; (b) a counter-city war, in which by attacking his population, one hits at the enemy's *will* to make war; (c) a counter-force war, in which one attacks the enemy's *means* of making war.

The logic of the first case is simple. Few weapons are needed, as long as they are secure from a first strike. Paradoxically though, it would appear to pay a country with this kind of nuclear force to appear rash and aggressive in peacetime, because the value of the weapons lies in the appearance of being about to use them. One can only fire them at the point of death, and if fired against a major nuclear power they guarantee death soon after. Therefore, logically, the weapon is never likely to be used because, while there is life, there is hope. So a country with this kind of deterrent must appear irrational.

The second kind of war needs more weapons, but they need not be any more accurate. This is perhaps the kind of war we imagine when we have nuclear nightmares: a hail of rockets directed against our cities and, after that, the end of everything. This is indeed one way of bringing an enemy to his knees, by so hurting and frightening his population that he capitulates. It is important to notice that the actual *instrument* of war in this case is the fear, panic and disruption suffered by the *survivors* and the pressure they bring to bear on their government to end the war. In other words, they are forced to revolt against their government. Hence civil defence also embraces counter-revolution. This argument also suggests that it may be very important to the attacker to preserve the enemy government simply so that there should be someone who *can* surrender.

This is the kind of war airmen began to plan in the 1920s and which the RAF and the USAF tried to wage against the Third Reich. In the Second World War two dynamic processes were balanced against each other: the rate at which Britain and America could make and man aircraft, and send them to bomb Germany, and the rate at which this bombing reduced German war production. In fact, as we have seen, the pressure on the population had very little effect.

It seems obvious to extend the principle to nuclear war. There can be no lack now of deaths and disruption among the enemy people. But the change has had a counter-balancing effect. The Second World War was a hand-to-mouth business. Almost everything that was needed by the combatants was made during the war, often only months before it was used. Civilians and cities were an extension of the supply organization to the front line.

But nuclear war is likely to be so short and violent that there will be no opportunity to make or distribute anything useful during its course. All that will be needed for the Third World War has been made and stored these five, ten, fifteen years. As vital war elements civilian populations are now irrelevant. This presents some difficulties to anyone planning a counter-city war. In destroying cities, he is having little military effect. America, Britain, the NATO countries of Europe could fight just as well, or badly, with or without their cities.

The destruction of the West's cities *may* produce collapse, surrender and the achievement of the Russians' basic war aim by unopposed occupation of Europe and America, the capture of the West's remaining nuclear weapons and our means of producing more. But in attacking populations alone, the existing weapons, commands, communications and military–economic base of the West are left more or less undamaged. If the attack fails to produce surrender – and there is no reason why it must – we remain almost intact as a military force while Russia has used up a good proportion of her weapons. She would be, in terms of striking power, in a *weaker* position, with her ultimate aims little nearer achievement. And as soon as the western powers had cheered up their surviving populations – or subjugated them – they would be in a position to reopen the war.

To be sure, a democratic western government might capitulate under heavy strikes, but it might not. Once the damage had been done, there would be more reason to continue to resist, to fight back and cripple the conqueror.

When one is planning a major war, it is a good idea to choose a strategy that *must* succeed, not one that might work. On these grounds alone city strikes seem an unattractive procedure for the Russians, or indeed anyone else. This is confirmed by a reading of *Military Strategy*,[14] a book written in 1962 by 15 leading Russian strategists and senior officers. The editor, Marshal Vassily Sokolovsky, was Chief of the Russian General Staff from 1953 to 1960, and the book sets out the basic primer of Russian strategical doctrine. The first edition created enormous interest in America, and stimulated a good deal of comment and analysis. A second edition of Sokolovsky was published 18 months later with a few interesting differences from the first. A commentary and analysis will be found in Wolfe's *Soviet Strategy at the Crossroads*.[15] A third edition was published in 1968.

At first Sokolovsky makes odd reading, because all the paraphernalia of American nuclear thinking, to which we have grown accustomed, the 'city trading', 'megadeaths', 'escalated responses' and so on are ignored. Some American writers put this down to military conservatism and naïveté on the part of the Russian authors, but, looking at it as an amateur, the explanation seems to be more fundamental. Each side describes war in terms of its own experience, and what it knows instinctively will defeat it. The Americans, richly populated, turbulently political, think in terms of war against populations. The Russians, to whom the individual is a servant of the state to live or die as may be necessary, who survived the loss of 25 million people in the Second World War, and only won because of superhuman efforts to evacuate and increase their military–economic base, think in terms of a counter-force war.

So, as Garthoff, the American editor of the translation of the first edition cited here, reads Sokolovsky:

... 'counter-force' versus 'counter-city' strategies are not ever opposed and discussed as they are in this country [America]. The long standing Soviet view, expressed again here, clearly places primary emphasis on strikes against Western nuclear delivery systems, but also includes attacks on the main administrative, economic and transportation centres. The pattern is one of an all-out attack in which tactical rather than political restraints give priority to counterforce strikes but give no 'sanctuary' to cities.

In fact the Russian authors several times speak slightingly of attacks on populations alone.[16] A favourite device of Russian writers, whose words may be cited against them out of context, is to put tricky arguments into the mouths of the ideologically contemptible, where they can be demolished with credit. Thus:

> The western press has also discussed what should be the main objective of the first nuclear attacks: nuclear devices (rocket-launching sites, air bases, nuclear stockpiles, etc.) or political centres and economic objectives. Certain authors consider it necessary to deliver the most powerful blows first at large cities, industrial regions and other military and economic targets where the peaceful population is concentrated. They believe that such objectives do not require special reconnaissance – their locations are known – and an unexpected nuclear attack on them could result in tremendous loss of morale among the population.
>
> At the same time certain western theoreticians justifiably consider that such a method of unleashing war is practically impossible under present conditions.[17]

Earlier the authors remarked of Second World War experience:

> Another aim of the American–British air strikes, viz. the demoralisation of the German people, was not accomplished. True, the German people suffered relatively high losses from air attacks, but their ability to resist was undermined not by these attacks, but by the operations of Soviet troops in German territory.[18]

They go on to quote Brodie, one of the leading American experts: 'The urban area bombing of World War 2 must be set down unequivocally as a failure',[19] and finally, Sokolovsky:

> Enormous damage can be done even to large countries, especially when mass nuclear strikes are made on the most densely populated industrial regions. But in order to achieve complete victory over an enemy, it is still necessary to eliminate his ability[20] to resist, to destroy all his nuclear weapons and naval bases. This can be done only by completely defeating his armed forces and occupying his territory, including those regions where his safely concealed strategic weapons are located.[21]

In the ten years since this passage was written and published, both sides have moved away from the idea of an all-nuclear war to strategies in which conventional weapons play a larger or, indeed, perhaps the only part. It is not unreasonable to suppose that, however much counter-city strategy has developed in America, the Russians' ideas are still basically the same.[22]

These considerations would seem then to make massive attacks on populations alone, if not completely unattractive, at least a less rewarding way of waging war than one usually imagines. There is, however, a way of fighting this kind of war without the disadvantages outlined here. That is, paradoxically, by *not* shooting at populations, but only threatening to. This strategy was proposed, rather invertedly, by MacNamara in a celebrated speech at Ann Arbor in June 1962. 'Principal military objectives,' he said, 'should be the destruction of the enemy's military forces, not of his civilian population . . . giving the possible opponent the strongest imaginable incentive to refrain from striking our cities.'

Schelling, one of the ablest exponents of the idea, gives this gloss:

> Cities were not merely targets to be destroyed as quickly as possible to weaken the enemy's war effort, to cause anguish to surviving enemy leaders or to satisfy a desire for vengeance after all efforts at deterrence had failed. Instead live cities were to be appreciated as assets,

as hostages, as a means of influence over the enemy himself. If enemy cities could be destroyed 12 or 48 hours later and if their instant destruction would not make a decisive difference to the enemy's momentary capabilities, to destroy *all* of them at once would be to abandon the principal threat by which the enemy might be brought to terms. . . . Live Russians and live Russian cities might be our most valuable assets.[23]

And

If the inferior side cannot hope to disarm its enemy, it can survive only by sufferance. It can induce such sufferance only by using its capacity for violence in an influential way. This almost surely means not exhausting a capacity for violence in a spendthrift orgy of mass-massacre, but preserving the threat of worse damage to come.[24]

There are odd consequences to this line of thought. The first is that he who shoots first loses the round. Thus, if the American government say to the Russians, 'Do this and that, or we will destroy Moscow', and the Russians don't, and so the Americans do destroy Moscow, what do they do next to get the Russians to comply? In fact, to be brutally realistic, the *Americans* suffer most, because (a) they use up a threat, (b) they use up some of their weapons, while the Russians do not, (c) the Russians are relieved of the need to go on making concessions to defend Moscow. The strike may hurt the Russian leaders a great deal emotionally. But they cannot restore the city by doing what the Americans want. The threat may be bad for morale, but once it is carried out it is likely to stiffen resistance, as did bombardment of German cities. Brodie remarks that the lesson of strategic bombing against Germany shows that the ability of an attacker to influence morale, and the effect of morale on behaviour, when the enemy government has all the reins, is much less than had been supposed.[25]

A city-hostage strategy is like the actions of a burglar who breaks into your house, picks up one of your dozen priceless Ming vases, and says: 'Do not attack me, do not call the police, but give me all your vases or I will drop this one.' If you do as he says, you lose all your Ming vases. If you go for him or ring the police you certainly lose one, but maybe you save the rest.

So far we have considered the Russian people and the Russian government – or the American – as one. Would a city strategy be more useful if it attempted to separate one from the other? In this view, when one threatens a city strike, one is either appealing to the sentiment of the opposing government (assuming that it is physically well protected) *or*, trying to convert the enemy population into allies with the same interests as yourself. As to the first point, one might observe that the sentiments of governments are notoriously changeable and rarely conflict with their self-interest. And at this stage in the conflict, a government's interest in the safety of its populations would be no more than sentimental, faced as it would be with the urgencies of an implacable attacker and a mutually destructive war. The preservation of cities can do the defending government little military good; their loss is no military harm. The threat cannot be guaranteed to produce results. The other case poses grave difficulties in conveying the attacker's interests to the defender's population. An obvious defence would be to deny communication – by radio jamming, shooting down leaflet-dropping aircraft, press censorship. But suppose that the attackers' demands have been got across to the citizenry. They then have to exert pressure on their government, which has presumably retired inside its anti-nuclear carapace. If the government can withstand nuclear bombardment, *a fortiori* it can ignore civil commotion. In this situation the ordinary mechanisms by which pressure is brought to bear on government – adverse voting at the next election, parliamentary criticism, hostile press comment, street demonstrations, riots – would be all irrelevant. With all preparations made for war, a western government would probably rather see law and order completely collapse than give in to an attacker's demands. Even if the defender's population manage to exert real pressure on their government, then carrying out the strike is to kill allies of the attacker – which the defending government by this stage might appreciate; if they do not manage it, then there is no point even having threatened to kill them, let alone in doing so.

Finally, as Schelling again pertinently remarks, if the enemy has inviolable counter-city weapons of his own, you might as well fire yours at your own cities as his, for retaliation will be certain.

One tends perhaps to think of the Third World War as, in the jargon of ten years ago, a 'spasm' war, in which both sides shoot all their weapons as quickly as they can at each other's cities and then resign themselves to what fate wills. But the present inviolability of nuclear rockets changes all that. Sure of the security of their weapons, there would be no need for an instant response, even if among the nuclear powers a city was hit in days of piping peace. There could be time for the most careful inquiries, to write formal notes asking for explanations; and, if necessary, to wait a day, a week, a month before firing a retaliatory shot. This need not be an escalation: a smaller city could be attacked, or a military installation.

Counter-city strike: casualties

Although logic seems to suggest that a city-strike strategy is less attractive to an enemy than one might at first suppose, it is not inconceivable that a nuclear power might get so exasperated with the British that he determined to extirpate us – perhaps as an example for the others. We calculate rough casualty estimates by judging visually how many weapons are needed to cover each of the 16 largest cities (see Table 6, page 81).

The strike on those cities kills only 16 per cent of the British. The next 35 cities in size – those with between 100 000 and 300 000 inhabitants – offer 4 million more casualties, and the 84 with between 50 000 and 100 000 people hold another 6·3 million.

So for an expenditure of 143 weapons (240, allowing for misfires) an attacker could kill 20 million or slightly more than a third of us. It seems very difficult to do more than this.

Table 6: *Number of casualties caused by a strike on the sixteen largest British cities*

City	Population millions	Area thousand acres	Radius equivalent circle(s) miles	Population density thousands sq mile	Number of weapons 1-MT	Number of weapons 5-MT	Casualties per cent	Casualties millions
London	8·25	397	4×7·1	13·3		4	41	3·4
Birmingham	1·1	51	2×3·6	13·8		2	85	0·94
Manchester	0·62	27	2×2·7	14·8		2	93	0·57
Sheffield	0·53	45	2×3·3	7·6		2	89	0·47
Liverpool	0·70	28	2×2·6	16	2		75	0·52
Leeds	0·51	40	2×3·2	8·2	2		62	0·32
Hull	0·30	14	2·6	13·5	1		74	0·22
Nottingham	0·31	18	3	11		1	95	0·29
Leicester	0·29	18	3	10·3	1		66	0·19
Coventry	0·33	20	3·2	10·6	1		62	0·24
Stoke-on-Trent and Newcastle-under-Lyme	0·34	32	4	6·7	1		45	0·16
Bristol	0·43	27	3·7	10·2	1		50	0·22
Cardiff	0·29	23	3·4	8	1		56	0·16
Newcastle-upon-Tyne and Gateshead	0·35	15·7	2·8	14	1		71	0·25
Glasgow	0·96	40	4·5	7·1		1	74	0·71
Edinburgh	0·47	35	4·2	8·5	1		41	0·19
Totals	15·8	830·7	—	12·1	12	12	56	8·85

It is surprising that the Americans set so much store by the theory of counter-city war because their own experience seems decisively against it. The US Strategic Bombing Survey investigated on the spot, immediately after the Second World War, what the political and economic effects had been of the massive Allied bombing of Germany. It came up with rather depressing conclusions; production in bombed cities tended to rise, as is well known; also the death rate tended to fall because the very young and very old were evacuated. In Düsseldorf, a city of half a million people and 50 000 houses, 15 000 houses were destroyed in 1943 but only 1300 people killed and wounded. Morale had little relationship to the weight of bombs dropped.

Table 7: Relationship between morale and weight of bombs dropped

Tons of bombs	Morale (per cent)		
	High	Trusting leaders	Willing to surrender
30 000	44	48	59
6000	42	44	59
500	51	52	54
0	59	63	51

The effect of area bombing was negligible, or even negative:

City houses destroyed (per cent)	Low morale (per cent)
60–80	53–5
40–59	56–9
20–39	59

It was concluded that the Germans feared the Gestapo more than the bombs, because the bombs were random, but the Gestapo highly selective. In fact, heavy bombing tended to *reduce* the chances of a successful revolution because it disrupted the opposition parties, who were without protection, while it left the government relatively untouched. As long as the police held, a regime on the defensive had nothing to fear.[26]

One of the leading American experts writes: 'The urban area bombing of World War 2 must be set down un-equivocally as a failure',[27] and finally, Sokolovsky, the author of the Soviet strategic manual says:[28]

'Enormous damage can be done even to large countries, especially when mass nuclear strikes are made on the most densely populated industrial regions. But in order to achieve complete victory over an enemy, it is still necessary to eliminate his ability[29] to resist, to destroy all his nuclear weapons and naval bases. This can be done only by completely defeating his armed forces and occupying his territory, including those regions where his safely concealed strategic weapons are located.'

In the years since this passage was written and published, both sides have moved away from the idea of an all-nuclear war to strategies in which conventional weapons play a larger part. It is not unreasonable to suppose that, however much counter-city strategy has developed in America, Russian ideas are still basically the same.[30]

Swiss civil defence
However, counter-city strikes cannot be ruled out in the future, and it might well be worth protecting ourselves against them.

As an example of what can be done, here is an account of Swiss civil defence excerpted from an article by the author in the *Sunday Times Magazine* of 28 March 1976.

The Swiss are as keen on insurance as other nations are on football, but all things considered the cost of their premiums is not all that high. They spend 1·7 per cent of their GNP on defence – about a third as much per head as we do, and about a quarter of that on old-fashioned civil defence – an art which many people in Britain thought had been lost. They have had a nuclear civil defence programme since 1962, when a large majority in a national referendum set it going, and plan by the end of the century to have a blast and radiation proof shelter for everybody and everything of value in the country. Every new building has a nuclear basement; every household is required to build and stock its own private shelter; and there are generous community shelters, with hundreds of command posts, barracks, equipment stores and hospitals tucked away underground.

For instance, in the centre of the village of Veyrier, a small suburban commune to the south of Geneva, there is a long concrete ramp sloping down into the earth. At the bottom huge steel and concrete doors protect a vast garage full of fire pumps, trailers, tools and clothes for the local section of the rescue organization. It is all brand new and must be worth at least £100 000. Next to it is the commune's brand new command post and communal bunker – warm, brightly lit, cheerfully painted, animated in the evenings by the lightly moustached *jeunesse* of Veyrier who use it for table tennis. Here is an immaculate kitchen, full of gleaming stainless steel, a dormitory for the school above, and a command post with a telephone exchange, radios and an elaborate *planification* of the commune's inhabitants, resources and hazards.

In the Swiss political system, the commune is perhaps the most important level. Sometimes the country seems not so much an uneasy confederation of 22 (or 24) cantons, as of several thousand communes. Each finds 20 per cent of the civil defence budget, and exercises considerable autonomy over how it is spent. Veyrier decided to hire its own civil defence chief, who doubles as village policeman, and proudly wears the village's uniform. A brisk, intelligent, self-made man, M— admires the Beatles and Rolling Stones, and proudly shows off the completeness of the underground arrangements. Village individuality obtrudes even here: the commune did not like the military-style mattresses issued by the federal civil defence office at Berne – a city which, in their eyes, is the mother of inconveniences – and decided to buy their own much more luxurious Dunlopillo ones. They had the blankets for the shelter specially woven in the village colours: green with a yellow stripe.

This bunker with its own well, its own diesel generating

plant, air filters, and stores for two months' sealed-up existence, will stand an overpressure of three atmospheres – the blast from a 1-MT warhead 1 mile (1·6 km) away. It is just a fragment of the second, underground Switzerland. Since 1962 every new building must incorporate a blast and radiation-proof shelter for its occupants and some more. The new main railway station at Berne, for example, has wide steel doors at the end of the ticket hall. Beyond them are shelters for 4000 people – as it might be travellers caught in mid-journey on the day – and everything they will need during their stay underground. Beneath a new ice-skating rink in the same city there is a vast shelter. It has room to house 2000 more strays, Berne's civil defence command post, the barracks of a detachment of engineers and firemen, and a magnificently equipped 400-bed hospital behind blast-proof doors big enough to admit ambulances. The whole thing is complete down to an entryphone, so that latecomers, trudging through the fall-out to find the doors shut, can explain their predicament to those within. Inside, you open the cupboards to find blankets, pillows, sheets, knives, forks, spoons, drugs, bandages, lancets, syringes – the whole thing could be in business within an hour. And this is only one of 600 hospitals just like it, spread around the country.

Eric Alley was until recently the Civil Defence Officer of Birmingham. He is one of those open, kindly souls who thrive on disaster as an opportunity for doing good, driven into exile by the reckless sloth of his countrymen. He is now deputy director of the International Civil Defence Organization, a UN sort of operation with its headquarters in Geneva, and lives in Veyrier. His glasses gleaming with enthusiasm, he says 'Veyrier, with only 6000 inhabitants, has a better built and equipped control bunker than we had for the whole of Birmingham.'

Civil defence in Switzerland does not just concern itself with people. There is a parallel organization for industry which protects vital processes and staff; systems for the railways, telephones, broadcasting, and a huge programme for micro-filming documents, ranging from electoral rolls to ancient manuscripts. There is a department which photographs old buildings in minute detail, so that the historic monuments of Switzerland shall rise as good as old from the ashes.

The mind boggles at the scale, the thoroughness, the standardization. It is evidence of paranoia of a very high and determined order – using the word in no insulting sense, but rather to mean the art of ignoring the reassurances of those who do not necessarily mean you well. Paranoia in this sense is something history has taught the Swiss – a people who only exist as a nation because of their own prickly defensiveness. Put simply, Switzerland consists of two chunks of beautiful but quite inedible mountain – the Alps and the Jura – with some fertile lowlands around and in between. Without the lowlands the country is impossible, and the Swiss only wrested and kept them from their much more powerful neighbours by being ready, ever since their first confederation in 1292, to be perfectly bloody to anyone who argued with them.

Their present military posture is simple. They point out that in a Europe of much bigger powers, most of who have nuclear weapons, she could never be an aggressor. Apart from the important north–south road and rail links through the Alps, there are no nuclear targets in the country. She has to fear involvement in a war between third parties, who might want to use her soil and air space for manoeuvre, or who might just be careless with their rockets and clouds of fall-out. The most likely scenario would be a Russian invasion of NATO. The Swiss Army gives itself six days between the first signs from radio traffic analysis of tanks massing on the Hungarian border 200 miles away, to the first T52s crossing their own border with Austria. The army plans to give ground slowly along the central valley between the Alps and Jura, halting the invaders for a while at five pre-prepared blocking zones. Then they withdraw into the mountains to make the enemy's occupation of the lowlands as expensive as possible.

There, in the Alps round Zermatt, one is told they have many a burrow. There are stories of surrealistic retracting radio stations on mountain tops. Look at the cliff face above the Castle of Chinon, say the well-informed, the regularity of the cracks in the rock betrays formidable gun emplacements. There are underground aircraft hangars giving on to mountain runways, hangars big enough to hold the 300 aircraft of their air force. All these installations will resist at least nine atmospheres, or a megaton at half a mile (0·8 km). Getting to them may prove awkward too, because more than 2000 bridges, passes and tunnels are permanently mined, including the alpine tunnels, which the Swiss would probably cut themselves to preserve their neutrality. There is an elaborate air defence system run by computers deep in the mountains.

You do not need to know much about military matters to imagine that this might be a hard nut to crack, and it is a nut full of one of the oddest armies in Europe. The country has a mere 3000 full-time soldiers – maintenance staff in the mountain fortresses, training staff in the army schools, and commanders of divisions. Everyone else is part-time – Hans Mummenthaler, the young director of federal civil defence, for instance, commands a battalion when he is not at his desk in Berne. Four adult males out of five are fit for the army. They train for short periods every year, and still keep their weapons and kit at home. This makes for a lot of army for little money – they spend about a third as much per head as we do, and their expenditure on civil defence is, for a population a tenth of ours, no more than we give to underdeveloped countries.

Yet there is no doubt that if there is a war in Europe, we shall lose most of our resources and 40 per cent of our people, while the Swiss will be almost unscathed in everything that matters. Assuming the major powers cripple each other – as they have the means and the will to do – post-war Europe will be run by the Swiss and the Swedes, the only countries with respectable civil defence. The mind boggles at that, too.

Counter-force war
The third mode of nuclear war, which requires weapons in greater quantity and with much greater accuracy than either

of the other two, is generally called a counter-force war. There are indeed gradations here, according as one side has the ability to destroy completely the other side's arms, or only to 'blunt' his attack by destroying the more vulnerable sections. But the essence of the matter is to devote one's efforts simply to destroying the enemy's means of organizing, supporting and delivering an attack.

Consistently, throughout the 400 pages of Sokolovsky, one sees described a counter-force war in the broadest sense, with over and over again the targeting litany: '. . . the enemy's strategic weapons, his military and economic potential, the governmental and military control system and his troop units.[31]

One passage sets out, almost completely, the Russian recipe for defeating NATO:

> These ends [undermining the power of the imperialist coalition] can be achieved by attacks on selected objectives by nuclear missile and aircraft strikes using nuclear weapons. The most powerful attack will be the first nuclear-missile strike by which our armed forces will retaliate against the imperialist aggressors [etc., etc.] . . . we can destroy military bases (air, military and naval), industrial targets (including atomic, aircraft, missile, power and engineering plants), communications, ports and control posts, etc. But the main targets will be strategic air bases which are very vulnerable since they occupy a great area and are essentially well known.[32]

The reader must remember that in 1961–2, when this was written, America's Strategic Air Command was the West's main instrument of nuclear war. Installation of the present system of hardened Titan and Minuteman sites had begun and this was noted by Sokolovsky, who forecast the missile armaments of America much as they are today.

Since then, according to the late Chief of USAF Intelligence, Major General G. J. Keegan Jr, the Russians have persevered with their plans to put themselves in a position to fight and survive a nuclear war. In an unusual outburst[33] he attacked the complacency of the American intelligence community, which he accused of consistently underestimating the Soviet ability and will to win the Third World War. In a long and interesting article, he said among other things that:

> The United States today lacks the firepower, lacks the accuracy and lacks the yields to overcome the enormous advantage in terms of neutralizing our retaliatory punch which the Soviets have engineered for themselves at great cost. They have removed their civilian leadership from our ability to cripple it. They have removed their military command and control from our ability to destroy or cripple. The nuclear chain of command from the General Staff to the lowest regiment is now beyond the reach of American retaliatory weapons. There is no physical way that we can destroy underground installations which now exist in the tens of thousands, that are now 1000–2500 p.s.i. [70–175 kg/sq cm] blast hardened – the hardest man-made structures in the world. They have put their strategic communications underground. They have put their nuclear weapons underground. They have hardened most of their fighting capabilities – particularly in the defense area.
>
> The entire industrial population of the Soviet Union, it would seem from the evidence which we examined, and the human sources we spoke to, are now 100 per cent protected. Every daytime working industrial shift in the Soviet Union has within a few feet a vast underground bunker hardened to 145 p.s.i. [10 kg/sq cm]. Now unless you get a direct hit against one of these, the incumbents or the occupants are going to survive, and that's precisely what the Soviets have done.

And that:

> I think that a Soviet war planner today, in the Warsaw Pact, given the forces, the capabilities, the combined arms doctrines, the chemical nerve gas weapons, the communications jamming capability, the hardness and survivability of his forces, the great masses of fleet armor, the

development of the new armored personnel carrier regiments, supported by the world's most advanced self-propelled guns, and a nuclear arsenal visible to anyone who will walk over there and pry around, that makes ours blush by contrast, would have every reason for believing that he could take Europe by force of arms, with a minimum of fighting in 24–36 hours, with or without the use of nuclear weapons. That's the posture that they have been placing themselves in.

As we have already noticed, the USAF has a vested interest in Russian armaments, but at the same time, one must admit that Keegan is in a position to know what he is talking about. His assertion in the last paragraph tallies with the British Army's view of itself as 'trip wire' – destined to be used up in the first couple of days of a nuclear conflict, but useful if that extra time gives the Americans a chance to deploy their complete forces.

It is surprising but true that the Americans only began to aim their missiles at point military targets (not silos, but airfields and communications centres) in 1975. Until then they had reserved these targets for their bombers and air-to-surface missiles.

As we have noticed earlier, a counter-force strike would seem likely to divide naturally into two phases: an immediate attack with nuclear missiles against urgent targets, which would be followed up, if successful, by a more leisurely and thorough working over by manned bombers and air-to-surface missiles. This passage seems to define the targets for the first strike:[34]

Naturally the task of eliminating the enemy's means for nuclear attack must be successfully carried out. Up to date and reliable intelligence regarding air bases, missile-launching sites, strong sites for nuclear warheads and the locations of fuel stores and control posts are particularly important.

The targets for the second strike are suggested in general by this passage.[35]

The military and economic foundation of the imperialist bloc is highly susceptible to nuclear attacks. The main economic foundation of imperialism is located in the United States. Here are concentrated the basic production facilities of the imperialist camp, where nuclear weapons, missiles, planes, tanks, ships and other weapons and supplies for military operations are manufactured. The second most important base is West Germany, which has a considerable production capacity. Britain and France are also highly industrialised to a certain extent. The vulnerable features of the economy of the imperialist bloc includes its high concentrations in limited regions, its dependence on imports, and the defencelessness of its communications [across the Atlantic and Pacific]. The United States depends on imported atomic raw material and nonferrous and rare metals, while Britain depends on imported iron ore, petroleum, atomic raw material, foodstuffs, nonferrous and rare metals etc.

In British and American thinking it is generally assumed that industrial production after the beginning of a nuclear war would be either irrelevant or impossible,[36] but the Russians, perhaps remembering the crucial role of tank production in the last war, are not so sure. Thus:

It is possible that a situation might arise in a future war where nothing else will be required apart from the previously established stores of weapons and military equipment. But it would be dangerous to count on such a possibility; industry must be prepared in peacetime to replace possible heavy losses in the armed forces.[37]

This passage is significant as suggesting an intention to attack the West's industrial centres as if they were military targets. Altogether one can draw out of Sokolovsky a fairly convincing targeting doctrine and, from two passages,[38] résumés of the NATO countries' preparations for war in terms of weapons, communications and strategic industries.

The course of the Third World War, as foreseen by the Sokolovsky authors, would run something like this:[39] a heavy nuclear exchange in the first few minutes would use most of the rocket forces in being. This might end the war immediately, but it might not; so Russian planning anticipates theatre campaigns in Europe and elsewhere that may be prolonged for some time. To assist in the defeat of land forces in Europe, an important step would be the cutting of communications with America by destroying ports and sinking ships at sea. After the occupation of Europe, Soviet ideas understandably seem to peter out. There are passages in Sokolovsky that look forward to the invasion of America and the achievement of lasting security through the possession of her 40 000 stockpiled nuclear weapons and the means of producing more, but the actual mechanics of invasion are sketchily described.

However, that is what the Russians seem to have in mind, and from Sokolovsky we can write a list of targets in descending order of urgency. These are:

  (i) Nuclear missiles; strategic bombers.

 (ii) Air-defence systems; radar-control centres, fighters and rockets. These categories would have to be attacked with rockets.

(iii) The instant means of waging conventional war; seats of government and high command, army and naval communication centres, troop concentrations and naval bases.

(iv) The future means of waging war; the military– economic base – factories for nuclear weapons, storage sites for completed weapons; aircraft, tank and explosive factories, shipyards, petrol refineries.[40]

In earlier editions of this book I tried to make some sort of estimate of the number of targets in Britain and the forces that might be brought against them, in order to make an estimate of civilian casualties. On reflection, the argument seems so tendentious as not to be worth repeating. All one can say with certainty is that there are a lot of targets here, and a lot of weapons there, and no particular reason why they should not get together. Britain is so densely populated that the casualties to be expected from a counter-force strike are hardly less than from a counter-city strike (page 80).

Ending a war and the problem of uninvolved allies

These complexities by no means exhaust the strange logic of nuclear war. If such a war were fought, and unless it was an outright spasm war, it would probably proceed by a more or less stately series of blows at military assets or the smaller cities, interspersed with frantic negotiations. It would almost certainly be very much easier to begin than to end, and the necessity of preserving someone on the other side to negotiate with might put each side in difficulties. If Sokolovsky is to be believed, the Russians, and presumably the Americans, plan to destroy the other side's government and high command (if they can get at them). But, as Schelling remarks, 'If we are to get any influence out of our enormous capacity for violence, we had better be sure there is some structure capable of being influenced, and capable in turn of bringing the war under control.'[41] Thus, the USAF decided not to mount a personal attack on the Emperor of Japan in 1945, so as to avoid putting Japanese backs right against the wall, and to preserve a central authority with whom to negotiate.[42] For this reason alone, the enemy capital might be surprisingly low on the list of target priorities – something to attack only when all hopes of persuasion had been exhausted. This opens some interesting possibilities. One of the best ways a British government could defend London might be to sit in their offices as usual, and hold the Polaris missiles in reserve. (As we shall see, protected accommodation in London would anyway be of little value.)

If there is to be negotiation at all, it is also necessary to preserve the means of communication. In all wars until now messages have been able to filter through embassies in neutral countries, spies, special messengers, newspaper stories and so on at a rate which was fast in comparison with the rate of development of campaigns. But now communications within seconds is essential to deal with peacetime accidents as well as the exigencies of war. Hence the 'hot line' between Moscow and Washington via the Atlantic cable TAT 3, London, Copenhagen, Stockholm, Helsinki, Moscow, backed up by TAT 2, Paris, and a radio link via Tangier.

In anything but a spasm war, it is likely that these places will enjoy some immunity, as will the combatants' long-range radio transmitting stations.

If America and Russia only were involved in the war, another tricky problem would arise towards its end. If both the combatants had exhausted their arsenals of nuclear weapons and done, as they must have, a good deal of damage to each other's conventional forces, then they would both be inferior to the powers that now only command negligible nuclear strength. These countries – Britain, France, China, Israel, India, Brazil – would dominate the world, and could, if they acted quickly enough, prevent the late superpowers from rearming by carrying out relatively easy strikes on their weapons factories and stores. So if, in the course of the Third World War, the superpowers found their strength approaching parity with the minor nuclear powers, there might be a strong temptation, even to our allies, to carry out a counter-force strike against us if we had refused to fight.

It is very difficult to foresee the balance of power in the post-war world. The shifts and stratagems *then* might be a good deal more tiresome than those which would have preceded the Third World War. The German joke at the end of the last war may well be relevant: 'Enjoy the war, for the peace will be frightful.'

NOTES

1. Overpressure-distance from Wilfred E. Baker, *Explosions in Air*, p. 128.
2. Richard D. English, Dan I. Beloff, *New Scientist*, 4 July 1974.
3. *Aviation Week and Space Technology*, 11 July 1977, p. 17.
4. *Aviation Week and Space Technology*, 15 May 1978.
5. *Aviation Week and Space Technology*, 7 November 1977, p. 19.
6. Kosta Tsipis, *New Scientist*, 16 January 1975, p. 145.
7. Russia's 60-MT device has been mentioned; on occasion civil-defence planners in America invoke 100-MT weapons, which are assumed here.

8. *Effects of Nuclear Weapons*, pp. 205, 207.

9. R. P. Haviland, *Handbook of Satellites and Space Vehicles*, New York, 1965, pp. 41, 45. A Polaris submarine can fire her 16 missiles no quicker than one a minute. In principle this means that the defender can work back from radar plots of the first missile's trajectory to find the boat's position. Sokolovsky in *Military Strategy* claims that such a submarine would be destroyed after launching only a few of her rockets. But if there is no anti-submarine ship or aircraft near by with the specialized equipment necessary for this kind of detection, the job would presumably have to be done by land-based radars of the BMEWS type, and attack carried out by 'sniping' with IRBMs. Again we have a number of balancing factors. The longer the radar plot continued, the more accurately could the submarine's position be found, but the more missiles it could release. Then it would be necessary to target the retaliating weapon – which would take at least several minutes – and launch it. At a conservative estimate this would take about ten minutes, so the submarine could fire two or three missiles and then move off at high speed, reducing, as we see above, her chances of being hit. Or, if she were firing at extreme range and took no evasive action, the time of flight of the retaliating rocket would be comparable with the time taken to loose off a complete salvo. Since the Russians are making energetic efforts to get a Polaris type fleet into commission, one must suppose that they do not take this problem very seriously.

10. Thomas C. Schelling, *Arms and Influence*, Yale, 1966.

11. G. Trevelyan, *Blenheim*, London, 1965, Appendix C.

12. See p. 159 for a résumé of the damage to Russia.

13. F. C. Ikle, *Social Effects of Bomb Destruction*, Oklahoma, 1967.

14. V. D. Sokolovsky, *Military Strategy*, London, 1963.

15. T. Wolfe, *Soviet Strategy at the Crossroads*, Boston, Mass., 1964.

16. The third edition, a translation of which was made available to me by the kindness of the librarian of the Institute for Strategic Studies, contains a new, long passage criticizing the idea of counter-city war and rejecting the Americans' proposals for rules to put populations out of bounds. In fact both sides are considering their self-interest. The Americans, who can deliver four times as many nuclear warheads to Russia as the Russians can in return, would prefer the Third World War to be a counter-force affair which they might win. The Russians, who have only 15 per cent of their population in large cities, are indifferent to city-sparing rules, and would prefer to hit at, among other things, America's sprawling megalopoli.

17. Sokolovsky, p. 274.

18. Sokolovsky, p. 257.

19. Bernard Brodie, *Strategy in the Nuclear Age*, Oxford, 1965.

20. Not his *will* [PL].

21. Sokolovsky, p. 223.

22. An impression confirmed by the 1968 edition of Sokolovsky.

23. Schelling, p. 191.

24. Schelling, p. 196.

25. Brodie, *Strategy in the Nuclear Age*.

26. S. T. Possony, *Strategic Air Power*, USSBS, Washington, 1949.

27. Brodie, *Strategy in the Nuclear Age*, Oxford, 1965.

28. Sokolovsky, *Military Strategy*, London, 1963, p. 223.

29. Not his *will* [PL].

30. An impression confirmed by the 1968 edition of Sokolovsky.

31. Sokolovsky, p. 288.

32. It is interesting to note that the official maps of Russia have apparently been grotesquely and purposefully distorted, so that hills, lakes, railway junctions, etc., are shown up to 10 miles (16 km) from their true positions (*Guardian*, 21 January 1970). Up until the 1967 edition of the British Ordnance Survey, military airfields were not marked.

33. *Aviation Week*, 28 March 1977, pp. 38–48.

34. Sokolovsky, p. 287.

35. Sokolovsky, p. 288.

36. cf. Brodie.

37. Sokolovsky, p. 324.

38. Wolfe, pp. 89–92, 97–107.

39. See Wolfe.

40. See also a somewhat similar list based on Sokolovsky by N. Hannunian in *Dimensions of Survival*, Rand Corporation, Santa Monica, 1966.

41. Schelling, p. 213.

42. Possony, *Strategic Air Power*, USSBS, Washington, 1949.

4 Revolution

We now turn the coin of violence and consider the obverse of nuclear attack: internal revolution. The rather limited repertoire of a nuclear weapon makes it possible to be fairly precise about the assaults that defensive structures have to withstand, even if one is unclear about where the blows will fall. By contrast, the problem of defending government against its own citizenry is extremely nebulous.

Although it is estimated that about half the world's states have changed their governments by unconstitutional means since the last war,[1] very few of these events have taken place in sophisticated western countries where the forces involved bear any resemblance to those likely to be engaged in Britain. One has to rely on conjecture. A recent pamphlet by a senior army officer who has specialized in civil order sets out this rather unhelpful scenario of a possible revolution in an industrialized western state:[2]

> There would be four phases. The first would be one mainly devoted to recruitment [to the revolutionary party], training and minor aggro on a countrywide basis. The second would be to concentrate on marches and riots leading to demands to change the government. No significant swing in government policy would be expected at this stage but it would lead naturally to the third phase which would involve the use of firearms, explosives and general disorder to attempt to force the government out of office and replace it by one acceptable to the Party. The fourth phase, which was regarded as inevitable, was one of total revolution and seizure of power by force.

It is during the third stage that the hardware we are

discussing will be useful, and one would like to know as much about it as possible. Unfortunately, in spite of the mass of literature on the theory of revolution, there is very little on how to make one work on the day.

Sorokin examined 1622 historical events which one can describe roughly as revolutions. Only 5 per cent happened without overt violence. But the average duration was very short – 'these social crises passed their acute stages within a period of a few weeks'.[3]

Evidence of a different sort is presented by Edward Luttwak.[4] He reviews the history of 381 attempts to change government by unconstitutional means between 1946 and 1964. He finds that of the various methods – civil disorder, coup, military revolt, etc. – civil disorder was the most frequently attempted (40 per cent), with a coup second (23 per cent), but that coups were far more often successful than other methods, with the chances of a clear win over the regime in power of only 4:3 against. Although most of his examples are taken from underdeveloped countries, and so appear not completely pertinent to our problems, it seems the progress of technology tends to favour the coup as against civil disorder. Even by 1917 the firepower of soldiers with machine guns made it quite clear to Trotsky, though not to Lenin, that mob-revolution was, by itself, most unpromising. And the firepower of the soldier is now three times as great. But, in contrast, the sophistication of modern armies makes them far more dependent on technicians as well as officers, and these technicians, who may be civilians, are necessarily drawn from a quite different political background and may be much easier to subvert or circumvent.

Classically one organized a revolution by raising the mob and going to see the king, emperor, caesar, shah-in-shah or whoever the temporal authority might be. He was traditionally to be found in his palace surrounded by regiments – who, having superior firepower, were usually able to decide the outcome of the day. A prudent revolutionary would try to come to some composition with the soldiers beforehand. To raise the mob, it was necessary to take advantage of 'widespread social unrest', and that too was traditionally provided by the regime in the form of food shortages, inflation, lost wars or oppressive taxes. Thus, the French Revolution was precipitated by state bankruptcy manifested by a bread shortage in Paris, and its first overt act was the descent on Versailles by the Paris mob, subtly led by its women – infiltrated by agitators in disguise, it is sometimes said – who asked the King in plaintive tones for bread, and on whom the soldiers were unwilling to fire.

This was the scheme proposed by Lenin for the Russian Revolution in 1917. The necessary social unrest was provided by the defeat of Russian arms by the Germans. St Petersburg was filled with deserters from the routed armies. The streets were alive day and night with shifting crowds. Kerensky, the Prime Minister, acted properly according to the best ideas of the time, and defended the exteriors of the Winter Palace, the Tauride Palace, the Ministries, the telephone exchange, with parties of Cossacks and student officers who waited for the mob to charge down the avenues and impale itself on their bayonets.[5]

Trotsky had other ideas in mind. He planned to take advantage of the general strike which was to be called as a prelude to conflict, to infiltrate the technical seats of power – the infrastructure of the state, as we might now term it. His targets were the telephone exchange, the electricity generating plant and district distribution stations, railway signal boxes, telegraphs and controls, water and sewerage systems. He argued that it was unnecessary to take the buildings where the government functioned if one could prevent officials issuing orders and receiving information. Also, if one could make life in those buildings intolerable by denying water, electricity and sewerage to their occupants, success would be assured within a week.

Of the two revolutions in contemplation, Lenin's classical and Trotsky's technical, it was Trotsky's which happened first. It was so stunningly successful that it made the second almost unnecessary. However, his method, though so decisive at the time, seems little help as a precedent now. The opposition was so feeble, and his technique so undreamt of, that assault parties were able to train against their operational targets: his sailors were able to wander over the central telephone exchange unchallenged in the days before the attack. Outside the Cossacks watched for the massing mob. So distracted were the defenders of the state, that, when on the day, Trotsky's three technicians arrived at the electricity generating station, the Director greeted them warmly, taking them for the guards he had requested to keep off the revolutionaries. Under these conditions the dramatic success which was achieved was not very surprising. It is more instructive for our purposes that Trotsky used the same weapon of technical paralysis against Stalin ten years later in Moscow, and failed dismally, for the Georgian had profited by the lessons of 1917 as it seemed their author had not. So have successive governments in every developed state. When today, in London, you see a sign in the entrance of important telephone exchanges advertising that admission is by pass only, you have Trotsky to thank.

Modern states take great care to protect the technical necessities of government and urban life. It is relatively easy to make them impenetrable to casual callers, more difficult to guard against subversion by those who are legitimately there. So, the main technical danger a modern government has to fear which might prevent its own proper working – as a virus paralyses the nervous system of its host – is the recruitment of parts of its own armed forces to the insurrectionary organization, the conversion of its technicians into saboteurs, or the translation of its civil servants into spies.

The 1943 generals' plot against Hitler is perhaps the nearest example in a technically modern state we can draw on. In spite of the fact that Giskes, the head of the Abwehr's signals organization, was one of the plotters, they failed to seize complete control of the communications system. The insurrection depended on a genuine, though slightly disingenuous, plan prepared by the army and authorized by Hitler to seize key points in major German cities to forestall a popular uprising. It relied only on the Abwehr, and would therefore be as effective against the SS as any other revolutionary group. And the SS were obviously the group most likely to resent Hitler's overthrow. Unfortunately there were five communications centres at Hitler's Rastenburg HQ: three accessible to Giskes, which he shut down after Stauffenberg had planted his bomb, and two controlled by the SS which he dared not touch. Furthermore, he dared not send the order to initiate the countrywide seizure of control by the Abwehr. Consequently, during Stauffenberg's two hours' flight to Berlin after he had planted his bomb in Hitler's map room, nothing concrete was done by his fellow conspirators – the heads of the Abwehr there. In the evening of that unfortunate day a small contingent of troops with some armour and artillery were sent to take control of the Nazi Party Headquarters, where Goebbels, as Gauleiter of Berlin, had charge. He adroitly invited the obscure major in command of the assault party to telephone the Führer at Rastenburg over SS lines. By an extraordinary coincidence this man had recently been personally decorated by Hitler and could therefore recognize his voice. At that the insurrection was over. On Hitler's orders the major arrested his own superior officers, who suffered the usual penalties attendant on the failure of such an enterprise.

The moral one can draw from this unhappy episode is that the seat of government must be defended from assault and infiltration. It should be physically remote and difficult to enter even for those entitled to be there, and it should have diverse communications – apparently, if the SS telephone lines had been cut, there would have been no other way of warning Hitler of what was afoot. Furthermore, communications should not only be multiple, but should pass through the hands of different organizations so that, for example, subversion of post office staff would still leave military networks intact.

The generals' plot was decisively over when Hitler managed to broadcast to the Germans on the evening of the same day, proving conclusively that the plotters' main selling point – that the Führer was dead, the regime collapsed and that they were in charge – was false. So another lesson is the vital importance to a regime of securing its broadcast links to the people.

Some broad conclusions can be drawn from this material about a revolution-proof seat of government:

(i)   It must be physically remote, difficult to find and enter. It must be defensible against assault by guerrillas or paratroops.

(ii) It is much improved by being split into small parts: this makes it easier to defend, and renders conspiracies among the central government staff – particularly the technical staffs – more difficult because their communications between separate elements would have to pass over links controlled and possibly monitored by the regime.

(iii) Communications must be diverse – in both mode and route. Multiple channels of telephone, HF, VHF and microwave radio should be provided.

In fact, there is little difference between these specifications and those for a nuclear stronghold.

Given these precautions, how likely is a revolution to succeed? Katherine Chorley, in one of the first modern studies of the subject, writes:[6] 'The rule emerges clearly that governments of the status quo which are in full control of their armed forces and are in a position to use them to the full effect have a decisive superiority which no rebel forces can hope to overcome.'

So much for the practical preparations of governments to defend themselves against a coup d'état – or nuclear attack. We examine the arrangements made in Britain in more detail later on.

What about the political relationships between governors and governed in these situations? We must first make a distinction between a revolution or coup d'état and a nuclear war, for if there is little difference between the two threats as far as the infrastructure of government goes, they are very different from the point of view of the people at large. To put matters simply: there are four major possibilities:

(i)   a revolution which sweeps its leaders into power;

(ii) a coup d'état which transfers power from one small group to another – by technical, political, or other means;

   (iii) a counter-force war in which the civilian population is irrelevant;

   (iv) a counter-city war in which it is the means of making war (page 80).

In case (i) the people at large must be regarded as the potential enemies of the government. As the British Army's *Land Operations Vol III: Counter Revolutionary Operations* (cited by Bunyan, page 277) succinctly puts it, the following measures are necessary:

   (i) the passing of Emergency Regulations to facilitate the conduct of a national campaign;

   (ii) various political, social and economic measures designed to gain popular support and counter or surpass anything offered by the insurgents;

   (iii) the setting up of an effective organization for joint civil and military control at all levels;

   (iv) the forming of an effective, integrated and nation-wide intelligence organization without which military operations can never be successful (was this drafted by a member of the Intelligence Corps?);

   (v) the strengthening of indigenous police and armed forces so that their loyalty is beyond question and their work effective (this is often easier said than done); and

   (vi) control measures designed to isolate insurgents from popular control.

As Bunyan remarks in *The Political Police in Britain*, since the Second World War, the British Army has dealt with some fifty colonial insurgencies (cf. (v) above), of which Northern Ireland is the longest running. In a home revolution, he estimates that the government could dispose of about a million men on security duties (page   ), which, setting aside those already in the armed forces, is about 1 in 10 of adult males. However, as Northern Ireland shows, it is one thing to deploy troops and another to extirpate revolutionaries.

Just as the body is always host to diseases which only occasionally break out and cause illness, so every state at every time has had people in it who would, if they could, overthrow it. Their part is to point out grievances, to make the people conscious of oppression, and one credits them with many advances in civilization, because the easiest defence against them is for government to adopt the most appealing parts of their programmes, gaining popularity with the people by redressing wrongs. However, when the government is in serious trouble – as it seemed to be in Britain in the mid-1970s because of the world recession – then this course of action is no longer feasible. The revolutionaries find they have real grievances to work with which the government cannot redress. So it is now their part to stir up strikes, demonstrations, stoppages, go-slows, contriving always to put a reasonable face on the matter so that the government is cast as the villain. In turn, the government does its best to make the revolutionaries seem the blackguards of the piece. The miners' strike of 1972 is an excellent example: it was not hard to present their case for higher wages in a good light; but, however willing the government might have been to settle, it could not for fear of massive wage increases in many other industries. In order to shift the blame on to the miners it was announced by the government that there were insufficient coal stocks in the power station yards to last the winter,* and that the country would therefore have to reduce its consumption of electricity. This was imposed through control of the distribution system: most factories, offices and homes were allowed electricity for only half the week. Possibly it was hoped that the resulting irritation would raise public opinion against the miners and force them to settle.

This was an ingenious reversal of the conventional revolutionary tactic of the General Strike. In Britain half the

---

* There is some doubt about this point. I was then a journalist with the *Sunday Times*. To test the matter I proposed that we should hire an aerial survey plane and take stereo photographs of the coal heaps at a sample of power stations, from which the volume of coal could be calculated. My editor said there was no need to waste money on so frivolous an inquiry; he had been personally assured by the Prime Minister that there was not enough coal. When I put the same idea to the editor of the *Daily Mirror* I was told not to be silly: the miners' leaders had personally assured him there was enough.

population lives in towns of 100 000 people or more. Urban life is impossible and rural life uncomfortable without electricity, gas, water, sewerage, food, fuel and transport. It is one of the major duties of government to provide or assure these services, and it is a tactic of the revolutionary, by calling all workers out on strike, to demonstrate the government's unfitness to govern by making it impossible for it to deliver the goods. The generality of a general strike demonstrates in a symbolic fashion the breadth of popular support for the movement, but its practical value to the revolutionary is that it makes urban life impossible, thus proving to the people that they need a new government which *can* control the situation – i.e., him. It also provides, or it is hoped that it will provide, confusion under whose cover he can mount his technical coup d'état, taking over the government whether the people will it or no.

The government's first counter to a general strike is to prevent it happening by the time-honoured methods of buying supine trade union leaders and encouraging the internecine quarrels of the more active ones. The revolutionaries who might foment and take advantage of it are identified, monitored and where possible frustrated, run over or pensioned. If a general strike seems inevitable, then governments try to provide essential services themselves – as was done in 1926, with undergraduates running the tube trains and sailors firing the power stations (see page 20, above). As the machinery of the modern state becomes more complicated, this course of action looks less and less promising. The thought of Royal Navy stokers trying to run a nuclear power station is enough to give anyone pause and the performance of the army as firefighters during the firemen's strike at the end of 1976 was far from satisfactory. However, as industry, and particularly the public service sector, becomes more automated, so its demand for manpower goes down; it becomes possible to treat the small number of those that are left as special cases. They are encouraged to think of themselves as an élite apart from the mass of the working class, who therefore can be isolated from the issues raised by the mass agitator. A particularly vivid example of this is to be seen in the data-processing business: a leading security consultant advocates the creation of an élite to manage computers who will be indifferent to the lures of crime and sabotage that so beset the ordinary workman.[7]

A prelude to a general strike will often be active attacks on servants of the regime – kidnappings of politicians, judges, businessmen, bombings of police stations, barracks, clubs, etc. The point of this activity – apart from releasing the aggressions of those who carry them out – is to provoke repression in self-defence by the government. This must necessarily be general in effect – curfews, searches, surveillances, raids – and is designed to enrage the citizen against his masters. The counter to that is to protect important parts of the state's machinery and to be gentle with such counter-measures as are necessary. The British government seems particularly skilled at this, and often disappoints its internal enemies by the mildness of its reactions.

However, there is no doubt that the West in general, and Britain in particular, is getting ready to fight more intensive internal battles than have been seen for many decades. The miners' strike of 1972, when enormous numbers of pickets prevented the police from opening a coke depot at Saltley, near Birmingham, demonstrated that the police alone might be no match for the workers. A National Security Committee was set up about then, part of whose work was no doubt the quotation at the beginning of this chapter. Its functions also include the building up of intelligence about industrial subversives,* the perfection of emergency control schemes for regional and local government liaison with police down to police station level, so that troops are available – as in

---

* The Ministry of Defence is reported to be considering a large new computer installation in central London to handle classified data, using two ICL 2980s and a 2960 supported by 100 on-line EDS 200 disc drives. One might guess this to be an extension to the UK of the computer system in Northern Ireland that is said to hold security data on half the Province's population (*Computer Weekly*, 9 February 1978, p. 1).

Such an installation would be able to store and process a 1000-word dossier on every adult in the British Isles. It may well use a program

Northern Ireland – to support police action of all sorts. An element of the civil defence control system – the provision of secure communications for government and the denial of them to civilians under the Telephone Preference Scheme will make the revolutionary's life very difficult. As Bunyan points out:[8]

An insurgent force would find itself with no telephones, no mail and state controlled news on the radio and television. Only direct personal communication would remain as an option and this would entail the use of the public highways where patrols could stop and search at will.

One might also add that the use of radio for communication rather than broadcasting would be more dangerous than doing without, because of the monitoring activities of the Composite Signals Organization. The location of any transmitter would soon be fixed, the contents of many coded signals soon read. The motorway system which can be comparatively easily closed to unauthorized civilian traffic, will be a great asset to the government, giving security forces, in effect, internal lines of communication, while the insurgents must move slowly on external lines through the old road system. As we shall see, there is a suggestive closeness between many sites of the civil control system and motorways.

A deeper analysis of counter-revolutionary strategy and tactics is rather beyond the scope of this book, which is to do with hardware. The reader is referred to Frank Kitson's *Low Intensity Operations* and Tony Bunyan's *The Political Police in Britain*, which has an extensive bibliography.

---

developed by Computer Technology Ltd, ostensibly for the Metropolitan Police Criminal Intelligence computer. The difficulty with data handling for surveillance and intelligence is that some of it may be wrong. You may think you are looking for a red-haired activist named Rudi who drives a yellow Cortina and has a girl-friend called Sally, when in fact the man you want has ginger hair, is called Rod, drives a pale green Escort and has a girl-friend jokingly known as 'Silly'. A computer program to deal with these errors is no simple matter.

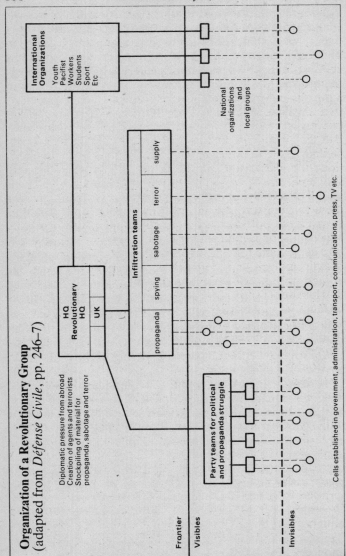

Organization of a Revolutionary Group
(adapted from *Défense Civile*, pp. 246–7)

Diplomatic pressure from abroad
Creation of agents and terrorists
Stockpiling of material for
propaganda, sabotage and terror

International Organizations
Youth
Pacifist
Workers
Students
Sport
Etc

National organizations and local groups

HQ Revolutionary HQ
UK

Infiltration teams
propaganda | spying | sabotage | terror | supply

Party teams for political and propaganda struggle

Frontier

Visibles

Invisibles

Cells established in government, administration, transport, communications, press, TV etc.

Just as it is hard to think of cases (i) and (ii) (p. 102) in isolation, so cases (iii) and (iv) are likely to happen together. My own feeling is that the Russians will not feel they have 'won' the Third World War until they have successfully executed a counter-force strike on America and NATO. In the process many civilians will be killed. They would probably not rely on a pure counter-city strategy if only because they do not allow their civilians to interfere with affairs of state, and so would not rely on producing victory over their enemies by this means. But they would no doubt not be unwilling to create and use civilian panic to interfere with the West's military preparations for war. Although the Third World War is usually spoken of as a 'spasm war', the month before it happens will be full of activity: outfitting mothballed formations, moving them to their war stations, preparing cities for evacuation, clearing the ports of shipping and a million and one tasks which must be carried out to put the country in as good a posture as possible for war. In previous wars this process relied heavily upon civilians, for instance, in the railway system. It is argued that the civilian stands in so much risk in nuclear war that his cooperation may not be entirely relied upon. It would be much in a potential enemy's interest to remind the shunter who couples the trucks which carry the tanks to reinforce the British Army on the Rhine that megatons of retribution may soon visit him in Pinner, or Warrington, or wherever he lays his troubled head and that carelessness in this matter, which results in the tanks arriving at Barrow-in-Furness rather than Harwich, will not go unnoticed.

It is no doubt with such considerations in mind that the military send large sums of money to remove their operations from the public sphere. Their communications are maintained by their own people. Their heavy armour is carried across the Channel in days of peace. Their 75 000 reservists go to Germany not by train, but by aircraft conscripted from British Airways, whose crews are willy-nilly reservists, and depart from RAF bases.[9] Their stores are bought years before and wrapped in airtight tins, so that ill-feeling on the shop floor shall not hold up war production and therefore the war.

However, it is hard to imagine just how the government proposes to ready itself for war in the midst of millions from whom war preparations can hardly be concealed, but who lack even the most rudimentary shelter from its effects. One can visualize – only too easily – mass panic as people try to leave the cities they fear will soon be devastated, and in the process making any sort of movement by road or rail quite impossible. It would not need much organization by an unfriendly power at such a time to produce quite spectacular interventions in the government's plans. There are signs that such questions are beginning to be considered by the Ministry of Defence, though whether any simple remedies are possible is open to doubt. The very fact that Britain has not even a cosmetic civil defence programme for its citizens makes it unlikely that we shall take any active part in the Third World War.

The Russians in their civil defence programme – and perhaps the Americans if they decide to take the same precautions – have removed their essential industries and the workers in them into the depths of their hinterland. There the factories can be spread out to present a large number of low-value targets each of which has to be attacked separately. Perhaps it is more important that these installations are removed from the city populations who might be stirred up by fear of attack to overrun them. In effect civil defence forces a government to winnow out what is vital for survival in society, stockpiles, depots, communications centres, research establishments, etc., and to put it out of the reach of the rest of the people.

This is a strategy of defence which we, living in a small island, are not well equipped for. But still we can do our best, and indeed something of this sort of segregation is to be seen in the preparations of the military and civil authorities. It is a trend which I think will continue over the next few decades, arising out of the direction in which technology and economics are going.

So one can expect that the preliminaries of a nuclear war will be much occupied with attempts to subvert the mass of the people, and to build up secret networks for sabotage and

propaganda within them. By the same token the defenders
must be vigilant to reassure, to prevent promises of retribution being received in the homeland, to track down and
unmask the agents of the enemy. The whole process is
admirably described in Michael Foot's *SOE*, in the context
of the invasion of Europe. The same basic material is
represented in an interesting light in Antony Cave Brown's
Bodyguard of Lies – an essential book for anyone who wants
to understand the reality of war.

It is a pertinent question, not just how far the civilian
population, with a little organization, may be willing and
able to interfere with the preparations for and conduct of the
next war, but also how well the numerous staffs of the civil
and military control systems – let alone the soldiers themselves – may be expected to perform when their families and
all that they are fighting for may be hourly vaporized. 'Better
red than dead' may become a widely fashionable point of
view. As we have seen, things at the beginning of the Second
World War seemed much as they do now. The prospect of a
million casualties in London alone must have made a
majority of those actively involved in the war effort wonder
whether it was wise to continue. And yet people faced this
risk and fought. (Of course, it was soon discovered that the
risk was greatly exaggerated, but that does not invalidate the
willingness to face it at the beginning.) So there is nothing
new in the physical prospect of mass destruction waiting for
the persons and families of those who help the war effort.
This was the risk you ran if you stood up against Rome, and
yet many did. The Jewish rebels in AD 60, when finally
besieged in Masada, killed their children, their wives and
finally themselves rather than surrender, inflicting a
propaganda defeat on the Romans which was taken very
badly.

The missing ingredient in our picture of the Third World
War is morale. At the moment it is hard to conceive of any
cause worth fighting for, so it is hard to imagine anyone
willing to fight. And this squares with the facts, for as far as I
know there is no cause worth going to war about and therefore no imminent prospect of the war happening. When a

cause appears, we shall see whether people are willing to run the risk for it.

Certainly, a military planner thinking about going to war tomorrow must expect that the civilian population of Britain, once they properly understand the issues, will not be anxious to help. And he must make preparations accordingly to avoid the malice of civilians.

So scenarios of both internal and external attack include 'Traîtrise, défaitisme et pacifisme, propagande et déclaration d'amour', as the Swiss Civil Defence Handbook puts it, and many other terrors which somehow look much worse in French, which the government must counter, and in whose plans the civil defence system will play a large part.

Of course these threats are the bread and butter of Britain's political police: the Special Branch, MI5, Military Intelligence. It is interesting that back in the peaceful 1960s the Intelligence Corps was organizing counter-intelligence exercises in which subversives were winkled out of their civilian cover.[10] Successful armies have always paid attention to this sort of business. The British government has a centuries-old tradition of espionage and counter-espionage: the freedom we enjoy today to say some of the things we like, is due to its success in the past at stifling, sidestepping, neutralizing threats to its authority. It worries some people that the increasing preparations for internal war undertaken by such bodies as the National Security Committee will mean that the government is better informed about dissent, and readier to view it not as legitimate political disagreement but rather as a threat to law and order, incipient revolution, treason. The sad fact is that, so long as your words produce no effect, you will be perfectly free to utter them. When they start to produce results, you will be gagged. This is how governments work.

NOTES

1. Richard Clutterbuck, *Protest*, p. 141.
2. Anthony Dean Drummond, *Riot Control*, RUSI, 1975.
3. Sorokin cited by Peter Calvert, *Revolution*, London, 1970, p. 129.
4. Edward Luttwak, *Coup d'Etat*, London, 1968.

5. C. Malaparte, *Technique du Coup d'Etat*, Paris, 1948, pp. 23–44.

6. Katherine C. Chorley, *Armies and the Art of Revolution*, London, 1943, p. 20.

7. Peter Hamilton, *Computer Security*, London, 1972, p. 38.

8. Bunyan, *The Political Police in Britain*, p. 284.

9. *Aviation Week*, 20 February 1978, p. 11.

10. See, for instance, the unmasking of the Ancient Order of Druids operating as a front for the Welsh People's Republic in the *Intelligence Corps Magazine* of 22 December 1960, pp. 36–8.

5   *British civil defence and the H-bomb*

The chapter that follows gives an account of British Civil
Defence as it was in 1967, based on interviews, information
and facilities given me by the Home Office and other government departments in aid of an article I was writing for the
Sunday Times Magazine.[1] In the Spring of 1968 spending on
civil defence was drastically cut, and the Civil Defence
Corps disbanded. However, the skeleton of the organization which was in being then still survives, as do the installations which housed it, so this material is still relevant to our
subject.

The Civil Defence Corps
The Civil Defence Corps was a 'slightly metaphysical con-
ception being a voluntary organization to assist local authorities in carrying out their statutory duties'.[2] The corps built
on the A R P expertise of the Second World War to produce a
body of esoteric practice in rescuing the trapped and suc-
couring the injured after nuclear attack. Through the 1950s
the corps was a moderately flourishing organization. It was
then settled that the business of shepherding, nourishing
and generally looking after the survivors of nuclear war was
the business of local authorities, who raised and partly paid
the corps, their executive arm in this task. The enthusiasm
with which individual local authorities took up the corps idea
differed considerably, usually in inverse ratio to their experience of bombing during the war. Thus Coventry, for
instance, resolutely refused to have anything to do with it,
until considerable government financial pressure was
applied. On the other hand, mild bribery by Whitehall
spread the word. Since each authority had to nominate a

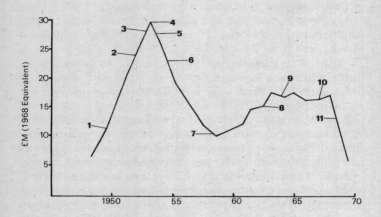

Fig. 16*

1. *Start of urgent CD preparation against Russia's A-bomb.*
2. *Deep government shelters being dug at Holborn and Whitehall.*
3. *V-bomber force operational. Select Committee on the Estimates finds incomprehensible delays in CD preparation.*
4. *Elm trees felled in Kensington Gardens (see Figure 33, page 219).*
5. *Explosion of first American H-bomb.*
6. *First Russian H-bomb.*
7. *First British H-bomb. American and Russian ICBMs begin to come into service.*
8. *Reorganization of CD to cope with H-bomb attack begins.*
9. *Home Office advertises completeness of national CD preparations.*
10. *Rescue and First Aid sections of the CD Corps abolished.*
11. *Rest of CD Corps abolished.*

The annual published totals for civil-defence spending 1949–69, corrected to 1968 values. Two phases are seen: an intense effort between 1949 and 1958 to prepare for the A-bomb, and from 1958 to 1968 a more steady effort of adaptation to prepare for the H-bomb. Since 1969 spending has remained at a low level.

1955: ROC equipped and trained to report radioactive fall-out.

1956–66: rebuilding of posts underground, and reorganization into 29 groups.

1967–69: rebuilding of Group Operations' Rooms.

Information from 'Royal Observer Corps' (pamphlet), HMSO, London, 1970.

'war controller', an official who would take executive charge of all government in its area in the absence of any higher organization, and part of his salary was payable by central subvention, the Home Office found itself feeing many a town clerk from the Civil Defence Vote.

But, from the first, one can detect an air of vacillation about the whole business. On the one hand, it was a good and necessary idea, there were many honest people passionately convinced of its usefulness, and the parent organization had done marvels during the Blitz; but long-term, passive preparations for war are often a waste of time, money and effort because methods of war alter before they are used. This was the fate of much early civil-defence work. So at the top preparations were often contradictory and half-hearted. There is a story, perhaps apocryphal, of a senior civil servant in the 1950s who saved the nation £20 million by forgetting to buy reserve fire-fighting equipment for civil-defence stocks. His negligence was the subject of an inquiry, he was severely reprimanded – and the next year got a knighthood.

Four years after the formation of the Civil Defence Corps, Parliament's Select Committee on the Estimates examined the totality of civil defence with a critical eye.[3] But if preparations were, as they found, dilatory the attack expected was derisory. The intercontinental rocket was then only a dream of Werner von Braun in America, and his late colleagues in Russia. The H-bomb had not been brought to its present pitch of perfection. It was expected that an attack on Britain would be mounted by aircraft carrying Hiroshima-type atom bombs. Three out of four would be shot down by the RAF, and altogether ten 10-kT bombs were expected to burst over British cities. To deal with the resulting disruption the wartime regional commissioners were revived, but they were now to be given radiation- and blast-proof war-rooms, and their job was mainly operational co-ordination of rescue services.

The Committee noted:[4]

The war rooms are approximately 7500 square feet [700 sq m] in area and of two storeys around a Central Map

Room extending the full height of the building. When possible the lower storey is partly underground. Dormitory and light refreshment facilities are provided to allow 24-hour shift working. The ventilating plant will be designed for the later incorporation of gas filters which have been designed and produced by the Ministry of Supply. The average cost of these war-rooms will be about £65 000 each, including £12 000 for the required protection. In most cases suitable sites have been found close to existing Regional office buildings on the outskirts of towns.

So far so good, but the Committee found numerous examples of sluggishness. The war-rooms had been given high priority in 1950, but no start had been made until 1952, and the programme was then not completed.[5] In 1948–9 a national civil-defence plan had been produced, based on strategic guidance from the chiefs of staff. This was estimated to cost £260 million over the period 1951–5. But by 1953 only half the estimated sum had been spent, although the original plan was 'not [even] a comprehensive scheme of preparation for war'.[6] The committee noted: 'Such plans as they [the civil departments] had were destroyed by successive budgetary reductions and policy decisions regarding expenditure on equipment and capital works.'[7] For instance, a tentative London County Council scheme to require all new buildings to have basements strong enough to support the weight of debris that might fall on them was held up by two years' argument with the Treasury, although the cost would only have been £2 million.[8]

There were 'incomprehensible' delays of five years and more in assuring the nationalized industries that their civil-defence schemes would be paid for by the government.[9] On the evidence assembled here it would be reasonable to suppose that the Treasury was unconvinced of the usefulness of civil defence, but there is another explanation. It now seems likely that the government was spending at least £9 million on digging an elaborate bomb-proof headquarters under London. Since this is 11 per cent of the total actually spent[10] on civil defence from 1951 to 1955, some penny-pinching is understandable.

Other more positive preparations noticed by the Committee were the rehabilitation of the Second World War system of petrol pipelines and storage tanks across the country, the mass production of an improved civilian respirator, the building of protected duplicate control rooms for the electricity grid, the building of protective walls round the larger generating sets, transformers and switchgear. The gas industry was encouraged to continue with its national pipeline grid. Various preparations were made for ports.

After 1953 the V-bomber force became something to be reckoned with, and pre-emptive counter-strikes on it entered civil-defence calculations. Fall-out became a problem for the whole country, and the corps was accordingly instructed in the complexities of monitoring, warning and sheltering.[11] The war was still seen as a spasm affair which would be over in a fortnight; during it, control over the community would in effect pass from the local authority – the town hall and the police – to the Civil Defence Corps. But towards the end of the 1950s it became apparent that the Third World War would not be an afternoon's picnic that could be superimposed to ordinary life. During its rigours people would still have to be housed, fed, sanitized, watered and doctored. Realistic preparations for war meant developing the Civil Defence Corps into a completely parallel set of social institutions which could perform every function of local and central government in the shambles of nuclear conflict. This was a lot to ask of a voluntary organization when professionals could hardly do the peacetime job. But the organization into regions, with hardened seats of government, was still oriented towards a spasm war whose main civil-defence problem would be as it was in 1941: rescue of those trapped in collapsed buildings. The subordinate organs – the sub-regions and groups – were designed simply for this purpose and had no relationship to the continued life. of the communities they served.

By 1962 this idea of an all-embracing Civil Defence Corps had to be abandoned. Already there is the material for an archaeology of civil defence: relics of the atom-bomb phase – massive blocks of concrete – are to be seen standing desolately in odd places. At the Lawnswood government site to the north of Leeds, for instance, a fine control, one of the 1953 war-rooms, is to be seen from the road. Heavily protected and now deserted radar stations stand disconsolately at Wartling, near Eastbourne, and Bolt Head. There are air-defence control rooms at Epping Forest and Cardiff on the Wenallt, which last also shows the distinction between the military and civil powers, for the city's civil-defence control is housed in a similar concrete building a couple of miles away, next door to the GPO's training school.

The next scheme envisaged far more continuity between peacetime and wartime control. The basic duties of looking after the citizen in war were to go on being the local authority's job, as they were in peace. The regions, which until then were designed purely for the operational task of rescue, were completely reorganized to follow county and city boundaries. They were split into sub-regions on the same plan.[12] County, borough and town councils were to develop within themselves a hardened core – much as central government had done long before – so that they could still function after an attack. Emergency legislation would allow them to delegate their powers to an emergency committee of three or so people, who would, if necessary, be able as well to wield all the powers of central government in their area.

Reorganization involved considerable expenditure on new bunkers to house all these fragments of government, but this time, perhaps remembering the fiasco of the 1950–3 war-rooms, which were now useless for their intended purpose, few controls were purpose-built either for the sub-regions or local authorities. There was great emphasis on adaptation of existing structures.

In 1962–3 the Estimates Committee took another look at civil defence as part of an examination of the whole Home Office.[13] Their scrutiny was less than searching this time, and partly obscured by the members' inability to understand the principles of carrier-wave signalling over telephone land-lines. However, they discovered – significantly for our purposes – that civil-defence communications caused one of the largest outlays of any of the Home Office's multifarious responsibilities, amounting to £1·6 million for lines, and £300 000 for radio, in the then current year. Since the Post Office spent £2·8 million on trunk cable in 1962–3[14] it seems that more than half their efforts were not, as represented, directed towards improving the telephone service, but towards improving the government's citadel.

The Committee's main strictures fell on a pamphlet issued by the Home Office called *Advising the Householder on Protection against Nuclear Attack*:[15]

> Although primarily intended as a training publication it is written in the form of advice to the householder, to whom however it is not readily available . . . In the opinion of your Committee the average householder who reads what to do in the event of imminent nuclear attack, and is told, if driving a vehicle, that he should 'Park off the road if possible; otherwise alongside the kerb', will not form the impression that the civil defence measures taken by the Government are of any value whatsoever.[1]

With the general deployment of hardened nuclear missiles by the superpowers, and as the realization of the very heavy pre-emptive strikes that would be sent against Britain as the island base of the NATO alliance bit into the official and the public mind, so the usefulness of the Civil Defence Corps, as it was originally conceived, became difficult to accept. The idea of rescue was the first to collapse. A counter-city strike like that imagined in Table 3 (see page 46) would leave some three million people trapped in their houses. Blitz experience showed that a rescue party of eight men can dig out 2½ people in an eight-hour shift, which means 400 000 teams working one shift on and one shift off for 48 hours. This demands 3·2 million men, or one in three of all the active male survivors. Even if fall-out would permit work in the target zones, it would be quite impossible to organize, equip and concentrate them in time.

So in 1967 the Rescue and First Aid sections of the corps

were abolished, leaving it, in effect, as a cadre of organizers and communicators at local-authority level. (The corps, being an open and public affair, had never had a place in the secrecies of government and regional organization.) And in the spring of 1968, in response to the continuing financial crisis, the corps was abolished completely. A Home Office circular of late 1968 said:

> The Government's decision should not be construed as implying the abandonment of all civil defence measures. The objectives of the care and maintenance policy are to retain the very considerable physical assets of operational value (such as the existing sub-regional and local authority controls and their communications, and stockpiles of essential supplies and equipment) which have been built up since the last war; to maintain amongst senior staff of local authorities some general knowledge of the basic facts of nuclear warfare; to maintain a nucleus of knowledge about civil defence techniques, and to continue with essential central and local government planning to enable the level of civil defence preparations to be raised again should the need arise.

It seems that in the present scheme, subordinate positions in the regional and sub-regional controls would be mainly filled by the police. In other words, future civil-defence activity should consist primarily of planning how to raise the level of preparations should the circumstances demand it (e.g. during a period of international tension) rather than of making physical preparations against the contingency of an imminent war.

The appropriate central government department will continue with the development of emergency plans in matters for which they are directly responsible, including the arrangements for the government chain of control in war, emergency ports and shipping, communications and broadcasting, the Warning and Monitoring Organisation and the due functioning of the power industries, but without incurring capital expenditure on the creation of new physical assets. Local authorities retain the civil-defence functions prescribed in those regulations made under Section 2 of the Civil Defence Act, 1948, which still remain in force.

Planning now posits two pre-war phases: a period of 'international tension' during which time civil-defence measures would be 'reactivated', lasting two to three weeks, and a forty-eight-hour warning period during which dispersion of people and resources would, one hopes, be carried out.

Although the suppression of the Corps and the ending of active preparation causes a lot of agony among civil defenders – those who remain after two decades of public contempt and government attrition are passionately devoted to their creed and see in it all sorts of remedies for peacetime as well as wartime ills – a great deal is left. In particular the country has the hardware for two elaborate networks of observation and control.

The ROC and UKWMO

The Royal Observer Corps (ROC) is staffed by volunteers who must train for a minimum of eighteen hours every six months, and during a national emergency, devote not less than twelve hours a week to their duties.* They are equipped with 873 bunkers[16] at intervals of roughly 14 miles (22 km) all over the British Isles. Each bunker is large enough for four men. It will protect them against moderate blast and intense fall-out, and is equipped with simple devices to monitor the position of bursts, the strength of blast and the intensity of fall-out. The readings of burst direction and blast pressure from two or more posts, reported to one of 27 Group Controls, give the position and yield of bursts. Some of the Group Controls have an electronic burst position indicating system called AWDREY. Radiation meters allow the development of fall-out plumes to be monitored and enable countrywide predictions of the fall-out situation to be made by the UK Warning and Monitoring Organization (UKWMO). The sector controls report to five 60-man sector controls. At this level information about the attack is brought together and passed to the military who need it in order to assess the threat to their people and installations,

* 'Royal Observer Corps' (pamphlet), HMSO, London, 1970.

and also to the government which needs it for strategic purposes, as part of the input to whatever bargaining process is going on, or to order appropriate retaliation, and finally to the Home Office system of civilian control (which I have already described in broad outline) so that people can be evacuated from the paths of fall-plumes. An essential element is the huge computing power of the Meteorological Office at Bracknell.

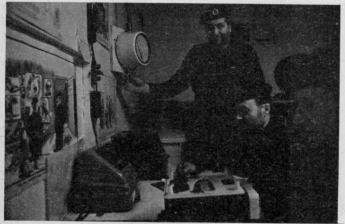

Fig. 17 Crew of an ROC bunker on exercise.

Air defence

The air defence problem is to monitor all air activity in a country's airspace and as far out on every side as may be possible – to identify friend and foe, detect radar jamming and pinpoint the transmitters responsible, compute interception courses for fighters and missiles, launch them at the right moment and then to recover the fighters safely. The wider the area of insensitive sea or land around your borders, the easier the job becomes. Thus America, with the whole of Canada between her and the Russian threat, has ample time to deploy her defences; Holland, which can be flown across in six minutes, needs to react quickly.

What makes the whole job very difficult is the enormous number of civilian aircraft which may mask or disguise a secret enemy attack. For instance, at any one moment there are some hundred civilian and six military aircraft on British radar screens – and any one of them could be an attacker. What gives the problem urgency is not just that an attacker may slip through and bomb a factory or a railway station, but that he may catch your airforce on the ground and completely destroy it (as the Israelis did to the Egyptians in 1967). An efficient air defence system is therefore not just a luxury for civilians, but an integral and essential part of every modern state. Aircraft are safe only in the air. But they cannot spend their entire lives flying and have to be launched at just the right moment to escape attack and hit the attacker, whether they are fighters or bombers.

It is easy enough to state the air defence problem in these broad terms; it is much less simple to decide how to carry it out. First, you have to decide on the threat. Britain and NATO are menaced (or not, according to how you see the strategic situation) by some 640 out of a possible 860 Russian bombers, all of which are capable of low-level attack and all of which carry nuclear weapons. They may fly high or they may fly low. The may come down the Norwegian coast and over Scotland, or dash across the Baltic, Denmark and the North Sea. Then there is the possibility to be considered that the Russians may opt to make a sneak attack using an airliner adapted to operate as a bomber.

These possibilities are, of course, all rendered rather unlikely by the theory of deterrence. More likely, in practice, is that they may make probing flights into our airspace to test defences, and they may operate electronic intelligence (ELINT) and electronic counter-measure (ECM) aircraft to analyse and confuse the defences.

Historically speaking, the threat at the end of the Second World War and into the early 1950s – when the pattern of Britain's air defence was set – was an attack by relatively few nuclear bombers coming from the east at a sensible height, say, 40 000 feet. The prime object of the British system was to get our bombers off their fields in East Anglia, Lincolnshire, and Yorkshire and away to attack their targets before they were bombed on the ground. Hence the air defence system built was a screen to the east of these areas. Because any likely war was expected to be only a spasm affair, the control centre, so long as it was to the west, did not need to be protected. Thus we have Sector Operations Centres (SOC) with radars, at Neatishead near Norwich, Boulmer in Northumberland, Staxton Wold in Yorkshire and Buchan in Aberdeenshire; each has a range of 300 miles (480 km) against aircraft 60 000 feet (18 000 m) (the limit set by the horizon). There are similar radars at Patrington, a satellite (dependent) radar at Saxa Vord at the north tip of Shetland, a radar in North Uist, and a radar in the Danish Faroes to cover the gap between the Hebrides and Iceland, where, no doubt, the Americans maintain several stations. The UK air defence system also has inputs from most of the civilian air traffic control radars, which are at Lowther Hill in the Borders; Bishop's Court at Killard Point in Northern Ireland; Clee Hill in Shropshire; Burrington near Barnstaple; Ventnor in the Isle of Wight; Ash near Canterbury. The controls for all these are at West Drayton, and the Air Defence operations centre is at Strike Command Headquarters at High Wycombe.[17]

Similarly, NADGE (NATO Air Defence Ground Environment), which is a homogenized and computerized revamp of the earlier air defence systems of the border nations, has a chain of some 17 high-power radars with overlapping coverage right along the Iron Curtain, from the Turkish border to the north of Norway. Another 68 sites are involved in the system, which must include smaller gap-filler radars and link sites for data transmission – cable, microwave and a chain of tropospheric scatter stations from Greenland to Turkey. Computers are installed in 37 of these sites.

Unhappily, while air defence systems have settled into this simple mould of a fence along the borders of the 'free world', air war has changed. Low-flying bombers that refuel on their way have opened Britain up to the north; for even a Linesman-type chain of radar stations right across the North

Sea would not protect us against aircraft flying at 100 feet (30 m) or less. In fact, the radars in that part of the world are somewhat patchy.

When one comes to think about it, land-based radars are not what are needed. The Americans, while they still have a vast array of additional systems, are in the process of scrapping their massive original and expensive SAGE system for the defence of the US and are now building four Over-The-Horizon (OTH) radars, each scanning one quarter of the compass out to several thousand miles, and a fleet of Airborne Warning and Control (AWAC) aircraft. These last are Boeing 707s with 20-foot (6 m) radar scanners on their backs, which look down and pick out low-flying aircraft from the doppler shift in their radar returns, and direct friendly fighters on to them. But even the Americans with their enthusiasm for new military hardware are jibbing slightly at the cost of AWACs, and their susceptibility to jamming. The Americans are trying hard to sell the system to the RAF and other European airforces – on the reasonable grounds that we need it even more than they do, being, as they are, nicely protected by Canada.

Over-the-horizon radar

An important development in early warning, yet one which is proving hard to perfect, is Over-The-Horizon radar. The principle is simple enough and is fundamentally the same as microwave radar with which we are all familiar. Instead of using radio waves in the centimetric region, which travel in almost straight lines and limit radar ranges against aircraft to 300 miles (480 km) or less, one uses waves in the high frequency band (HF) (3–30 MHz) which are normally used for intercontinental communication. They bounce alternately off the ionosphere and the earth's surface to give ranges of

---

Fig. 18 *Some of America's past and present Over-The-Horizon radar sites which ring Russia and China. They can operate either alone using backscatter, or with a second receiver site using forward scatter. By way of illustration, the coverage of the pair Dyabakir-Tokyo is shown. Various target sites in Russia and China are also indicated. (After Owen Wilkes,* OVER THE HORIZON RADAR, *SIPRI, Stockholm, 1978.)*

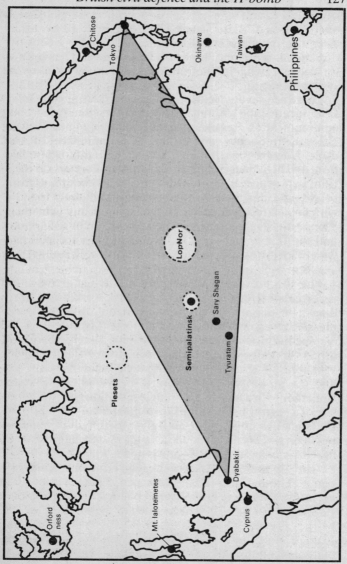

several thousand miles. A powerful, directional transmitter emits pulses of these waves which are reflected by distant aircraft targets and which are then detected in a sensitive directional receiver. This much is obvious and has been so for decades; what has not been obvious is how to make the system work.

There are several snags. The first is to secure good ionospheric reflection without too much absorption. Again, as in communication frequency management, it is necessary to tailor the frequency used to the time of day and the sunspot cycle. Low frequencies are necessary at night to get reflection, and high ones during the day to avoid excessive absorption. In practice, an OTH radar needs a secondary, vertical, sounding radar to test the ionospheric weather, together with an HF receiver to search the band for quiet channels. The best radar frequency is then calculated by a computer and the transmitters and receivers adjusted accordingly – which, for installations as powerful and complicated as these are, is in itself quite a performance.

The second snag is that signals of interest arrive at the receiver at extremely low vertical angles. Aerials which produce a beam only 2–4° above the horizontal are necessarily massive structures whose most important feature is a good conducting ground plane extending some 3 km in the forward direction. This can be, and has been, done on land by laying vast areas of wire mesh, but it is much easier to use the sea, and the majority of OTH are to be found on the coast. Together with a need for low angle radiation goes the necessity of a narrow beam in the horizontal plane – this improves the signal-to-noise ratio and gives better discrimination between targets. To produce a beam 1° in the HF region an aerial array about 1·5 km wide is needed.

Already the difficulties seem staggering but worse is to come. The majority of the returned signals will be from ground and sea; a 50 kW OTH radar at the Appleton Laboratory at Slough, where much of the early theoretical work was done, showed about 1 mV signals on the aerial from ground clutter, while returns from aircraft were predicted as one hundredth of this voltage. Happily, picking these out is not as difficult as it might seem, for if HF radars are imprecise about distance and bearing, they are acceptably accurate when used to detect radial motion through doppler shifting of the returned echo. At 20 MHz, it is possible to resolve a 1·5 knot difference in target speeds, while ground and sea clutter is easily filtered out.

Ranging is not so good. Since the signal is busy bouncing off the ionosphere for the first 1000 km out from the transmitter or receiver, no echoes can be returned from this region. Range resolution is apt to be 20–40 km and relative to a known target, an accuracy of 2–4 km can be achieved. This is for signals on the first bounce – that is, out to a distance of 4000 km. Signals that have arrived by two bounces, will show worse resolutions.

The real difficulty in making these devices operational, however, has been in understanding the mechanics of the bounce off the ionosphere. This layer is the interface between two fluid layers and is disturbed as the surface of the sea. One can see the lower manifestations of ionospheric waves in the occasional bands of high cloud that look like breakers. These waves, together with more random swirls and twists, distort the returned echoes like mirrors in a funfair. Professor E. D. R. Shearman of Birmingham University, who uses an ingenious aperture synthesis technique to apply OTH radar to the study of sea waves far out in the ocean, likens the result to the 'undulating, warped view we see of the bottom of a swimming pool when looking down at it through the rippled water surface'. [18]

What has made OTH radar a useful tool both for the military and for oceanographic and ionospheric studies, is real-time computer processing of the echoes, using the distorted pre-doppler filtered ground returns as a guide to the state of the ionosphere, so that appropriate corrections can be applied to active targets. (Interestingly enough, the same problem occurs in processing the returns from the huge low-frequency sonars that survey equally vast areas of ocean for submarines, and for the same reason – that is, waves on the sea surface.) One ionospheric disturbance that, it seems, no amount of computer processing can correct is when the ionosphere is punched in by blasts of electrons from the sun to form aurorae. So OTH radar paths ought really to avoid latitudes higher than 60°.

The first thorough description of an OTH radar with military potential appeared in June 1974.[19] The paper described the US Navy's Project Madre radar at Chesapeake Bay, Virginia, which can look south to Cape Kennedy to get experience with returns from rockets and their ionized wakes and across the Atlantic to follow commercial aircraft. As long ago as 1961 it was tracking flights out to 4000 km with 50 kW of power. The aerial array consists of a double row of dipoles in 90° corner reflectors, and measures 93 by 43 metres. A large, low-angle HF aerial of some interest was built in Australia at Rockbank, 20 miles (32 km) north-west of Melbourne, in the early 1960s. It consisted of several slow wave structures lying parallel on a bearing of 306°, each four wavelengths long, including the large ground plane. Altogether the aerial used some 25 miles (40 km) of wire. It worked at a fixed frequency near 20 MHz and could be steered by phase shifting the feeds to the different sections to cover Singapore, Calcutta and the UK.[20]

The one great advantage that HF radar has over centimetric radar is that targets of military interest give returns by resonant, rather than optical reflection – since their dimensions are often comparable with a half wavelength ($1/2\lambda$ at 20 MHz is 7·5 metres). This means that they re-radiate as well in the forward direction as backwards to the transmitter. Consequently, OTH radars can be employed in both forward- and back-scatter modes. Thus near targets can be examined by having a receiver near a powerful slewing transmitter, and far targets can be studied by placing another receiver at the far end of a great circle through the area of interest. This makes sense on economic grounds as well, since one transmitter, which tends to be a heavy and expensive item, can cover twice as much ground. A constant satellite link would be needed to co-ordinate frequency shifts at the receiver and transmitter.

So far nothing much has been published about the military applications of OTH radar, but we can make some intelligent guesses by extrapolating from the Madre results. The basic radar equation says that if the aerial gain, noise conditions, target reflectivity and frequency are constant, the minimum transmitter power needed to produce a usable return varies as the fourth power of the range. One can adapt this to the forward-scatter mode by saying that the transmitter power (P) is equal to $Kd_1^{-2}.d_2^{-2}$ where the target is a distance d_1 from the transmitter and d_2 from the receiver. Inserting the Madre result that 50 kW successfully illuminated aircraft targets at 3000 km, the constant turns out to be $6 \cdot 17 \times 10^{-10}$ when d is in km and P in watts.

The known OTH radar sites are Orford Ness in Suffolk, built by the Americans and operated until recently by joint British and US staff; Cyprus, built by the British and operated by the Americans, probably on the eastward facing coast at Cape Greco – where there has been a spur of the NATO ACE HIGH tropospheric scatter communication chain working to Adana in Turkey since at least 1969 (see Figure 13). Another OTH site is at Dyarbakhir (another ACE HIGH station), a third at Ching Ma in north-west Thailand, and others at Tokorazawa in the suburbs of Tokyo (where it causes the ultimate twentieth-century crime – television interference), Chitose, Hokkaido in northern Japan, Awase in Okinawa, Shemya in the Aleutians. Taking Cyprus and Okinawa for the moment, one sees that the cover to be expected would take in many of the areas in central Asia which must be of interest to British and American intelligence. (As well as detecting aircraft and missiles, OTH also reveals nuclear bursts, which focus or diffuse the radio beam, producing unusually bright or dim echoes from ground about as far away again.) One of the areas 'visable' would certainly be Tyuratam, the Soviet Union's main rocket launching station; others would include the Kara Kum desert and the Semipalatinsk regions where the Russians are reported to have tested nuclear weapons, the Sary Shagan ABM development centre, the Tarim desert where the Chinese are reported to test missiles, as well as their Lop Nor nuclear proving ground. Lop Nor lies exactly on the great circle joining Cyprus to Okinawa.

A back-scatter radar in Cyprus running only at 33 kW (many ordinary broadcasting stations run at higher powers than this) would just illuminate Tyuratam, while a transmitter broadcasting with a power of 300 kW would nominally cover the whole area in Figure 19; in practice about four times as much power would be needed to allow for absorption on the second bounce. (The coverage for 200 kW is shown to illustrate how much more rapidly forward-scatter coverage increases with power than one would expect from the fourth law for back-scatter radars.)

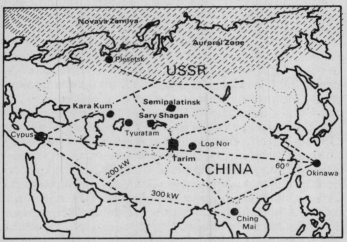

Fig. 19 OTH radar coverage between typical stations at Cyprus and Okinawa for transmitter powers of 200 and 300 kW.

No doubt the victim of OTH intelligence cover would like to take steps to stop it by jamming the receiver. Although a relatively low-powered transmitter in the receiver's beam working at the right frequency would obliterate target returns, to do this operationally might be difficult. It would perhaps be possible to shield a particular site from a particular receiver by putting a jammer between them, but the problem of tracking and imitating the radar frequency would remain. The intruders would anyway be able to re-site the receiver, which is not a very expensive item, particularly if it only had to watch in one direction.

Although the Cyprus-Okinawa path gathers in a rich harvest of sites, doubtless the Americans and British would like to watch the other areas – particularly Russia's northern rocket launching site at Plesetsk, near Archangel, and their northern nuclear testing ground in Novaya Zemblaya. It is significant that Orford Ness lies very close to the great circle through Plesetsk and Okinawa. We were told when it started operating that Orford Ness was for the study of HF propagation in high latitudes through aurorae. One can now see that this was perfectly true, though the Ministry of Defence was careful not to say why they should wish to spend so much to learn about this recondite subject. One must assume that the experiments were a failure, since the station was closed down in 1972 after a year's operation. It may be a coincidence, but Orford Ness lines up with Tyuratam and a point on the north-west Australian coast not far from the US Navy's controversial station at North West Cape for controlling Polaris submarines. It is possible that there is, or was, an OTH receiver there also. Or, again, it may have been intended to work with the Australian Army's low angle array at Rockbank. But since the path would have been 14 000 km or more and the power demanded at least 1·2 MW, one must assume that the returns were too weak to be useful.

However, the Orford Ness array is of some interest, since it is the only known military site to have been photographed in enough detail to make some guesses about the design. It consists of a fan of 18 aerials, 8° 40′ apart, spread over 150° whose axis bears 60°T.

Each aerial consists of a curtain of vertical wires about 450 m long, 60 m high farthest from the sea, tapering to 13 m at the front. It is not immediately apparent how the electronics work. The vertical wires may act as a broad-band slow-wave structure – rather like a TV aerial – to give directivity, but in that case one would expect the height from front to back to vary logarithmically rather than linearly. On the other hand one could interpret the sloping wire at the top of each curtain as half of a conventional long wire V, with the curtains being

switched in pairs by the equipment visibly at the front of the
fan, to straddle the desired azimuth. An aerial of this sort
needs a terminating resistance of about 430 ohms, and this
may be the purpose of the two metallic mushrooms – about
ten metres high and one metre in diameter – at the centre of
the fan. If one imagines that they dissipate heat at about the
rate of a domestic fan heater, they would cope with the
necessary 500 kW. In the horizontal plane one might expect
a beam width of 5° 30′. At the lowest frequency of operation,
6 MHz, the beam width would be about 26°. When the
transmitter was operating, everyone would have to be
cleared from the site lest their eyes be cooked.

If this interpretation is correct, Orford Ness is an odd
design and one not usually used for transmitters, since so
much energy is dissipated in the terminating resistors. However, there may be other economic trade-offs that are not
immediately apparent. For instance, the structure of the
masts that support the curtains is reported to be most
unusual, being made of concrete or earthenware drainpipes
cemented together. No doubt this is to avoid eddy current
losses in metal masts, and perhaps the guy wires are formed
from terylene. (ICI briefly marketed a synthetic non-stretch
rope for staying aerial masts; it was also offered as shrouds
for yachts but failed to perform well, and is no longer
available.)

It is unclear just how successful OTH radar is. American
air defence is said to be about to be remodelled using four
OTH radars and the DEW line to replace the chain of
coastal microwave sets. However, in 1975 four OTH transmitter sites and five receivers were shut down. A discussion
of the problem is to be found under the title 'Over the
Horizon' in *Jane's Weapons Systems 1977*. Recent reports in
the wireless press indicate the contrary, though. Radio
amateurs complain of extremely strong transmissions from
what must be an OTH radar in Russia operating somewhere
'near Gomel, in Byelo-Russia,[21] with transmitter powers of
20–40 MW.

Allowing for losses in bouncing the signal once or more
from earth and ionosphere, 40 MW is the sort of power that

would be needed to illuminate the centre of the USA. No doubt the Russians are interested in American aircraft and missile tests which are carried out in Utah just so as to be out of the way of surveillance. The range would be about 6000 miles (9600 km) and the time for a radio signal to go and return about $^1/_{10}$ second, which squares well with the Russian station's 10 pulses per second.

Recent work[22] suggests that it is possible to measure the size and shape of distance targets by illuminating them with signals of different frequencies. If this becomes operationally possible, it will give the defence warning of the numbers, type, speed of their attackers, with a rough indication of the range and bearing.

Home Office control systems

The development and purposes of the Home Office control systems have already been described; now we turn to the structure and organization of the controls. The country is divided into twelve regions: nine in England, with Scotland, Wales and Northern Ireland. English regions are further subdivided into two sub-regions each, Wales into two zones, and Scotland into three. Each of these has a sub-regional control (referred to after this as an S-RC). These are designed to give protection against fall-out, and some of their use of existing highly protected sites – like the one under Dover Castle – must give considerable protection against blast as well.

Under slight protest the Home Office was persuaded to take me round one of the S-RCs in the summer of 1967.[23] Accompanied by an Assistant Secretary and the civil-defence organizer for the region, we drove to a hill-top in a fairly remote part of the country. The concrete road, cracked and grassy, led through a broken-down gate and past a collapsing house. Cows lounged about; there was a rusting perimeter fence with holes in it. Round a corner of the hillside, a large block of concrete came into view. We parked on the broken hardstanding in front of it, and rang a bell beside the rusty metal grille over the door. It was obvious that no one ever came here.

But the peeling blast-door behind the grille was opened by a trim figure in a black double-breasted uniform. I was surprised to learn that the custodian was a retired Captain RN, and to see that the inside was as immaculate as a battleship. Large diesel generators kept the place light and warm; a communications room boasted high-speed teleprinter equipment and a locked cipher room, the telephone exchange was impressive, and upstairs, wall maps were set out for a large-scale exercise. There was a tiny BBC broadcasting studio connected by hardened lines to all the transmitters of the region.

I was told that the reel of tape visible on a console had a warning of attack recorded on it, and that in thirty seconds normal broadcasting could be stopped all over Britain, and the output from this tape substituted. I was not told precisely what form of words was used on the tape, and this reticence is not surprising, considering the confusion caused in Germany towards the end of the last war by British broadcasting of fake evacuation orders to German people on frequencies used by their own radio stations.[24]

It was evident that life here in war would be far from luxurious. Sealed tight as a submarine, this landship would have a complement of 400 souls. The regional commissioner and half a dozen subordinates had rooms of their own – the commissioner's was a small, bare apartment, with a bed, a table, a telephone and a combination-locking filing cabinet. There were no wardrobes – people will sleep in the clothes they come in. There was a dormitory with three-high bunks for everyone else.

Current plans for the organization of regional and sub-regional governments are quite elaborate. The commissioners of both will be 'persons of ministerial rank', nominated by the government in the period of tension before the day, and appointed by royal warrant. The sub-regional commissioners and their staffs would go immediately to their controls. I was told that the commissioners and their larger staffs would disperse themselves in odd corners of their regions. But on reflection, this seems hardly likely. The chain of command is constructed on a redundancy

Fig. 20a BBC broadcasting studio in an RSG in 1967. The reel of tape in the foreground was said to contain an attack warning for broadcast to the nation.

principle. If any element is knocked out the elements around can combine to replace it. Thus, if an S-R C is eliminated, the County and Borough controls below it and the Regional Seat of Government (RSG) above it can take over its function. It is likely that this principle applies with more force near the top, so that if the National Seat of Government (NSG) is destroyed, there is a replacement national government to be drafted together out of the RSGs. It seems that the RSG staffs are sheltered in the military's Regional HQ bunkers, forming a national government second team.

Fig. 20b   Communications centre in the RSG, showing Telex machines and tape readers. The door, right, leads to the cipher room.

After the attack, and when residual radioactivity permitted, each commissioner would set up his organization in some suitable location – perhaps a town hall, or a large office block in a town that had not been hit. So each region contains three or four potential governments, either protected or dispersed; it is most unlikely that all will be knocked out. Similarly the regional commissioners and their staffs, together with the surviving ministers, form a dispersed national government, in addition to the staff of the protected national seat of government.

The regional and sub-regional governments contain representatives of almost all government departments, with other useful undertaking: the police, fire service, electricity, gas, water, hospital service, the BBC, the GPO and also local leading figures in industry who are given authority to organize their surviving colleagues in petrol, transport, building and food distribution.

Lower level staffs of S-RCs will, one hears, be provided mainly by the police – a task which would absorb some 2000 to 4000 people. This use of the police may always have been the plan for S-RC manning; if it is new, it is interestingly in line with the role of the civil-defence control system in fighting an internal war.

Below the S-RCs there are 211 county and metropolitan county councils with smaller but roughly equivalent staffs who can, if necessary, govern their areas autonomously.[25] Each council has two controls, one in or near its peacetime headquarters, one in another part of its area. So, for example, Cheshire County Council has its principal control in the basement of County Hall at Chester, with its standby in the basement of the Municipal Buildings, Earle Street, Crewe.

Each headquarters is linked by telephone, teleprinter and VHF radio to its S-RC, neighbours and to its subordinates among more than 1000 smaller local authorities. Three-quarters of the cost of radio and land line communications is paid for by the Home Office.

In addition to the radio facilities provided by central government subvention, there is an organization of radio amateurs* called RAEN – Radio Amateur Emergency Network – who will put their VHF equipment at the disposal of police, ambulance, fire and local authorities. One correspondent suggests that in South Devon, for instance, RAEN would be the exclusive providers of emergency radio communication for the local authority.

---

* In Britain, radio amateurs have to pass a fairly stringent examination in order to get a licence from the Post Office. They form a somewhat exclusive and conservative group.

War Cabinet
Clwyd County Council War Planning

Wartime Appointment	Résumé of Duties and Responsibilities.	Chief Officer
Controller	To act on behalf of the Emergency Committee to employ and control all the resources at the disposal of the County to the greatest effect to preserve and maintain the life and morale of the population assuming such extra responsibilities as may be placed on him by the Government of the day.	Chief Executive Officer
Deputy Controller	To deputise for Controller as and when necessary. Staff deployment to Controls. Staff shelter and welfare.	Deputy C.E.O. and Director of Admin. & Management Services
Assistant Controller	Staff Officer to Controller. Control centres, staffing and admin. Allocation of Radiac Instruments. Telephone Preference Scheme. Provision of Scientific Advisers, Staff Training. Advice to public on Home Defence. Co-ordination of District Council War Plans.	Emergency Planning Officer
Legal Officer	Requisitioning (Legal) Summary Courts of Justice. All other legal matters.	Director of Legal Services
Emergency Meals Officer	Communal Emergency feeding. Emergency Feeding Centre. Emergency feeding staff.	Director of Education
Emergency Homeless Officer	Care of homeless persons. Setting up and manning rest centres. Control organization for homeless.	Director of Social Services

Information Officer	Dissemination of information to public from Central Government and Clwyd. News sheets, etc.	County Librarian
County Works Officer	Repair of roads, bridges, public utilities, etc. Advice on and co-ordinate available resources. Carry out individual works schemes. Maintenance of Essential Service Routes.	County Surveyor
Emergency Repairs Officer	Strengthening of Key Premises. Advice on Public Shelter. Repairs to damaged premises. Advice on temporary dwellings.	County Architect
Reconnaissance and Communications Officer	Field Reconnaissance. Maps and plotting. Control signals staff. Emergency communications.	County Planning Officer
Health and Hygiene Officer	Liaison with Area Health Authority on medical care and hygiene of population. Casualty Services. Advice to District Councils.	Occupational Medical Officer
Financial Officer	Financial Advisory Service. Salaries and Wages. Compensation.	County Treasurer
Transport Officer	Overall responsibility for all transport. Collection and disposal of Radiac Instruments. Emergency stores.	Transport Co-ordinating Officer
Requisitioning Officer (premises and land)	Requisitioning of ear-marked and other premises.	County Estates Officer
Fuels Liaison Officer	Liaison with Power Industries on provision of fuel and power.	Chief Officer Consumer Protection

Addendum I to Appendix D to minutes of the meeting of the Public Protection Committee held on the 4th October, 1973 – Clwyd County Council.

The legal position of the commissioner

In formal terms, if there is time to make the arrangements, the commissioner is appointed by royal warrant to represent the Crown and therefore the Cabinet. He brings with him all the government's ordinary and emergency powers. The text of proposed emergency legislation is not revealed, but if it is only a repeat of the Emergency Powers (Defence) Acts of 1939 and the No. 2 Act of 1940 he will be able to make any regulations he thinks fit to secure public safety, supplies, the defence of the realm and the maintenance of public order. He will be able to try offenders against these regulations, and detain people without trial if he needs to. He will be able to require that people put themselves, their persons and their property at the disposal of the Crown[26] – that is, the regional government. In fact, as long as he acts honestly and in good faith, he can do practically anything.

As an example of how he might use these powers, one can imagine that, as in blitzed German cities, bedding, furniture and cooking implements will be scarce in the post-attack Britain and he might requisition a proportion of each surviving family's household goods – so many chairs, so many blankets, saucepans, cups, plates, etc. He might send all the men to labour camps, and the girls to be nurses. But in reality, even in law, the commissioner's formal powers are unnecessary. If the emergency is so severe that he has none – perhaps because Parliament and the executive are destroyed by a surprise attack – then legal authority reverts to the Crown, and common law supplies the want of delegation. If the action of an enemy throws the kingdom into disorder then the Crown – and that means in practice citizens acting on its behalf – has a common-law power to do anything that is necessary to restore public order and secure the defence of the realm, and may, if necessary, treat citizens as enemies. 'Martial law', as this is called, is a state of affairs, not a set of rules, or the result of a proclamation. It is 'martial' because normally, when administration collapses, the army is the only executive arm of the state capable of taking over. But there is nothing magic about the army. The common-law powers that justify otherwise illegal actions taken under martial law apply to all citizens and only to soldiers because they are citizens, and would equally justify actions taken by the commissioners or local-authority controllers, or anyone who could see what had to be done and did it.

Martial law has not arisen in Britain since the civil war of the seventeenth century. But it has existed in this century in South Africa, Southern Ireland, Canada, Palestine and parts of India.

So, without any specific powers, a commander may lawfully give any orders that would reasonably contribute to removing the emergency. In the BBC's documentary film, *The War Game* (1967), which dealt realistically with what a nuclear attack and the recovery period will feel like, a commissioner was shown having looters shot by a police firing squad: this seems legally perfectly permissible, although in practice not likely to be necessary.

Seen from a prosperous, peaceful, civilian setting, it perhaps seems dreadful that the state should deliberately create the means of executing such policies. But one tends to measure the powers against the peacetime situation which is all around us. The chaos and confusion and despair that would exist after a nuclear attack are more difficult to imagine. Most people would then complain that the government had too little power and not enough means of enforcing its decisions.

Cooke writes:[27]

It must be remembered that the Commissioner will be working in conditions of extreme confusion and stress, with tasks of immeasurable magnitude, with little useful information but many false rumours. He will have no means whatever to coerce anyone [we examine this statement below] and will have no legal sanctions that he can usefully apply for disobedience. The mere possession of a legal power will not get things done. He can only get things done by co-operation from others, and no amount of legal machinery can enforce co-operation under these circumstances.

Experience shows that societies in fact display extra-ordinary cohesion and helpfulness, at least immediately after disasters. Cooke suggests that this will be the commissioner's real resource:

> In disaster a heightened degree of co-operation and unity develops within the community among the people themselves and among the organizations they belong to. Individuals and organizations are anxious to contribute their best and to sever, for the time being, any entangling affiliations that prevent or hinder their co-operative efforts. Officialdom is, for an appreciable time, 'clothed in a mantle of grace and benevolence'.

It seems that any sort of surviving organization acts as a focus of crystallization for the social impulses of the shattered community. For this reason alone it is worth protecting the tiny core of government that will find room in the controls.

It is a commonplace that disasters bring out the best and kindest in people, and indeed the commissioner's ability to *force* anyone to do anything will be limited. He will have the police, and the war plan is to call up the police reserve to augment the strength of the force by another third. Then about a third of the total will be dispersed into the countryside to escape attack. Thus, of the 120 000 policemen that should be available on the outbreak of war, 40 000 will be dispersed and should suffer fewer than average casualties, while the other 80 000 will probably suffer in the same proportion as the population at large. A heavy attack which killed 10–20 million would then leave 48 000–64 000 policemen, or one to every 340–400 people. Although this is higher than the peacetime ratio of one policeman to every 550 people, the slight increase will have little effect when set against the disorder of post-attack communities, and will hardly provide enough force to *make* people do anything they do not want to.

Police war duties are set out in a Civil Defence Staff College training memorandum that I was given in 1967. The principal peacetime responsibilities of the police – the prevention and detection of crime, the maintenance of public order, traffic control and general assistance to the public – will continue in war on an increased scale. Their first task in war would be the maintenance of law and order and morale of the public (a 'mass outbreak of hysterical neurosis among the civilian population') but they will also be responsible for a number of additional tasks connected with security and home defence. These are likely to include:

   (i) Taking special measures to maintain internal security, with particular reference to the detection or restriction of movement of potentially subversive people.

  (ii) The guarding of key points, the maintenance of protected areas, and the restriction for security purposes of movement by the public.

 (iii) Reconnaissance immediately after the attack to determine the extent of damage and radiation. (This would fill in the details of the ROC picture. See page 122.)

 (iv) Assisting in the control of the homeless.

Until 1968 there was a tenuous volunteer military organization which existed specifically to 'assist the civil power' in the event of emergency. This was the Territorial and Army Volunteer Reserve III. There were to have been 23 000 men who trained at weekends, but the cuts of 1968–70 abolished them. Presumably whatever is left of the Regular Army, the T & AVR II – the active 110 000-strong active reserve with a call-out commitment to serve abroad in peacetime – will assist the civil power. But since a nuclear attack on Britain will hardly happen without considerable military embroilment abroad, there is little point in looking to the army for much help.

And anyway a nuclear exchange would hardly end the war. There is explicit reference in Sokolovsky to the possibility of using paratroops to capture and destroy the enemy's remaining stocks of nuclear weapons, even when all the delivery vehicles – rockets and aircraft – have been used up. So the military would have the continuing and vital task of guarding nuclear installations and weapons throughout the recovery period.

So, having done as much as possible to preserve government – that is the first responsibility of the animal that governs – what should be done next in the way of civil-defence preparations for the public at large?

Mass protection for populations is far more difficult. One soon runs into astronomical costs, and if preparations are effective they introduce very awkward strategical problems for powers that also have nuclear weapons themselves.

Deep shelters
We can illustrate both of these points by reference to deep shelters, which people perhaps tend to think of as the best protection from nuclear attacks.

The first objection to deep sheltering is that provision has to be made for everyone in a city, while only those in a relatively small ring around ground zero are actually going to benefit. Take for example a 5-MT air-burst over London. If everyone had been in sufficiently deep shelters, the 15 per cent of people killed would have been saved. But this is a very small return for the cost of shelters for everyone. At £200 a place[28] – a very conservative estimate – shelters for the metropolis cost £1 600 000 000 and the cost per head *of those saved* is £1330. Realistic building costs, providing the shelters with many blast doors, and ventilation systems proof against gas, fall-out and firestorms, might raise this to £5000–6000 a head.

If deep shelters were only suspect on grounds of cost, perhaps we should not reject them so readily. But there is also the difficulty of getting people into them within a realistic warning time. The same problem was tackled when deep shelters were considered in 1939 by the Hailey Conference.[29] The members noted that 'shelter protection depended not only on strength but also accessibility' and that, since warning of an air raid would only be about seven minutes, those seeking shelter would only have time to travel about 300 yards (270 m) along congested streets by day, or half this distance by night.

Roughly the same warning is appropriate today,[30] though it may be far less. Even if we accept 300 yards as a realistic estimate of the distance people can move to shelter, this implies that each shelter entrance must serve a circle with an area of about 0·09 square mile (0·2 sq km), and that the 15-mile (24 km) radius circle of London would need nearly 8000 entrances. Each entrance must absorb an average of 2200 people, and it would be safe to assume that they will not arrive until two minutes after the siren. Experiments in 1938[31] showed that the highest flow of people through a door is 40 per foot (12 per metre) width per minute when lanes in multiples of 22 feet (6·7 metre) are provided. If this cannot be achieved, then the flow rate is significantly lower. So each entrance has to be 30 feet (9 m) or more wide. If the doors are 7 feet (2·1 m) high, then each set has to withstand a load of 140 tons at an overpressure of 100 p.s.i. (7 kg/sq cm). Four leaves weighing 1850 pounds (840 kg) each would be needed, yet it has to be possible to close them almost instantaneously, perhaps by a mechanism triggered by the flash of initiation of an H-bomb.

Finally it is necessary to note that although underground shelters with blast-proof doors and air intakes offer protection against air-burst weapons, their performance against ground-bursts depends very much on the medium in which they are tunnelled. London clay is almost useless: the lethal radius for 1-MT against a point structure is only 15 per cent less 600 feet (180 m) underground than it is on the surface. But even 600 feet is quite out of the question as a depth for mass shelters, if only because people couldn't get down the steps in time, and lifts would be too slow, and too expensive to install. If shelters were 100 feet (32 m) deep or less, it would be necessary to fire only three 1-MT missiles to be sure of scoring a hit, and each hit could kill up to 17 000 people. This is admittedly a great improvement on the 750 000 people the same weapons could kill if they were air-burst over London when no one was sheltering, but it is hardly the performance one expects from such an expensive system.

To set this sort of proposal in perspective, we may look at

Stockholm, where five shelters have been provided to accommodate the 10 per cent of the population who must stay behind in an evacuation. Even so, they take 20 minutes to fill.

But the real drawback to deep shelters lies in none of these discouraging calculations. It is strategic, and lies in the fact that, even if a country has nuclear weapons, its strength is still offset by the vulnerability of its people. The very fact that civil defence is in no country remotely absolute – that is, it can only reduce damage by a small amount, not prevent damage altogether – means that even nuclear powers can be hurt, and therefore present no real menace to their neighbours. But if a country with nuclear weapons provided itself with total protection for its people (either by active measures like ABM, or passive ones like deep shelters), then that in itself would be a hostile act. Construction alone would raise international tension and the likelihood of war, and it would tempt potential enemies into making a pre-emptive strike on the population before the shelters were complete and the people got out of reach. If in a period of 'rising tension' a country with deep shelters for everyone sent its people into them (to get round the difficulty of warning) this might itself be interpreted as evidence of an intention to launch a pre-emptive strike on the other side, and so draw down a blow that might otherwise have been averted. Even if the enemy did not react to sheltering with a strike, he would only have to wait, to hold the population hostage. People cannot live for ever in deep shelters. But they cannot come out until the war is over or things have gone back to normal. How long are they to stay? The war turns into a siege: the attacker can keep them boxed up until they surrender, or wait until they come out, calculate that they will ignore the sirens so soon after release, and pick them off with air-bursts.

But even if deep shelters in major cities were completely successful, the attacker could easily shift his aim to secondary cities, or to industrial assets like fuel refineries or power stations. Or he could ground-burst weapons upwind at fortnightly intervals, letting fall-out do his work for him. Since the strategy of nuclear war need not call for damage to any particular part of the enemy's society or economy, it will always be possible to do *unacceptable* amounts of damage until he has put almost everything of value underground. And this is quite out of the question.

What else?

If deep shelters are impracticable and something of a liability for a nuclear power, what do we do instead? Cost for cost, more lives seem likely to be saved by early warning, which gives people time to get out of the way of heat flash and flying glass, than by any other measure. This is achieved by connecting the British Air Defence Operations Centre[32] – which is fed with information about attacks by the BMEWS at Fylingdales early-warning and air-traffic control radars – to the Second World War sirens that still decorate police and fire stations up and down the country. In the last war these were set going by a complicated chain of telephone messages; today they are worked automatically by means of a 72 kHz carrier signal (inaudible in a normal telephone), sent over ordinary telephone lines from distribution centres – much of the long hauls being superimposed on lines from the speaking clock which radiate across the nation. This ingenious system cost some £4 million to install at the beginning of the 1960s, and cost, in 1968, about £1 million a year to maintain.[33]

Voice communication in the ROC chain is over ordinary telephone lines, with the long hauls being carried by inter-exchange links borrowed from the civilian network during exercises or crises. This needs to be set up by operating switches in exchanges, a process which takes an hour or so. Thus the ROC system has its trunk line needs served without the expense of laying cable specially for the job.

The next best precaution, in economic terms, is dispersal. The official scheme now provides for the evacuation of some 9·5 million people – the 'priority cases', mostly mothers with babies or school-age children – to some 20 miles (32 km) from the biggest cities.[34]

(In the last war official evacuation was confined to

children and mothers of infants. This was because winning the war depended on production in the cities: men without wives to look after them, and without the necessity to provide for their wives, cannot be relied on as effective workers. The inclusion of mothers of schoolchildren in the priority classes is therefore a tacit admission that production will be irrelevant in a nuclear war.)

The only preparations needed for evacuation are railway timetables, which cost some £250 000 to draw up, and a nominal amount to maintain (railways themselves are durable). The reception of the official evacuees, and whoever leaves the cities voluntarily will be in the hands of the local authorities and the WRVS. It is said there will be no policy, as there is in America, of forbidding egress, either in general or by specified routes. But when Spies for Peace searched Kelvedon Hatch, they found documents outlining a plan to prevent citizens leaving London by Eastern Avenue, the main road out of London in that direction, in favour of government traffic.[35] The homeless would initially be looked after in 'rest centres', which would be schools, church halls, etc. Over the country 15 000 of these have been identified and some preparations made for equipping them. They would offer no more than a roof, a cup of soup, elementary hygienic facilities. As many people as possible would be billeted on homes round the nearer rest centres, and the rest moved on, until, a month after the attack, it is hoped that the homeless would have been diffused across the country and been billeted on undamaged homes. Luckily peacetime British housing density is low: normally we have a national average of 0·75 people per room. After attack and dispersal, this might double, but would still be less than the normal local authority criterion for overcrowding in peacetime. Physical preparations for dispersal are fairly primitive. A small stock of blankets is held for shock cases; simple cookers for mass catering – which were designed for the Crimean War, but are none the less effective for that – and the WRVS has a scheme for instructing housewives how to care for themselves and their families in disaster conditions – which could be caused by fire or flood as well as nuclear war. This is one of the few public civil-defence activities which the government continues to subsidize, though it is nowadays in little demand. Three thousand housewives heard the talk in 1976 compared with 1½ million in 1969.[36]

Rescue after the attack, as we have seen, would be impracticable in any general, organized way. The remaining step is the identification, preparation and stocking of fall-out shelters. Since about 85 per cent of the British live in houses that give a PF (see page 44) of ten or more, this is an area that shows promise. If householders were intelligently advised in good time before the attack and provided with suitable materials they could doubtless do a good deal. But something more to the point is needed than *Handbook No. 10* if only because its proposals are so ambitious. If its recipe for building sandbagged refuges were followed to the letter just in the city of Hull, the entire national stock of sandbags would be used up. If its proposals for boarding up windows were followed throughout the nation, several years' imports of soft timber would be required. But television films and recorded broadcasts are held ready by the BBC for pre-attack briefing, and the Ministry of Agriculture is ready to issue tinned meat and biscuits for the 14 days people will have to spend in shelter.

A national survey of communal protection for the 15 per cent who live in houses too flimsy to give adequate protection factors was rumoured to have been completed just before the civil-defence cuts of 1968. It said that enough shelter spaces could be identified, modified and stocked at reasonable cost, and it seems that this would be something worth pressing slowly ahead with. But for the moment the plan is shelved.

A scheme of control has been worked out for fall-out areas. It used to be thought that the ROC system would give sufficiently advanced warnings of fall-out so that people could be evacuated from the threatened areas. The basic assumption behind this approach was that all the nuclear weapons fired by the attacker would burst at once – as in a spasm war. It is more realistic to assume that nuclear attacks may alternate with negotiation and periods of conventional warfare. Evacuation might make matters worse by moving people away from their homes, where at least they had some protection and provisions, into areas where they have none and are completely exposed to fall-out.

Current planning therefore assumes that people stay put, and are told to do so, both before and after attack, and that intensive sheltering will be necessary for a week or so, with exposure controlled after that for some time by limiting the number of hours a day people spend out of doors.

The details of this scheme would have to be passed on to its executants – the citizens – by a variety of methods, of which broadcasting would be one of the most important. A Home Office pamphlet[37] dourly remarks, 'Disregard of the rules suggested for public behaviour, whether from bravado or ignorance, would bring its own penalty; there could be little in the way of enforcement in the ordinary sense of the term since neither police nor wardens would be able to patrol the fall-out area.'

The success of the scheme depends so much on the training, calm and good sense of those who will have to carry it out – which means not only civil defence, but also enormous numbers of ordinary people – and luck on the day, that one can hardly make any constructive criticism of it now. But one point of interest is the heavy reliance on broadcasting for telling people what to do. 'Wireless broadcasting would need to be used to the fullest extent to explain to the remainder the plans being made to help them; only thus could they be kept in good heart and be convinced of the necessity to remain in their refuges until their turn came to be evacuated.'[38] We shall return to the crucial role of broadcasting in Britain's civil-defence system.

Medical care

In peacetime we believe that everyone who is ill has a right to medical attention; on the battlefield, or in Britain after a nuclear attack, this comfortable philosophy would have to alter. After nuclear war the supply of injured would be inexhaustible and medical resources very limited: it would only be possible to treat the most suitable cases. That means that the injured would be divided into three classes: those who could live without further treatment (in peacetime these would often be considered very badly hurt indeed); those who, if given some simple treatment, would live, but who would die without – people with lacerations that could be sewn up, or limbs that could be amputated; and those who would need complicated surgery to live at all (these would have to be put on one side, given morphia and left to die).

There is a plan for dispersing the essentials of the hospital service in the pre-attack phase. This envisages sending every hospital patient home who is well enough to walk – surprisingly, these amount to 75 per cent of those in hospital at any one time. Then staff and essential portable stores – bandages, blankets, drugs, hand instruments – will be evacuated from the big cities. The immovably ill will be left in the care of a skeleton staff. This will mean the closing of nearly half the country's half a million beds.

The evacuated staffs will augment those of the now nearly empty country hospitals, to give 400 000 beds, and 'auxiliary hospitals' will be opened in shops, halls, warehouses, etc., after the attack. These will provide another 450 000 beds, but with one trained doctor and one nurse, assisted by public volunteers, for every hundred beds, they may look – and smell – just like Florence Nightingale's hospitals in the Crimea.

So, altogether, there should be 850 000 beds empty on the day, and that, bluntly, is the number of injured that can be treated.[39]

While rescue was seen as the principal civil-defence task, that is up until 1963, there was an elaborate organization of Forward Medical Aid Units (FMAU). Each of these consisted of four doctors, four nurses, 36 nursing auxiliaries and 15 supporting staff. Their job was simply to sort patients into the three categories mentioned above. Those in the second would be taken by fleets of improvised ambulances to hospitals in the country. But since the FMAU organization makes little sense without an elaborate civil-defence rescue organization to dig bodies out of the rubble, it is doubtful whether it will be retained. In fact, if the evacuation plans for the hospitals work as advertised, there may be a surplus of beds after the attack, simply for want of means of getting people to them.

The Ministry of Health stockpiles three basic drugs; probably morphine, aspirin and penicillin. This is done simply by holding back Health Service supplies for six months or so: thus ensuring automatic turnover of the stock at small cost. Post-attack medicine will be extremely basic. The level of sophistication envisaged is shown by the refusal to stockpile other drugs. Diabetics, for instance, will have either to store their own supplies of insulin, or make do without.

NOTES

1. Published 10 December 1967.
2. Albert Cooke (Civil Defence officer of York, and Secretary, Civil Defence Officers' Association), *Local Governments in Nuclear War*.
3. *First Report from the Select Committee on the Estimates*, Session 1953–54, *Civil Defence*, HMSO, London, 1953.
4. *First Report*, p. 260.
5. *First Report*, p. xviii.
6. *First Report*, p. xx, xv.
7. *First Report*, p. xvii.
8. *First Report*, p. xx.
9. *First Report*, p. xxii.
10. *First Report*, Appendix.
11. cf. *Radioactive Fall-out: Provisional Scheme of Public Control*, HMSO, London, 1956.
12. Home Office Civil Defence Circular 17/63.
13. *Eleventh Report from the Select Committee on the Estimates*, Session 1962–3, *The Home Office*, HMSO, London, 1963.
14. GPO *Report and Accounts*, 1964.
15. *Eleventh Report*, p. xxviii.
16. *UKWMO*, HMSO, London, 1974.
17. *Flight*, 3 April, 1975.
18. *Spectrum*, No. 67, 1969.
19. J. M. Hendrick and M. I. Skolmick, *Proceedings of IEEE*, June 1974, p. 664.
20. J. F. Ward, *Nature*, vol. 205, p. 1062.
21. *Wireless World*, February 1977, p. 53.

22. Y. T. Lin, A. A. Ksienski, *The Radio and Electronic Engineer*, vol. 46, No. 10, October 1976.

23. It was a condition of my visit that I did not reveal its position or photograph the exterior.

24. Sefton Delmer, *Black Boomerang*, London, 1962, pp. 201–6.

25. See Clwyd County Council war organization, from *The County Warbook*, Mole Express, Manchester.

26. E. C. S. Wade (ed.), *Wade and Phillips' Constitutional Law*, 6th edition, London, 1960, pp. 673–4.

27. Cooke, p. 103.

28. Contemporary tunnelling costs in London clay are exemplified by the recently built Victoria Line. The running tunnels, 3·5 metres diameter, cost £150 per metre. Scaling up by volume to the 16·5-foot (5 m) tunnels of the 1942 London deep shelters, we get a cost for bare tunnelling and lining of £90 per foot (£295 per metre). The 1942 deep shelters could accommodate 8·3 people per foot (27 per metre) overnight, so 5 million Londoners would need an absolute minimum of 516 miles (830 km) of tunnel at a bare cost of £180 million, or £22 a head. (The 1942 cost was £35–42 a head.) But in addition to this there are the costs of entrances, blast-proof doors, ventilation with protection against drawing in hot air from fires, gases or war pathogens. Then, since it will be necessary to stay in the shelter for a minimum period of two weeks, we have to allow for cooking, sanitation, some medical facilities and a little space to move about. It seems that tunnelling alone is the least of the problems, or the costs. Estimates for American schemes vary from $505 per head (£220) (optimistic) to $1500 (£650) (realistic), at 1965 prices. See *Scientists and Citizen*, February–March 1966, pp. 13–15.

29. See O'Brien, *Civil Defence (History of the Second World War, United Kingdom Civil Series)*, London, 1955, pp. 13–15.

30. Fylingdales B M E W S gives a nominal 15 minutes' warning. But this is by grace of the attacker. He can easily lower this by firing missiles on depressed trajectories, by using S L B M S or fractional orbit bombardment systems (F O B S). In the last case, the warning would be 15 seconds.

31. C. W. Glover, *Civil Defence*, London, 1942, p. 230.

32. In case the Air Defence Operations Centre is knocked out (a virtual certainty) Home Office warning officers are stationed at R A F radar stations in the United Kingdom. They can pass warnings into the system via the R O C's Sector headquarters.

33. Private communication, Home Office Scientific Adviser's Department.

34. See Table 6, p. 81. Cardiff is the smallest city affected.

35. Personal communication.

36. W R V S Annual Report for 1976. For the syllabus, see *A Handbook on W R V S Emergency Welfare Work*, H M S O, London, 1968.

37. See *Radioactive Fall-Out: Provisional Scheme of Public Control*, Manual of Civil Defence, vol. I, Pamphlet no. 2, H M S O, London, 1956, p. 7.

38. *Radioactive Fall-Out*, p. 17.

39. At Hiroshima the ratio of killed to injured was 1:2 (F. C. Ikle, *Social Effects of Bomb Destruction*, Oklahoma, 1967, p. 51) which implies that an attack which incapacitates 9 million will leave 6 million injured. But only those near the edges of the devastation will be able to get, or be brought, to hospital.

6   Recovery from a nuclear war

As Herman Kahn chillingly observes, the winner in the nuclear game is the country which survives all the stages of war:[1]

   (i) The pre-attack phase of dispersion and sheltering (2 weeks?)
  (ii) The attack itself and its immediate consequences (1 day)
 (iii) The fall-out phase (2 weeks)
  (iv) The period of collecting and integrating what is left of the country's human and physical assets (6 months?)
   (v) Long-term recovery (2–5 years?)
  (vi) Long-term medical and genetic effects (20–50 years?)

Earlier chapters have discussed the first three. In this chapter we shall consider the fourth and fifth, the recovery period, from the point of view of what might be done, and what relevant precautions have been taken by the British government. The last two are perhaps the worst, certainly the least studied, and the most difficult to foresee.

The recovery period starts when fall-out sheltering is over. All nuclear weapons may not have been used up, so that further attack or conventional hostilities may continue for a while; but the basic problem will be that of reorganizing people and assets, and settling down for the long haul back to a normal economy. The main enemy is time, because the pre-attack economy may have been so damaged that it is difficult or impossible to rebuild it before many of the survivors have died. It is this element of desperate economic surgery against time that gives the recovery period a certain gloomy interest to the student of social pathology, but it must be admitted that the amount of damage done by nuclear war and its ultimate social effects are so difficult to predict that one can hardly say anything very authoritative. In one sense, the heavier the attack, the better the prospects for the survivors, because people are more easily destroyed than farmland. The same is true to a lesser extent of some other resources. A single 5-MT air-burst over an idealized London would slightly reduce the proportion of people to locomotives, motor vehicles and machine tools, so that the survivors would be *richer* in terms of these resources than they had been.[2] At the same time they would be *poorer* in terms of houses (by a factor of two and a half), bridges, factories, office blocks, railway rolling stock and trees. This, of course, assumes that all these things are evenly spread over the landscape. Since that is not in practice true, one can only use these results as a guide to the outcome of a counter-force strike on the economy as a whole.

Food
One immediately visible difficulty in Britain is that we have far more people than our farms can support. We import 55 per cent of our food, and so there are, at peacetime standards of consumption, 25 million mouths too many. This excess is quite comfortably fed because we have a sophisticated economy and a great deal of world trade. But in thinking about the post-attack period, we must pre-suppose that either there won't be any other countries in a condition to trade with us, or there won't be the ships and harbours to permit imports, or that, even if other countries are untouched, Britain will be so severely damaged that we could send nothing abroad to pay for our imports. We are then left with the problem of an over-large population with too little food.

Food is Britain's most serious recovery problem – as it is not in every country. To get some idea of the issues, we have to balance the likely number of survivors against the likely produce of the island. We can see if there is a gap, and if there is, whether it is small enough to be closed by strategic stockpiling. If so, one would want to know whether this corresponds with what the government has done.

Experiments in America[3] show that 500 calories a day protect one against starvation but make work impossible, that 1000 calories keep one physically healthy and that the minimum for sustained work is 1500 calories. Since many people in the West eat double this, there is evident room for economy. Moreover, we eat far more protein than we need, and since animals have to eat seven vegetable calories to produce one calorie as protein, here is another area for improvement.

The average man or woman weighs 64 kg and needs 19·2 grams of meat protein a day, or just over half an ounce. Since 100 grams of meat supplies 150 calories, a minimum meat ration gives 29 calories, leaving 1471 calories to be found from vegetables. An obvious agricultural strategy is to try to raise all the vegetable calories we need, and use the rest of the farm capacity for raising protein which, if not enough, can be more easily supplemented from storage.

In peacetime each acre (0·4 hectare) of western European farmland produces about 8000 plant calories a day. This high level of production depends on a good many other resources. A great deal of machinery is used in modern husbandry and after an attack fuel will be scarce. All major dairy farms use electrical milking machines and electricity may be short. Although fertilizers will be hard to get, it is thought that the soil already contains enough for two or three years. A more serious want will be pesticides and the intensive single-crop farming now in use will have to be abandoned, so that the pests of one year can be discouraged with an unpalatable crop the next. Imported seed will be wanting, so 10 per cent of each crop will have to be saved for the next year. We might assume that at the worst these difficulties will reduce farming efficiency by 50 per cent, but that land lost through ground-bursts will be replaced by land that is now unused being taken into cultivation.

We have 18·3 million arable acres (7·4 million hectares) in the UK. If each produces 4000 plant calories a day after the attack, and there are 40 million survivors, then 14·7 million acres (5·9 million hectares) are needed to supply them with plant calories, probably mostly as potatoes. The minimum meat ration calculated above needs 200 plant calories, so the 3·6 million acres (1·2 million hectares) left could in fact raise protein for 72 million people, or nearly double what is needed, though doubtless the extra would be eaten soon enough.

Deep-sea fish would be unlikely to be affected by fall-out. In peacetime 8 million tons are landed a year, or 2400 tons a day. If we assume that this would be halved in wartime, there is still minimum protein for some 64 million people there. It would be hard to distribute fresh fish, and one cannot count on the survival of freezing plants; but even so, fishing must make a substantial contribution to the post-war economy.

Enough food may exist in theory, but distributing it is obviously going to be something of a problem. However, as we shall see below, it is likely that railways will be essentially workable in some form over the whole country; and that there will be enough fuel for at least the most vital transport. In any case the food strategy outlined above has the useful effect that the great weight of food is produced actually in the countryside, where most survivors will be living. The protein rations, that are more likely to have to be distributed, will weigh only 2 per cent of the vegetable rations. The interval between the attack and the first harvest will have to be filled somehow. It is estimated that there is three months' food at at least a minimum scale of rations in the distributive chain, though this is slowly falling as the food industry is rationalized into larger units and faster methods of distribution. An attack may come at any time of the year, so there may be as much as nine months to fill. This would have to be done from strategic stocks.

The point of this quick analysis is not to devise an optimum way of managing the post-attack food problem, but to see whether it can be solved within the bounds of possibility. We have to conclude that people could be kept alive and active, but it would be a miserable diet, and additions would be welcome. But in case it could not be supplemented, it would be wise to store a year or so's supply of meat in case of unforeseen disaster. The small meat ration described here for 40 million people for a year would weigh some 600 000 tons. How does this compare with what one can guess of the Ministry of Agriculture's strategic stocks?

During the Second World War, by 1943, the then Ministry of Food had some 6½ million tons of food stored in numerous dumps around the country. There was a National Emergency Reserve, to feed people fleeing from bombed cities, of 2½ million rations in five dumps, at Ayr, Harrogate, Market Harborough, Chippenham and Tring. Also during the war the government built or acquired 15 million cubic feet (420 000 cu m) of cold storage (400 000 tons of meat) in 40 separate places,[4] and 16 grain silos were built to hold a total of 80 000 tons.

Strategic stocks of food held today are not discussed in detail. Arrangements are generally said to be similar to those at the end of the war. There are apparently stocks of sugar and flour in laminated plastic sacks, and also quite a large holding of corned beef in tins. Since this has to be turned over at ten-year intervals, and the elderly stocks sold, it is possible to estimate the total. Intelligent guessing from within the tinned-meat industry suggests that 1–2 million tons are in store.[5]

It seems that the former Ministry of Food's stocks are now kept in fifty or so 'buffer depots' spread around the country, administered by warehousemen and local firms of wharfingers. The addresses of these depots are listed in telephone books. Figure 21 shows the positions of those that are known.[6]

We can conclude that the amount of food that can be grown and stored in Britain would be roughly what seems to be needed. This could be vitiated if fall-out had a drastic effect on husbandry. But it seems that animals are affected less than humans. Livestock can be protected to some extent against fall-out by being kept indoors for a few days after the attack. Those that are irradiated are fit to eat provided they are slaughtered before they fall sick. Animals grazing on contaminated pasture in the month after the attack would be fit to eat provided that the carcasses were properly bled, and

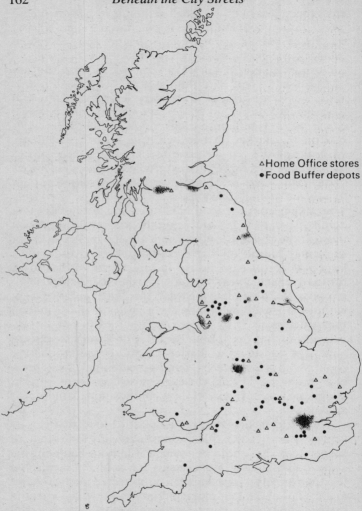

△Home Office stores
●Food Buffer depots

Fig. 21 Locations of the Ministry of Agriculture's semi-secret, privately run 'buffer depots' which contain the nation's stocks of food for nuclear war and Home Office supply and Transport stores which contain fire-fighting equipment, gas-masks, sandbags and probably supplies of C S and C R anti-riot gas, the cities are those most likely to be attacked.

the offal and bone discarded. Their milk would be dangerous, especially for children, but this could and would be
monitored. Fish, unlike animals, tend to concentrate radioactive isotopes in the flesh as well as the skin and innards. But
even immediately after an attack, deep-sea fish would
almost certainly be safe to eat. Fish from shallow fresh-water
lakes would be risky for some time, but these make little
contribution to the country's food stocks. Standing crops at
some stages of growth can be damaged by radiation, so at
certain seasons an attack would reduce the food available.
Otherwise crops are safe enough even in the month after an
attack as long as they are washed clean of dust. For some
years after an attack crops on contaminated soil would take
up minute quantities of isotopes, but the amounts would be
too small to be dangerous.[7]

In addition, arrangements have been made in case other
countries send us food after an attack in which our major
ports have been bombed. The Ministry of Transport has
provided a dozen or so emergency ports around the coasts.
These are no more than a trot of mooring buoys in sheltered
inlets that already have a railhead, a port-control bunker
with radio links to a regional port organization rather like
the Home Office's control system. This reports in turn to the
NATO Planning Board for Ocean Shipping, Eastern
Hemisphere, which has its headquarters at a secret protected site in Britain almost certainly Northwood; it will
have operational control over the merchant ships of all
NATO countries. As far as British food imports go, there
are stocks of grain handlers and mobile cranes to unload
cargoes. An extremely rough estimate would suggest that
this had a capacity of another 1–2 million tons, a figure
which, combined with the calculations above, would tend to
support the statement made to me by a senior official at the
Ministry of Transport: 'If everything works perfectly on the
day, we should just be able to squeeze by.'

Since it seems that, at 55 million, Britain's population is at
the limit of size beyond which survivors will not be able to
keep themselves alive, a policy of population limitation
would seem to be a valuable, basic civil-defence strategy. If

contraceptive techniques can be thoroughly disseminated through the population, it has been suggested that all the illegitimate babies, and half of the legitimate, would not be born. This would bring Britain's population growth to a stop as it has in the past year.[8]

Cohesion

People may be kept moderately active after an attack, but it is another matter to get the cohesion of effort that will be necessary to rebuild the economy. Since in times of physical crisis people fall back on the old emotional bonds of society, preservation of the Sovereign or a reasonably legitimate heir to the throne may be of the utmost psychological importance. Persuasion will be far more important than force, for as we have seen, the surviving government will have scant ability to coerce anyone. Rather than relying on coercion, it will have to manipulate the economy in quite subtle ways in order to encourage people into continued co-operative work once the first enthusiasm has worn off. The first essential is to control food. But since what food there is must, on grounds of democracy and social policy, be shared out according to need rather than personal value, it will not be practical to force people to work by the threat of starving them if they do not.[9] Withholding food from large numbers of people might only provoke riots which could not be suppressed with the forces at the government's command or might drive people into banditry or subsistence farming. It will probably be more to the point to manage luxuries, which are likely to take the place of money after an attack. This would either be because currency loses its value if there are not enough goods in circulation to balance money – a £5 note might be a poor exchange for a potato at H-day plus six months – or because pre-attack currency will have been withdrawn to discourage scavenging in bombed cities. (Though the experience of German cities does not suggest that looting will be a serious problem.)[10]

The Treasury is rumoured to have a subtle scheme to seize all the readily portable luxuries – whisky, cigarettes, chocolates, aspirin, coffee – that are to be found after the attack, and to store them under guard as titbits with which to manage the barter economy that will replace money.

People

If we take the worst likely attack, it seems that some 20 million will be killed. Although, as we have seen, bomb effects are markedly selective, killing far more of the old and young than those in their thirties, this is unlikely to have much effect on the surviving community. But since families are often split up for most of the day, a heavy casualty roll implies an even larger proportion of damaged families. Hannunian finds that an attack which kills 60 per cent of Americans would leave only 20 per cent of families intact. Since social life revolves round the family, and caring for one's wife and children is the strongest motivation of most workers, this could have serious economic consequences.

A more worrying aspect of an attack which included strikes on cities is that it would tend to kill the more useful and productive members of society. Hannunian finds that after a heavy counter-strike in the USA, people with 1959 incomes of $10 000 or more tend to survive at rates 75–85 per cent of those for the population at large.[11] Although these account for only 15 per cent of families, they earn and spend one-third of all income. De Kadt, in estimating the effect of a counter-city strike on Britain,[12] suggests that one-half to two-thirds of all the people in paper, printing, shipbuilding, law, teaching, medicine, general engineering, vehicle manufacture, local government and building will be killed, as will two-thirds to three-quarters of those in precision instruments, electrical engineering, insurance, banking, finance and national government (assuming no pre-attack dispersal). Skilled workers, the people who actually make things with their hands, are concentrated in cities,[13] while professional people who will be less useful in the make-do-and-mend of the recovery period, are more evenly spread. Although the balance of ages will probably not be very much changed after the attack, the state of the economy will possibly dictate changes in our attitudes towards non-producers. In particular the elderly, whose maintenance now represents almost pure altruism in economic terms, probably will not get their present pittance from the state. How many of the old will survive the first winter of the peace? Moderately mature children represent an almost immediately useful asset and will probably be well cared for: babies are more long-term investments, so although the state will probably continue to support them, there is likely to be considerable emphasis on contraception and abortion during the first few years of recovery. Fewer babies will mean more women at work, and fewer demands on the tattered health services. Another class which presents more difficulty is that of the insane. A post-war economy may well be unable to afford the food to keep them or the people to look after them, and this applies even more strongly to the criminally insane. Unfortunately from this point of view, few mental hospitals are in target areas. Some regional commissioners may be forced into a policy of euthanasia.

Disease

It is often said that mass disease and epidemics of plague will be one result of a nuclear attack. It is true that radiation does lower resistance to infection, but there is otherwise no evidence to support the idea. The experience of Germany towards the end of the last war is the nearest practical experiment we have. In spite of the very large amount of damage done in German cities, there were no epidemics after the bombing. The reasons for this, given by Mitchell in a study of the matter, were:[14]

(i) the Germans had a high standard of personal and domestic hygiene;

(ii) hygiene courses were given during the war as part of civil-defence training;

(iii) there was a well-organized public-health service;

(iv) the average German was very obedient in health matters;

(v) the country started out relatively free from disease carriers.

It appears that a good pre-attack vaccination programme,

such as we have here in Britain, will prevent most diseases
that might be expected to flourish. Tuberculosis, which is
latent in about 17 per cent of western people, may well break
out more frequently under the hardships of the recovery
period, but is unlikely to amount to an epidemic. Typhus was
a serious problem in wartime Germany – and Russia –
mainly because no DDT was available to control lice.
Although plague exists in pockets of Europe, and is spread
by rats, it was Hamburg's experience that rats were more
susceptible to bombing than humans. Cholera is a danger,
but can simply be kept in check by boiling drinking water and
cooking food.

The long-term genetic effects of radiation may be considered under the head of disease. Here one is on thin
ground, for this is a debate in which there is as yet little
information, but in which emotion plays a large part. (At the
time of writing, Autumn 1978, the most recent contribution
was from Sternglass.[15]) Sternglass claims that a laborious
analysis of infant and foetal mortality rates in America
shows that the states downwind, that is east, of the Nevada
test site for nuclear and atomic weapons showed a reduced
rate of decline of foetal mortality (which had been dropping
steadily since the 1930s) between 1950 and 1965 – the years
of intense bomb testing. He also, more impressively,
correlates the strontium-90 concentration in foetal bone
with excess foetal mortality; excess infant mortality with
strontium-90 in teeth; and the rate of strontium-90 production with excess infant mortality for the whole United States.
He writes:[16]

It is therefore clear that in the light of the long range
worldwide biological effect of nuclear weapons, all past
calculations as to casualties, 'loss-exchange ratios' and
chances of recovery from a nuclear war in the presence or
absence of anti-missile systems or shelters become utterly
and completely meaningless. In fact, even the threat of a
massive first strike by one major power against another
loses all credibility when the resulting release of fission
products into the world's atmosphere would be sufficient

to ensure that the children of the nation that launches the strike would die before reaching maturity.

At first sight, Sternglass's results are impressive but, as Stewart points out,[17] the argument depends throughout on 'excess' infant and foetal deaths relative to a steady decline, and a decline in a death rate cannot go on steadily for ever. If it did, in the absurd limit, it would pass zero, and more children would survive than were conceived or born. So the rates must sooner or later level off. Does this explain what Sternglass has found, or is it due to fall-out? Stewart writes: 'In practice infection deaths are so strongly correlated with sex, age, wealth, climate, density of population, chemo-therapy and so on, that any deviation from normality of related death rate and prevalence rates . . . can only be regarded as significant *after* these effects have been eliminated'; and this Sternglass had not done.

In spite of a decade of vigorous debate about the risks of low-level radiation, the picture is hardly less confused today. It is extremely difficult to discover whether or not there is a threshold radiation dose below which no damage is done; let alone to find out whether it is lower for the very young and very old than for healthy adults. So Sternglass may be right when he says that the 'biological poison' released by large-scale use of nuclear weapons could lead to the extinction of the human race by killing the children. On the other hand, supposing that there was such an effect, the variability of fall-out, and the variability of individual reactions to it, might mean that substantial numbers of children would survive. Humanity, like many another threatened species, would doubtless increase its birth rate to compensate. Species are very hard to kill; especially one as tough and determined as man.

Other resources

After food the next obvious stumbling block is motor fuel. In peacetime we import about 72 million tons a year and produce a few thousand from wells on the east coast. About a month's supply is at sea at any moment; and another month's in the pipeline, being refined and distributed in the UK. It would be unwise to count on much of the first winning home; half the second might survive an attack, giving us 5 million tons. The interest of Russian submarines and surface ships in North Sea oil and gas platforms makes it doubtful that they will not be attacked. In any case, the pipeline terminals on the coast are vulnerable targets. It would be unwise to count on much help from this source during the recovery period.

However, it is proposed[18] (1977) to excavate 19 caverns in rock at Cromarty to contain 2 million cubic metres of crude oil and petroleum products: this method of storage is said to be advantageous on aesthetic, safety, commercial and strategic grounds.

How much oil would we need to maintain the recovery economy? It is rather like asking the length of a piece of string. There is no easily visible cut-off point, as there is with food, below which any sort of life will be impossible. One way of guessing is to look at the situation in 1943 when fuel rationing was at its height. Then buses and lorries used 1·7 million tons per year of petrol and derv.[19] They were carrying not only minimal rations for the people of Britain, but also war materials, but if we equate this second activity with what will be needed to restore the economy, we may not be so far wrong. Another approach is to note that at the moment goods vehicles use 2·4 million tons a year. If we say, arbitrarily, that half of this is engaged on moving imports, exports and luxuries, we get an irreducible minimum of 1·2 million tons. We must add something to that for a minimum of public transport – for even in the reconstruction phase people will have to get to and from work. So if we put minimum reconstruction needs at 2 million tons a year, the natural storage in the distribution chain – well dispersed from attack – will last the necessary two years or more. Our native on-shore oil fields produce 87 000 tons a year of crude oil, or 4 per cent of post-war requirements.

As well as this, the Ministry of Energy keeps strategic stocks of fuel, probably mainly for the services, which are occasionally referred to in oblique terms. Kohan[20] mentions that a 6 foot (1·8 m) concrete roof was put over the Navy's oil tanks at Rosyth in 1938, and the 1953 Committee on the Estimates touches on the rehabilitation of the wartime petrol storage and pipeline schemes. And in the last 25 years there has been considerable effort by governments and the oil industry in building pipelines here and in Europe. Fuel pipelines are almost invulnerable to nuclear attack, as well as being cheaper in peacetime than any other method of moving fuel. Their strategic importance is subtly underlined by Section II of the Pipelines Act 1962, which provides that a person building a pipeline (for liquid fuel or gas) can, if he needs to, apply to the Minister of Energy for a compulsory purchase order to get the land he wants. This is said to be the *only* provision in British law giving private persons power to get compulsory purchase orders.

That this activity continues is shown by a recent news-paper report:[21]

> The Ministry of Defence proposes to lay a fuel pipeline from Falmouth to RAF St Mawgam as part of a NATO 'infrastructure pipeline system' to supply bases in Europe . . . A Ministry of Defence spokesman said last night that similar work was taking place all over Europe for NATO. 'It is both cheaper and more secure than using tankers,' he said.

Sokolovsky said in 1962 that the European members of NATO had 8000 kilometres of fuel pipelines and storage for 3000 million cubic metres (1560 million tons) of fuel. (This is about equal to 20 years' supply at *peacetime* rates, and seems a lot.)

We have two other indigenous power resources. Coal mines are naturally resistant to nuclear attack, and pro-duce about 20 times as much energy as we import in liquid fuel. Natural gas is also an important resource: distribu-tion pipelines cover the country and are again resistant to nuclear attack, though the wells in the North Sea and their feeders would be vulnerable. Again there are occasional indications that the demands of nuclear war are borne in mind. The Gas Council's North Sea terminal at Bacton, Norfolk (where the hot line enters the sea) is designed to process 4000 million cubic feet (113 million cu m) of natural gas a day.

Nature, in a report of the opening in 1960, said:[22]

> With so much of the British gas supply being channelled through Bacton, precautions are being taken to guard against mishaps. The Gas Council terminal is equipped with two independent power supplies, *one underground* [my italics] and each has a back-up system in case of failure. There is only one main feeder leading to the national grid near Rugby, but four others are planned for full operation in 1974.

Railways will be extremely important: happily their lines and bridges are almost completely resistant to explosions, except very close ground-bursts. Engines are fairly hardy, but rolling stock less so. An engine positioned randomly in London under attack from four 5-MT bombs would have an 89·2 per cent[23] chance of survival. Post-attack railways' viability will depend on the amount of stock in target cities at the time of attack. But since one doesn't know the aiming points, or the effects of the railway's dispersal plans, it is difficult to say anything precise. British Rail says that if the counter-city strike imagined in Table 6, page 81, were carried out at noon on a summer weekday, 30 per cent of locomotives, 50 per cent of passenger vehicles and 20 per cent of wagons would be made useless.[24] Losses on this scale would not cripple the recovery economy.

There is a pleasant rumour current that British Rail have quietly preserved some 500 of the 2000 steam locomotives discarded from service since 1966 for use after an attack. Although this would seem a sensible precaution – and one that has been adopted in Sweden – it seems to have no basis in fact.[25] The main job of the railways would be to distribute coal from the coalfields for power stations and to keep people warm (though this last would be helped by the gas grid), and their main problem would be the collapse of key bridges in target cities. But the same table shows how resistant bridges are. Track damaged by blast can be repaired at the rate of 20–30 miles (30–50 km) a day,[26] so

there would probably be little difficulty in running through
even completely flattened cities a month or so after the
attack. Luckily railway installations are much more
vulnerable to high-explosive attacks than they are to air-
burst nuclear weapons, or even ground-bursts unless they
are prime targets. So the extensive works carried out in
1942–5 would still be useful, as would the pre-war
'insurance' precaution of building a line right round London
from Cambridge, via Sandy, Bedford, Calvert and High
Wycombe to Staines.[27] The last problem, that of control,
has been attended to. The railways have hardened operating
centres and, as a back-up, control rooms on lorries with
portable radio stations which can be set up in unobtrusive
spots. One system is a development, as so much in civil
defence, of the Second World War planning. The Southern
Railway (now Southern Region, British Rail) had its headquarters in a cave in the grounds of a hotel at Deepdene, near
Dorking, and other underground divisional offices at
Woking, Orpington and Redhill. To this railway belongs the
credit of inventing the mobile radio controls – mounted in
half-ton parcel vans and moved about to confuse German
direction finders.[28] This system stays the same, and doubtless the more permanent installations are not so different
now, since all trace of the Deepdene cave and the Woking
tunnel have 'disappeared'.[29] The London and North
Eastern Railway (now Eastern Region, British Rail) had its
main headquarters at Luton Hoo, and hardened controls at
Gerrards Cross, Shenfield, Knebworth, Bawtry and Godly.
A refuge for a Scottish control was prepared in the disused
railway tunnel from Edinburgh Waverley north to Leith, but
never used.[30] There are said to be mysterious carriages in
locked sheds at Craven Arms, Shropshire, and at Springs
Branch, Wigan – which might well be mobile controls.

Electricity-generating is also, though for different
reasons, naturally resistant to nuclear attack. The cost of
land, if not considerations of passive defence, has forced the
Central Electricity Generating Board to site its newest and
largest power stations out in the countryside. Individually
not important enough to rank as targets, they have a very

good chance of survival. By the early 1970s 9 per cent of the installed capacity is due to be nuclear, though as atomic piles can produce the raw materials for nuclear weapons, these are likely to be prime targets in a counter-force war; 13 per cent of capacity will be oil, and therefore vulnerable, as well. About 2 to 3 per cent is hydro-electric, and independent of fuel supplies. For the same reason that the large power stations are in the country, so are the grid and supergrids and the large switchgear parks that connect different sections. The system is designed with considerable redundancy, so that most points in the middle of Britain are triply connected or better, though perhaps there will be some loss of power if links are damaged. Full power can be delivered everywhere with 10 per cent of generators and one transmission line out of action in each section.[31] It is worth remembering that at Hiroshima electricity and railways were working again within 24 and 48 hours of the attack.

Coal, electricity, gas and railways are long-term needs. Londoners did without all of them for days at a time during the Blitz. Water, though, is an absolute essential, and it must be available within hours of an attack. Happily again, supplies are distributed by underground pipes, which are apt to survive closer to ground zeros than people. But without electricity to work the pumps, or fall-out-proof sources, this is going to be little use. Pure-water supplies are said to have been secured by a countrywide survey of wells and bore-holes. Apparently there is enough capacity everywhere in the country to keep people going,[32] and in any case about half our water normally comes from safe, underground springs.[33] To counter damage to pumps and the immediate dislocation of electricity supplies, the Department of the Environment has accumulated stockpiles of pumps and pipe.

One can make a crude attempt to estimate how quickly Britain might recover. In peacetime we invest about a fifth of our national output. Let us suppose that a counter-force war (see page 64) destroys 40 per cent of the nation's replace-able capital assets – houses, factories, roads, etc. – and hence 40 per cent of our means of generating more capital. Let us suppose that, by dint of extraordinary efforts in the recovery period, the rate of investment can be doubled (i.e., consumption comes down from 80 to 60 per cent of output).[34] Since the peacetime rate of investment is about £4000 million a year (1968 pounds), this means that, allowing for loss of assets, recovery period investment might be £4800 million. In the ordinary year £2000 million is spent on replacing worn-out assets, but we assume that in the recovery period this is reduced to a quarter, and deduct £500 million on this head. We are left with a possible rate of investment of £4300 million a year. The nation's capital stock in 1968 was worth about £128 000 million and 40 per cent of that, the damage done by the war, is worth £51 000 million. So it seems that in something like twelve years we should be back to normal. In practice, of course, recovery will be likely to be slower than that because of damage not only to the parts of the economic machine, but also to the way they fit together.

Looked at from a severely practical point of view, the aftermath of a nuclear war is not wholly bad. This sort of attack would have these benefits at least:

    (i) it would demolish most of Britain's slum houses;

   (ii) it would reduce the population to 35 million, a level which some people feel would be quite comfortable for these islands;

  (iii) by the end of the recovery period the ratio of population to some fixed assets might be *higher* than it had been before the attack – the survivors would be better off;

  (iv) it would decentralize government; and

   (v) it would solve the balance-of-payments problem.

Recovery in other countries

Some study has been made, particularly in the United States, of the ways in which small sectors of the economy might survive a nuclear war. But it is difficult to jump from these to an accurate appreciation of what an attack will do to the economy as a whole, and to judge how it will affect the imponderables of the system. It may be that resources enough for the recovery period exist, but no way could be found to distribute them and get a new economic system going. On the other hand, it may be that even sophisticated countries (which in one view are more vulnerable, as being further removed from basic living) could recover quickly from even such enormous blows as these. One guide is to look at the recent experience of hard-hit nations.

Hannunian[35] briefly surveys three countries' experiences during and after the Second World War. Japan lost 25 per cent of her houses, 20 per cent of her electricity-generating stations, 70 per cent of petrol refineries, 80 per cent of cotton-spinning plant (then her main export industry). All in all she lost her complete gross national product for 1940 and a quarter of her stored, reproducible wealth. But her recovery was complete within ten years.

Poland lost 15 per cent of her people in each World War. After the Second she had lost 25 per cent of houses, almost all important bridges, factories and most farm animals. Warsaw, the capital, was completely razed. The Germans left no seed, no draught animals, no tractors, no fertilizers. Since the war a large part of her production, particularly of coal, has been sent to supply Russia. Yet today she is not unprosperous.

For Russia the Second World War was merely the continuation of struggles that had gone on almost non-stop since 1914. But in it she lost 25 million people, or 12 per cent of the pre-war population. Of her land, 40 per cent was occupied, and in that area every factory was destroyed or gutted, as were half the houses in towns and a third of the country dwellings. Altogether she lost 13 per cent of housing, and 27 per cent of her reproducible wealth. Yet the pre-war amount of fixed capital was reached again by 1950, and the 1940 level of production slightly earlier.[36] By 1955, living space was 170 per cent of the pre-war amount. These three countries suffered on the scale of the attack we have postulated here.

One cannot therefore say categorically that a nuclear war would be the end of everything. Certainly the Russian government does not believe so. A recent study of their civil defence by Boeing Aerospace[37] found that 98 per cent of the population could survive a US attack and its industry could probably be back on its feet three or four years later, because efforts were being made to site three-quarters of new factories outside cities, to separate factories so that one war-head could damage only one target, to stockpile materials and to develop simple methods of protecting large machine tools. (But one must remember that Boeing is a company that makes much money from military rivalry between the USA and USSR and has an interest in making the Third World War seem credible.)

NOTES

1. From Kahn, after an adaptation by Albert Cooke, *Local Government in Nuclear War*.

2. N. Hannunian, *Dimensions of Survival*, Rand Corporation, Santa Monica, 1966.

3. R. S. Pogrund, *Nutrition in the Post-Attack Environment*, Rand Corporation, Santa Monica, 1966.

4. See R. J. Hammond, *Food II* (*History of the Second World War, United Kingdom Civil Series*), London, 1956.

5. Personal communication.

6. I am indebted to Ron Bailey for this information.

7. Pogrund; UK Civil Defence Staff College, *Food Control Notes*, 1966.

8. M. Simms and J. Medawar, *Optimum Population for Britain, Institute of Biology Symposium*, London, 1969.

9. Superficially, the wartime situation in Russia might seem parallel where the rations issued to different classes of people varied enormously according to their usefulness to the state. But that was a settled society with large military and police forces available to quell unrest. Even so there were riots in Moscow in 1941. See J. Lawrence, *Life in Russia*, London, 1947.

10. Ikle, *Social Effects of Bomb Destruction*, Oklahoma, 1967.

11. Hannunian.

12. E. de Kadt, *British Defence Policy and Nuclear War*, London, 1964.

13. *Atlas of Britain*, Oxford, 1963, pp. 148, 149.

14. H. H. Mitchell, *Survey of the Infectious Disease Problem as it Relates to the Post-Attack Environment*, Rand Corporation, Santa Monica, 1966.

15. E. J. Sternglass, *Bulletin of the Atomic Scientists*, vol. 25, no. 4, April 1969, p. 18; *New Scientist*, 24 July 1969.

16. Sternglass, *Bulletin of the Atomic Scientists*, vol. 25, no. 6, June 1969.

17. A. Stewart, *New Scientist*, 25 July 1969.

18. *New Civil Engineer*, 1 September 1977.

19. C. I. Savage, *Inland Transport* (*History of the Second World War, United Kingdom Civil Series*), London, 1957, table 10, p. 655. Unfortunately the promised volume in this series on *Oil* has not yet been published.

20. C. M. Kohan, *Works and Buildings* (*History of the Second World War, United Kingdom Civil Series*), London, 1952.

21. *Western Morning News*, 11 October 1978.

22. *Nature*, vol. 222, 14 June 1960, p. 1020.

23. $(97 \cdot 2)^4 = 89 \cdot 2$ per cent.

24. Personal communication, 1967.

25. Personal communication from J. E. Baker, 1976, Hon. Sec. Railway Correspondence and Travel Society.

26. Neville Brown, *Nuclear War*, London, 1964.

27. Savage, pp. 106, 424–30.

28. Bernard Darwin, *War on the Line*, London, 1946.

29. Personal communication from J. B. Henderson, Chelsea Speleological Society.

30. Norman Crump, *By Rail to Victory*, London, 1947.

31. H. B. Dreyfus, *The Transmission of Electrical Power*, London, 1966.

32. Communication from Ministry of Housing and Local Government, 1967.

33. *Atlas of Britain*, Oxford, 1963, pp. 38, 39.

34. In 1932 Russia managed to invest 56 per cent of her gross national product.

35. Hannunian, pp. 6–18.

36. Lawrence found conditions *better* in Moscow in 1942 than they had been in 1935.

37. *Aviation Week and Space Technology*, 22 November 1976, p. 17.

7   *Government citadels in Britain*[1]

It would be interesting, if only to satisfy one's vulgar curiosity, to know something about the locations of the government's citadels: the national seat of government, the service headquarters, the sub-regional controls. We may be sure that our enemies have known them for years.

The inquiry which follows is made possible by two basic and interlinked characteristics of emergency preparations: economy and conservatism. As we saw in Chapter 1, the spirit of economy runs all through Britain's preparations for civil defence. Bluntly, money spent on protected accommodation and communications is money wasted unless there is a war or a revolution. If there is no emergency, every pound unspent on these things is a pound saved. This reluctance to spend on things that one hopes will be useless encumbrances for most of their lives, leads to the quality of conservatism. Because emergencies, by definition, happen rarely, planning to deal with them receives few tests. While the rest of life hurries along, this aspect of human affairs lies dormant for decades at a time, then is sharply exercised. If, in the crisis, it is overwhelmed, no further need arises; if it survives it has proved itself and is perpetuated. So the story of emergency planning in Britain is like an ultra-slow-motion film. While other institutions change out of recognition, emergency plans lie dormant through the centuries.

If this is true of paper plans, how much more so of buildings and machinery? So we find buildings being adapted for new but basically similar uses over a thousand years. Dover Castle is an example. Built in the twelfth century, it has been useful in the time of the arrow, the cannon, the rifle shell, the high-explosive bomb, and still protects an S-RC against the hydrogen bomb. This is not untypical. In the field of passive defence, nuclear weapons have made less difference than one might at first suppose. High-explosive bombs of the last war could penetrate 100 feet (30 m) of earth. A solid shield of rock was as comforting then as now. And many protected buildings of 1939–45 were designed with the atom bomb in mind. It was assumed that the Germans might use it (otherwise what was the point of the V2 rocket?) and steps were taken accordingly. In planning for the scale of attack, too, the assumptions made were, as we have seen, nuclear in scale. So, much of civil-defence thinking and hardware created for the Second World War will be appropriate to nuclear defence. That, combined with the peculiar conservatism of the subject, makes the last war's preparations a useful starting point for anyone interested in the field today.

The second avenue of approach exploits the tendency towards economy in communications. The point of hardened accommodation is to protect the brains of decision-makers. Mewed up in their concrete tombs, they are useless without a ready flow of information in and out. This necessitates a rich system of emergency communications. But since this may not be used for decades at a time civil defence relies for the most part on taking over the peacetime trunk systems when the need arises. As a former chairman of Cable and Wireless, the government-owned body which provides radio and cable communications throughout the Commonwealth, writes:[2] 'An emergency circuit consists primarily of a switchable portion, normally in use for the public system, which can be connected quickly to two local ends.' So the ordinary British trunk system contains within it the hardened civil-defence network.

The 'hardening' is almost automatic, since trunk cable runs in ducts some two to three feet (60–90 cm) below ground. That is enough to protect it from almost all air-bursts, and from those ground-bursts that do not actually cut the cable. The chance of this happening in open country is remote, and made less likely by the GPO's normal practice of guarding against line and equipment faults by providing at least two routes to most places in the trunk network.

A Home Office witness before the Estimates Committee of 1963 said:[3]

> Hitherto, or until recently, we have necessarily placed the main reliance on line communication . . . this has been developed in a very substantial way, and in quite, I think, an ingenious way, to provide a considerable number of routings of landlines avoiding the most likely target areas. We are now supplementing this by wireless [low channel capacity sets working with the peacetime police hilltop VHF radio system] but we have only in the last two years been able to embark on a programme of operational wireless provision on any substantial scale because we have not had the money until the revised civil defence programme began two years ago.

In a rare burst of frankness the next year the Home Office took full-page advertisements in several London papers to explain what it was doing. It was said then that 400 miles (640 km) of trunk cable had been relaid away from the likely targets to guard against nuclear attack[4] (a striking example is perhaps the underwater cable from Colwyn Bay in northern Wales across to Heysham in Lancashire bypassing the crowded Liverpool–Manchester conurbation which is almost certain to be a target in either a counter-force or a counter-city war) and that 750 miles (1200 km) of radio links had been installed to cover the breaks.

The system used is probably VHF or UHF links via existing Home Office hilltop radio stations. These are familiar enough objects in the landscape, sited rather prominently to give coverage to mobile units of the police, fire, ambulance and other local authority services. They have two types of aerial: dipoles to give all-round coverage for mobiles, and yagis to give tight beams to the controls. The characteristic hilltop station consists of two lattice self-supporting towers and a brick building housing the transmitters and receivers,

Fig. 22 Typical Home Office VHF radio site with yagi aerials – like fish bones – for point-to-point relays, and vertical dipoles for all-round communication with vehicles.

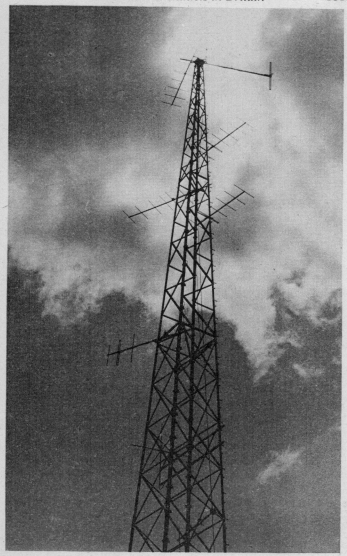

with another containing an emergency diesel-power genera-
tor. S-R Cs have much lighter stayed lattice towers, with yagi
aerials to repeaters and HQs if the link is possible direct. It
would be most interesting to have a nationwide survey of
aerials' shoots from hilltop radios. Most of them would lead
to police, fire and ambulance service HQs in towns. Those
that did not might point to secret sites.

Given duplicated routing, ordinary trunk cable is about as
'hard' as one would want it to be with the limited amount
there is to spend on civil defence. But special protection is
necessary at the ends. The exchanges and the organizations
they are to serve must be housed in well-protected places,
because they are the ganglia of the H-bomb-resistant brain.
If they are damaged, the government creature is blind, deaf
and dumb.

Bearing these general principles in mind, we find that a
study of precedent in hardened accommodation, and the
civilian cable system, is rewarding.

Citadels in London
One way and another, central London is honeycombed with
more or less bomb-proof holes and buildings, going back – as
far as one knows – to the First World War. The lack of
sophistication of the government citadel in 1916 is shown by
the practice of hiding King George V in his train in a railway
tunnel on Zeppelin nights, where he severely dislocated
railway traffic.[5] The major underground shelter used then
was the Post Office tube railway. Building was authorized in
1913,[6] and by 1917 two 9-foot (2·7 m) tubes had been dug
which ran, and still run, after modernization in the mid-
1960s, from Paddington Station–Wimpole Street–Museum
Street–Mount Pleasant–St Martin's le Grand–Liverpool
Street Station–Whitechapel. The first serious air raids in
London took place in 1917 (see page 16) and these tubes
were used to store the Elgin Marbles and other treasures.

In 1917 the eastern of the two short tunnels carrying
the Piccadilly Line spur from *Holborn* to *Aldwych* was
peremptorily closed.[7] Since this, at 130 feet (40 m), was one
of the deeper and therefore more bomb-proof sections of the

tube system, it is possible that it was commandeered as a shelter for the King, Cabinet and War Office.

A London Transport drawing of 1930, N/115-52/075 showing proposed remodelling of underground platforms at Waterloo, marks *six* underground lines: two each of the Bakerloo and Hampstead (now Northern) Lines and two called 'Aldwych'. It is not clear whether this was a proposed extension (which would surely be mentioned as such) or a description of how things actually were. If the latter, then one might suppose that at least one *Aldwych–Waterloo* bore was kept to provide the second river crossing in the government's deep shelter system.

No other use seems to have been made of the tube system during the First World War. The Post Office tube was completed in 1927, and through the 1930s there was a good deal of modernization of the passenger network to meet new traffic needs. Several stations were remodelled and repositioned on the Piccadilly and Central Lines, leaving empty accommodation deep underground that was shortly put to use.

When the Second World War started, a good deal went below. Seventy-nine deep tube stations were used as overnight public shelters. Tunnels for the Central Line east of Liverpool Street towards Bethnal Green, which had been dug and lined, but were otherwise unfinished, were used as an underground aircraft factory. The other Aldwych Line was closed in 1940 and used as a shelter, as were the two tunnels from King William Street in the City to the Borough High Street south of the Thames, which were 100 feet (30 m) deep and had been abandoned in 1900. Southwark Borough Council leased the southern half and used it as a shelter for 14 000 people. Although the Hailey Conference in 1939 had decided against deep shelters – for fear that workers might remain underground rather than face the bombs – in 1940 policy was reversed. Construction of ten deep shelters was begun at eight stations on the Northern Line and two on the Central (see Figure 24, page 191), although there seems to have been no pressing need for shelter space at the time: in November 1940 the tube stations had a capacity of 8 per cent

of Londoners, although only half this number actually used
them.[8] In effect, the new deep shelters added room for only
another 2 per cent. They each eventually provided shelter
space for 8000 at a cost of £35–£42 a head. Work at the Oval
was defeated by the underground springs that had made the
original construction of the Northern Line there so difficult.
Jackson and Croome say that work at St Pauls was also
abandoned[9] for fear of damaging the cathedral, but O'Brien
says only that 'considerable delay was experienced'.[10] Just
how far work was carried at *St Pauls* is difficult to say. While
the Cabinet Office papers, recently made available at the
Public Record Office, mention the deep shelters and the use
of *Clapham Common* and *Kingsway* as citadels, and the use
by the American Army of *Goodge Street*, nothing is said
about *St Pauls*.

The problem seems to have been resolved by copies of
London Transport engineering drawings which kind friends
procured for me at the end of 1978. A layout plan titled
'Home Office Tunnel Shelters – Shelters at St Pauls' is
annotated in longhand: 'Site abandoned, no works com-
menced,' with signature and dated 'Sept 45'. Drawing
C/113-52/005 dated 1940 shows what did happen: a new *St
Pauls* tube station entrance was built where it is today, and
the old *Post Office* station entrance on the north-west corner
of King Edward St and Newgate St closed. In two of its four
shafts a nine-storey deep national HQ was built for the
Central Electricity Board. It is not surprising that the south
side of Newgate St opposite this site is today occupied by
the Central Electricity Generating Board's headquarters
building.

The seven deep shelters actually built on the Northern
Line were: *Stockwell*, *Clapham North*, *Clapham South*,
Belsize Park, which were opened for public use during
the V1 and V2 attacks from the summer of 1944 onwards:
while the others, *Clapham Common*, *Goodge Street*,
with *Chancery Lane* and *St Pauls* remaining in government
use.

Part of *Goodge Street* was adapted in 1942 to serve as
Eisenhower's headquarters. The rest of it was used as a

military transit camp until May 1956 when it was badly
damaged by fire. It was re-equipped as a camp, fell into dis-
use and was offered for sale in 1974. I toured it then with a
BBC television team: it consisted of bare, metal-lined
tunnels with a mid-level deck and a narrower lower deck
furnished with bleak metal bunks and tables. It was
interesting that the air filters were those installed during the
Second World War. They were marked as effective only
against smoke: that is, they probably would not give
protection against radioactive dust or CB weapons. This
fact would suggest that the deep shelters were not taken
seriously as part of the government's tunnelling works of
the 1950s.

*Fig. 23 A typical shaft-head building for the deep shelters built in London
in 1940–43. This one is at Belsize Park.*

The nine shelters on the Northern Line are easily identified by the conspicuous brick stairhead structures on the
surface; these are equally conspicuously missing at *St Pauls*
and *Chancery Lane*.

It seems likely that the deep shelters were built in expecta-
tion of Germany's development and use of the atomic bomb.

The possibility of such a weapon had been described in the popular press in 1939, and by the middle of 1940 Frisch and Peierls, refugee scientists at Birmingham University, had written their crucial memorandum setting out the basic characteristics of a uranium-235 'super bomb'.[11] The shelters consisted of two parallel tubes 16½ feet (5 m) in diameter, 1200 feet (370 m) long, beneath the existing plat-forms. We are told that the idea was to join them up after the war to form an express line, but there may have been some intention to connect them on first construction, for the Frisch–Peierls memorandum said, 'Deep cellars or tunnels may be comparatively safe from the effects of radiation, provided air can be supplied from an uncontaminated area (some of the active substances would be noble gases which are not stopped by ordinary filters).' We now know that the radioactive isotopes of the rare gases, which cannot be removed from air by any simple filtration method, are not a particularly dangerous part of fall-out, and that sufficient protection can be obtained by 'buttoning down' a shelter for the first few hours, to take advantage of the high initial rate of radioactive decay. But it may have seemed in 1940 that it would be necessary to dig shelter tunnels several miles long so that air could always be drawn from a point well removed from a burst. Or it may have been intended to provide a deep escape route out of a devastated and radioactive London by way of tunnels that could not be flooded, crushed or invaded by the public.

If one accepts this theory about the Northern Line deep shelters: that they were planned early in the atomic bomb programme as segments of a deep escape route from London that later research showed was unnecessary, and were then converted into shelter accommodation, at least one puzzle remains. If you are a frightened cabinet minister standing in the centre of a flattened London, your immediate instinct is not to go either north or south, but west. The trend of official yearning towards safety is shown by the plume of important sites to the west of London: Harwell, Aldermaston, Air Defence HQ at Bentley Priory, Strike Command at High Wycombe, UK Land Forces HQ at

Wilton, GCHQ at Cheltenham, the huge underground site at Corsham and so on. So, one might imagine, the first priority was escape to the west, not to the north or south. And, indeed, one often hears rumours of a tunnel linking the centre of London with Heathrow. However, it is not necessary to suppose that such an ambitious work was carried out during the war, or that if it had been we would have heard nothing of it. It is not unlikely that such a tunnel existed some time before the war, built for quite a different purpose.

The Central Electricity Generating Board (CEGB) had, at the end of the war, some nine power stations between Woolwich and Fulham. They are all near the river, from which they draw their cooling water, and because they are surrounded by houses, their output cannot be carried away in overhead cables as is usual from power stations in the country. Instead they deliver their power in underground cables. Of course, most of it is consumed within a short distance because the population density of inner London is so high, but in order to guard against failures, they are also connected to the National Electricity Grid, and one would imagine that the connections are heavy enough to deliver at least one-third of the total power consumption. The Oxford Atlas of Britain (page 99) shows central London's generating capacity as being 25 500 000 000 kW hours in 1954, which is roughly 3×10^9 W hours, and a third of that is 10^9 W hours. Now the supply voltage in inner London was then 132 kV, so in emergency the central area might need to draw some 7000 A from the grid. The maximum practical cable capacity then was 10 kA, so at least one high-capacity, high-voltage cable would have been necessary to join the centre to the grid and super-grid terminals on the outskirts. In fact the grid approaches London from five directions: the south-west, with numerous terminals in the Weybridge area, from the east with connections in the Dartford area, from the north at Waltham Cross, from the north-west at Elstree and from the west at Iver, which is also the main feed from the super-grid. Although high-power cables can be laid in shallow gravel-filled trenches (the French installed the first one at 220 kV in 1930), these must be under roads simply because it is too difficult and expensive to buy wayleaves over private properties in dense urban areas. And road traffic has a very bad effect on cable – as heavy lorries drive along they produce ripples in the ground which gently urge heavy cables forward in the direction of traffic flow. This force is quite capable of straining or breaking them, with consequent heavy maintenance costs. Moreover, shallow high-power cables are vulnerable to sabotage and if damaged can wreak considerable violence on neighbouring lives and property. If the Post Office found deep cable tunnels worthwhile in central London during and after the war (see page 191) it is even more likely that the CEGB did so before the war. It would not be surprising to learn that they had, by 1935, a system of tunnels linking central London with the outskirts, particularly with the west, in which direction lie the largest power stations. These tunnels would probably be 12 feet (3·7 m) in diameter to make it easier to handle the heavy armoured cables, and would be fitted with some sort of railway. They would have excellent ventilation to prevent the cables overheating, and so would need little adaptation for use as a government bolt hole.

Since the grid circles London both to north and south, and the super-grid lies well away from it, we do not have to postulate through tunnels to make sure of grid continuity. One, or perhaps two, links with the exterior would be enough, and the evidence of the Northern Line tunnels might suggest that these were to the west and – possibly – to the east.

As well as avowed, specially constructed accommodation, which did not become available until 1943–4, odd bits of war machine were tucked away in spare spaces underground,[12] mainly on the Piccadilly and Central Lines, where several stations had been redesigned so that access to the platforms was by escalator rather than lift. This often meant moving the surface buildings to one side of the underground station, with the effect that the old lift shafts became available for accommodation or access to other things underground. In other cases complete stations were abandoned. Thus, for an odd example, I had to write an article about the Parachute Brigade in the early 1970s. The Brigadier, Farrar-Hockley, quite naturally wanted to have a look at me first, and kindly proposed a rendezvous in London to save me a possibly fruitless journey to Aldershot. I was surprised to find him in the abandoned surface buildings of the old *Brompton* station, next to the Brompton Oratory, which then housed a Territorial Army centre. So the abandoned station at *Down Street* (0·31 miles – 500 m east of *Hyde Park Corner*) was used as the headquarters of the Railway Executive Committee, and occasionally as a safe place for the Cabinet Office to meet, and for Churchill, with his family, to sleep. He writes:[13]

Towards the middle of October [1940] Josiah Wedgwood began to make a fuss in Parliament about my not having an absolutely bomb-proof shelter for the night raids. He was an old friend of mine . . . his brother was the Chairman of the Railway Executive Committee. Before the War they had had the foresight to construct a considerable underground office in Piccadilly. It was 70 feet below the surface and covered with high, strong buildings.

The neighbouring abandoned station at *Dover Street* (made into *Green Park* in the 1930s) housed some of London Transport's staff, who were also accommodated at *Holborn*, *Hyde Park Corner* and *Knightsbridge*. Control staff of the Great Western Railway were in the relatively deep Bakerloo Line at *Paddington*, and London Transport's emergency engineering staff were in a pair of abandoned station tunnels at *South Kensington*, built in 1903 for a never-completed deep District Line.

British Museum, between *Tottenham Court Road* and *Holborn* on the Central Line, was closed in the 1930s. The bricked-off station platforms are visible from trains, and the surface site is still empty, a weed-grown plot on the north-east corner of New Oxford St and Bloomsbury Ct. The old spiral staircase, 110 feet (34 m) deep, still gives access to the structures underground, and its top seems to be housed in a small brick building in the north-east corner of the plot. There are no visible doors or windows, so entrance is

presumably through the disused warehouse to the east of the
site, which is itself entered through an anonymous door in
Streatham St behind. When asked who owned the warehouse, neighbours said 'The Department of the Environment'. I must confess that any undeveloped site in central
London arouses my suspicions, since the pressure on land
since the Second World War has been so great. There are not
now many left, and most of them seem to stand over secret
underground sites. This particular site has been disused for
nearly 45 years. It may be significant that Centre Point is a
few hundred yards to the west, and *The Oasis*, where
Military Intelligence is said to have an office, not far to the
south-west.

Churchill had a second protected headquarters in
London, called 'Paddock'. Neither Jackson and Croome
nor O'Brien mention it, and the only reference seems to be
by Churchill himself. He writes:[14]

> A citadel for the War Cabinet had already been pre-
> pared near Hampstead, with offices and bedrooms and
> wire and fortified telephone communications.

He described a dress rehearsal for the autumn of 1940:

> We held a Cabinet Meeting at 'Paddock' far from the
> light of day, and each Minister was requested to inspect
> and satisfy himself about his sleeping and working apart-
> ments. We celebrated this occasion by a vivacious
> luncheon, and then returned to Whitehall. This was the
> only time 'Paddock' was used by Ministers.

'Paddock' was – and is – under the GPO's research station
at Dollis Hill, Hendon, north London, and is almost certainly what Kohan[15] refers to in his list of wartime capital
projects as 'Hendon ring main telephone exchange'. I was
told this by an anonymous caller from Dollis Hill, who said
that the rooms are now used to store table tennis equipment.
Confirmation comes from the Cadogan diaries, 10 March
1940: 'Cabinet met in the Dollis Hill War Room.' Since
Churchill was not present, this seems to have been a
different occasion from the one he describes above.

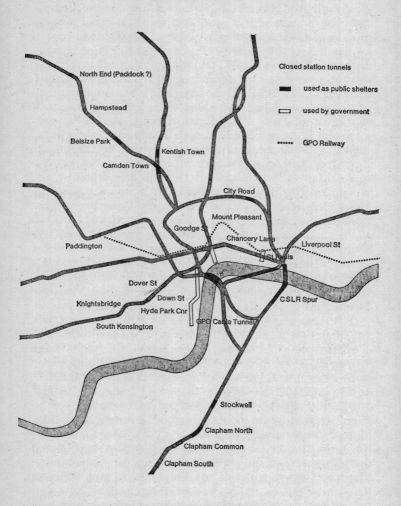

Closed station tunnels

used as public shelters

used by government

GPO Railway

North End (Paddock ?)

Hampstead

Belsize Park

Kentish Town

Camden Town

City Road

Mount Pleasant

Goodge St

Chancery Lane

Paddington

Liverpool St

St Pauls

Dover St

Down St

Knightsbridge

Hyde Park Cnr

C S L R Spur

South Kensington

GPO Cable Tunnel

Stockwell

Clapham North

Clapham Common

Clapham South

Fig. 24 *During the Second World War a good deal of spare space in the London Underground system was used for public and government shelter. This map shows diagrammatically the two G P O cable tunnels dug under Holborn and Whitehall.*

As well as making use of fortuitous holes in the ground, the government built a good deal of bomb-proof accommodation. O'Brien mentions a 'few' alternative war-rooms built in the suburbs after 1939 in case central London had to be evacuated. The major buildings in Whitehall were given strengthened basements. Churchill himself spent most of the war under 6 feet (1·8 m) of concrete in the sub-basement of the annexe of the new public offices in George Street.[16] During the first half of 1941 four fortresses, generally known as Citadels, were built in central London.[17] Two can be identified with some confidence as being among the following: Montagu House 'Fortress', the Admiralty blockhouse in Pall Mall – Churchill called it the 'vast monstrosity which weighs on the Horse Guards Parade' – the Rotundas in Horseferry Road, on the site of the old Westminster gas-holders.[18] 'In 1937 the gasholders were removed. In 1941 their tanks were converted into two heavily reinforced underground strongholds each equipped to house several thousand Government officials in absolute safety from enemy attack for up to three months. These were joined by tube railway to similar strongholds in Whitehall [Montagu House] and the Mall [The Admiralty Blockhouse].

The Rotundas were in use in 1967 as an ROC school. For the other two, we can choose among: the ground floor of the Department of Education and Science in Curzon Street (formerly Beaverbrook's Ministry of Aircraft Production, with its own self-defence force), now said to house MI5's registry, Citadel telephone exchange at Faraday House, and the London Civil Defence War-room just to the south of the Geological Museum (now, as are the Rotundas, the foundation of a new building on top).

During the first half of 1941 some strong steel-framed buildings were erected in central London with the intention that they should resist, if not direct hits, at least the blast from near misses.[19] This was because Churchill says that he refused to use 'Paddock' except as a last resort, and insisted that safe accommodation should be available not only for the Cabinet and its immediate staff, but also for key members of major ministries. So he writes,[20] 'Lord

Beaverbrook was thus entrusted with the task of making a large number of bomb-proof strongholds capable of housing the essential staffs of many departments of state, and a dozen of them, several connected by tunnels, survive in London today.' These buildings, identifiable by their utilitarian bleakness, seem in the main to stand in New Oxford Street, and between the Strand and the Embankment.

In view of the description 'bomb-proof' and Churchill's mention on the next page of a bomb that had penetrated to 80 feet in marshy soil, we may take it that these buildings covered considerable and deep underground structures. 'Tunnels', in this context connecting 'bomb-proof strongholds', sounds like tunnels people can walk through, not just cable ducts, though at first, since bombardment was intermittent, movement of people was less important than providing bomb-proof runs for telephone cables.

This mention of tunnels is almost the only reference in the commonly read literature to the extensive system of burrows that was constructed under London during the war, though specialized books and journals mention them quite freely.[21] In fact there seem to have been two interconnecting, but basically distinct, tunnel systems which still exist and are in use. The first was the network of Post Office cable tunnels. To begin with, there were two small bores which served to protect important cable runs against aerial attack. The first was dug in 1939–40. It lay 100 feet (30 m) below ground, parallel with and slightly to the south of Holborn, linking *Holborn* telephone exchange with *St Martin's le Grand* and *Faraday House*. At the eastern end, just before it reached *St Pauls*, it divided into two, so it looked like a T on its side. The southern arm of the T ended under *Citadel* exchange, housed in a monstrous block of concrete at the north-east corner of the *Faraday* building. It has walls 7¼ feet (2·2 m) thick, its own artesian well, and was built in six months of 1940 at a cost of £250 000. The tunnel was 7 feet (2·1 m) in diameter, lined for the most part with concrete segments, and had 650 feet (200 m) of iron.[22] The northern limb of the T ends where one might expect to find *St Pauls* (page 191), just south of G P O H Q at *St Martin's le Grand*.

Another writer, Boryer, describes[23] the digging of this tunnel from shafts sunk at the three ends, and from a fourth in Warwick Lane, west of St Paul's Cathedral. It is not hard to see why a protected cable run was needed on this alignment. *Faraday*, at the eastern end, was then the international trunk exchange, Electra House, where all our overseas telegraph cables terminated, was only a few yards away; while *Holborn*, at the western end, was one of London's major trunk exchanges. Through a thousand yards of wire flowed the control of a war that spread round the world.

The other original tunnel ran from Trafalgar Square down Whitehall, swung to the west of Parliament, and then continued on a parallel alignment to terminate on the Rotundas. It was again of small diameter designed to carry cable between military headquarters buildings and *Federal* exchange under the old War Office (according to an old map I found in the GPO HQ Library; under the Rotundas according to more modern sources). A map showing the two tunnels as thus described is given in Harbottle (see Figure 25).[24]

A London Transport engineering drawing of 1939 (B/129 31/001) shows the construction of a new cable shaft at the junction of Whitehall and Trafalgar Square, with cable runs coming from the north and southbound train tunnels, and going away down Whitehall (drawing B/129 52/010 of 1950).

During the war the tunnels seemed to have developed space. Boryer says that the 'original concept of the system' was a cable run linking the major service departments. In May 1941 there was 1 mile (1·6 km) of it, by 1942 there was 1 mile 740 yards (2·3 km), and by the end of the war 3 miles (4·8 km). After the war the system remained secret, since it still provided the capital's major defence-communication arteries, but was also developed for civilian as well as defence purposes. The Post Office found that, although cable tunnel at £250 a yard (£270 per metre)[25] was expensive to dig, in the long run it was cheaper than the usual method of burying cable in shallow ducts under main roads. In the subterranean quiet of the tunnels the watertight outer skin of cables seldom breaks, so maintenance is much reduced, and

and it is simple to lay new cable or rearrange the existing
network. In 1967 the system was taken off the secret list,
though the map given me in 1969 by the Press Office of
London Telecommunications Region did not show the
tunnel under Whitehall. It is hard to believe that this is
not still used. The Post Office tunnels in London are now
15 miles (24 km) long; in 1976 extensions were being driven
at Waterloo, Dartford and Shepherds Bush.

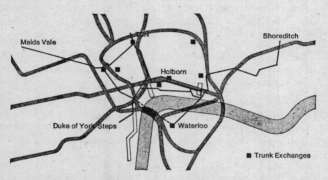

*Fig. 25 As well as the network of shelter tunnels under modern London
there is a system of GPO cable tunnels which extends from Maida Vale and
Shepherds Bush in the west to Shoreditch in the east.*

At the beginning of the 1930s, long before these tunnels
were dug, or perhaps even thought about, the Post Office
had begun to run the London ends of about half its
long-distance trunk cables in deep Underground tubes
(Northern, Piccadilly, Central).[26] This network, much of it
devoted to the needs of the Services after war broke out, was
interconnected with the GPO cable tunnels, and cables
running in the Post Office railway tunnels. As an extra
precaution, a ring main was thrown round London to
guarantee through communications even if the entire centre
of the city was flattened. Kohan[27] notes that the Hendon
Ring main exchange cost £90 000 (but see also page 190) and
Harbottle says that the cable ran under the Thames via the
pilot bore for the Dartford tunnel.

The BBC, which works, as we shall see, in close collaboration with the GPO, also safeguarded its operations in
central London. Bishop writes:[28]

> . . . an exceptionally strong building was built near
> Broadcasting House to provide for small studios, a con-
> trol room and a number of offices for use in extreme
> emergency. Line and radio communications were pro-
> vided to Brookman's Park and Daventry. It was for-
> tunately never necessary to use the building for its original
> purpose. This was in the northeast corner of Broadcasting
> House.

There may have been another protected BBC site in
London. Bishop says that before the war the recording
equipment was sited in the Maida Vale studios – a long
corrugated iron building, originally a skating rink, in
Delaware Road. This means that every programme to be
recorded was routed through Maida Vale, so it was already
something of a focal point in the system:[29]

> In the months that preceded the war, some of the
> recording channels were moved to other centres as part of
> a general policy of dispersal, whilst those that remained at
> Maida Vale were moved to a better protected part of the
> building.

In 1969 concrete blocks two stories high stuck out of the
roof at either side of the southern end. One had an air intake
grille and a whip aerial. By 1975 they had been demolished.

The London telephone system

Direct evidence of the tunnels is thin after the burst of publicity in the euphoric postwar period. We will return to what
little there is, but for the moment it is worth examining the
London telephone system for whatever evidence it may
contain.

In the first edition, I put forward a theory of the telephone
system which would have been elegant if it had been true,
but those who know more about telephones than I do have
demolished it.

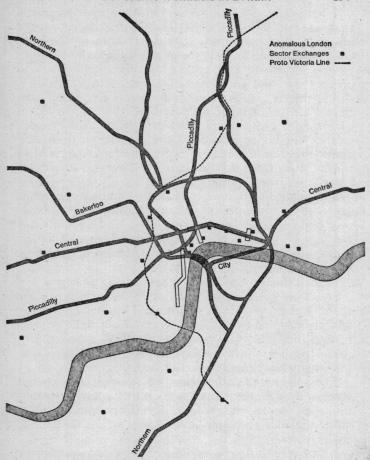

Fig. 26 *During the 1930s a large part of the central network of telephone cables was run in the deep tube lines. Traces of this network, used both for peace and war, seemed to survive in the organization of the exchanges of central London. Those shown here are connected together in 'sectors' that stretch right across the city. It will be seen that the geographical relationship between the exchanges and the old tubes is fairly loose. It is interesting that the Victoria Line passes underneath no fewer than six, as well as other important buildings, including the Post Office Tower.*

What I think one can still say, with some confidence, is that in about 1935, during the period of preparation against air raids, the government started to run their telephone cables in the deep tubes. It seems likely that, as is usual with emergency cable, this system was also partly given to civilian use, and connected exchanges across London – those, that is, which stood conveniently near deep tube lines. For after all, unless the government had its own system of telephone exchanges (and in fact it had only one, *Federal*, in the War Office Rotundas) the problem of protecting communications in the city resolved itself into the problem of protecting cable between certain exchanges – those that served essential government offices.

One might imagine there was a certain amount of shuffling about at this time, so that important offices in out-of-the-way buildings were moved into those which could easily be served with protected communications, while less important units of government were moved into more vulnerable accommodation.

During the war the cable tunnel system was begun, and cables were gradually moved out of the deep tubes into them. But since this was a piecemeal job, the association with the deep tubes remained, so that we might now expect to find that important government offices are served by exchanges near the deep tube lines, even though there is no longer any functional connection with them.

The cable tunnels offered many advantages: much better security (remember the CIA coup in Berlin, when they tunnelled across the border, and intercepted Russian military cables), a better environment for the cables, and easier maintenance.

If this were true, some oddities of the system would make sense. For example, the extension of the tunnel to Maida Vale – not in itself an important communications centre – would tend to confirm the identification of the BBC's studios there as the site of a protected war headquarters.

To get a cable to *Victoria* and *Tate Gallery* it would indeed be possible to use the known Post Office cable tunnel as far as the Rotundas. But when one looks at the 1969 tube map of

London something very odd leaps to the eye. The Victoria Line, which was only completed in 1969, not only passes under this exchange building, but also provides an excellent deep cable run to *Battersea* and *Brixton*. In fact, without the Victoria Line, these two are hard to fit into the system at all. One hears occasional rumours that this tube line is somehow connected with the government tunnels under London. On the face of it, this is preposterous: its construction was not begun until several years after the H-bomb and the abandonment of the London tunnel system. But we do not have to invoke timewarp to explain the connection. Such is the leisurely pace of progress that the Victoria Line implements a plan that was first devised in 1946. This was the work of the Railway (London Plan) Committee, set up by the Minister of War Transport in 1944, when doubtless questions of defence were not far away from his mind. (Preparations against the potentially A-bomb-tipped V2s began in the summer of 1943 – see page 25). The only difference from the Victoria Line as it is today was that 'Route 8', of 1946, swung west of Buckingham Palace and *Down Street*, going by *Hyde Park Corner* and *Bond Street*.[30] The idea is rather attractive that, when the tunnels were extended in 1942 or thereabouts, a pilot bore at least was driven in this alignment (see Figure 26). If this were so, it would connect *Museum* telephone exchange (now the GPO Tower, but since the early 1930s the national distribution centre for the BBC's programmes), the BBC itself, the bunker in Curzon Street, Churchill's early hole in the ground at *Down Street* and Buckingham Palace.

This could join up with an extension of the Post Office cable running at the north end of Vauxhall Bridge, and, passing under the Thames, go close below an odd nexus of officialdom at the other end of the bridge. There are annexes of Scotland Yard and the Foreign Office, and the headquarters of the London Telecommunications Region. We know that the original intention to build a deep shelter at *Oval* was frustrated by springs of water there. If the chain of these shelters, ostensibly intended to be connected after the war into an express line, were intended to be linked during the war, the trouble at the *Oval* would be circumvented by the proto-Victoria Line's detour to *Stockwell*. Some support for this idea is given by a London Transport engineering drawing of the Victoria Line station at Stockwell (N/147 52/010 dated 1970). It shows, parallel to the northbound station tunnel, an odd structure labelled 'Existing cast iron tunnel previously backfilled with concrete'. It is only 7 feet (2·1 m) in diameter – what one would expect. Nothing similar is shown on the Home Office drawing of the deep shelter.

The second tunnel system

Cables in the deep tubes and the cable tunnels provided communication that was secure against conventional and even atomic bombs, but it is evidently equally important to protect the communicators. We have already seen some of the ways in which the wartime government burrowed into existing holes in London. But a system of scattered holes that would serve very well as protection against two or three raids a day with high-explosive bombs (in between which people would come out and move about), would not be at all useful if the enemy used nuclear or biological weapons. Then it would be necessary not only to be able to shelter from blast for the duration of the raid, but also to survive contamination of the surface for a period of several weeks. One can detect a new and modern approach to the problems of protecting the central government and high command from as early as 1942 when Allied intelligence began to get whispers about the V2 rocket. In Britain and America the atom bomb was already well under development, while two years before, Gruinard Island had been sprayed with anthrax. It must have seemed likely that the German rockets would be tipped with atomic or biological weapons, and equally obvious that, to counter this threat, the centre of the war machine had to be housed in a much more coherent, self-contained underground system.

Some time in the 1930s the central government telephone exchange, *Federal*, was installed underground. Shortly before war broke out, the system of man-sized tunnels with offices off them was built under Whitehall. A correspondent sent me a story told him by a friend who went in 1939 to the Labour Exchange to get a job. He was set to work fastening tables to the floor in rooms off a tunnel under the Horse Guards. The tunnel went a long way, with many branches, some guarded and inaccessible. There was rumoured to be a branch at Charing Cross, so that the government and Royal family could catch a tube to Paddington, a train to Bristol and away to Canada if there should be an invasion. Curiously enough, the man who installed central heating in my present house had worked for a cleaning company which had the contract to do the housekeeping in these same tunnels. An air intake for the Buckingham Palace–Whitehall spur is just outside the gents' loo at the Institute of Contemporary Arts in the Mall.

I stumbled on what might be an amusing reference to the tunnel system as recently at 1975. I was in the press office of Camden Council seeing the people about a story. To make conversation, I asked what was holding up the second phase of the Brunswick Centre – an architecturally interesting complex of flats and shops just south of St Pancras. The answer given by a young public relations officer was that the developers could not get possession of a Territorial Army Hall in Handel Street which had to be demolished, because there was 'a gun in the cellar defending London' which would have to be moved, and as yet there was nowhere to move it. It sounds as if an access to the tunnel system was meant, for the danger in tunnels is fire, and the civil service and Post Office have strict rules about multiple exits. Naturally these exits must be into buildings owned by the government, and in the sticky state of the property market it may not be easy to provide a new one to replace one that might emerge into the TA Hall.

One of the next steps in the programme to protect the government seems to have been the burial of a central international exchange. Kohan[31] mentions in his sparse list of the GPO's major wartime schemes, that the *Holborn* exchange (tunnel scheme) cost £15 000. The tunnel in this case was the two 16½ foot (5 m) bores under *Chancery Lane* tube station, and it seems likely that the cost far exceeded the sum he mentions. A series of drawings titled 'Home Office Shelter Tunnels' are kept by London Transport among their station plans. These drawings are undated, but have a 1939 look to them. One of *Chancery Lane* (unnumbered by LTE, but probably filed at C/115 52/010) has some interesting manuscript notations on it. One is: '? About £300 000', which seems a more realistic value, even at 1940 prices. At the same time some deep-level excavation was probably done to house elements of the central government, but nothing more is head of this tunnel system until the early 1950s. Then, in the first post-war spasm of civil-defence spending (see Figure 16, page 115), which prepared against Russia's unlooked-for development of the atom bomb, a great deal more digging was done. In 1951, Frank Gullett in the *Daily Worker*[32] reported mysterious excavations in Holborn and Whitehall. He said that 'some 2000 building workers are engaged in building a network of atom-proof tunnels under London stretching from Holborn to Westminster a mile away. These secret tunnels are designed not for London's population, but for Cabinet ministers, top civil servants and defence chiefs.' He went on to describe two shafts in Furnival Street and another outside the War Office in Whitehall. We can now, almost 30 years later, see the fruits of this labour – at least at the Holborn end. The excavations in Furnival Street were to provide air shafts and an equipment lift for a large extension to the Holborn deep shelter to house a 500-line automatic exchange called *Kingsway*. The new tunnels opened into the pair of tubes dug in 1942, and were fed with cable from the 1939 cable tunnel which ran nearby. The first NATO transatlantic cable – TAT1 – terminated there. There is an Act of Parliament about *Kingsway* and its two brothers in Birmingham and Manchester, which mentions that two agreements dealing with the London tunnels were concluded between the Ministry of Home Security and the

Fig. 27a Kingsway telephone exchange underneath Chancery Lane underground station. Part of the Post Office cable tunnel is shown at the bottom.

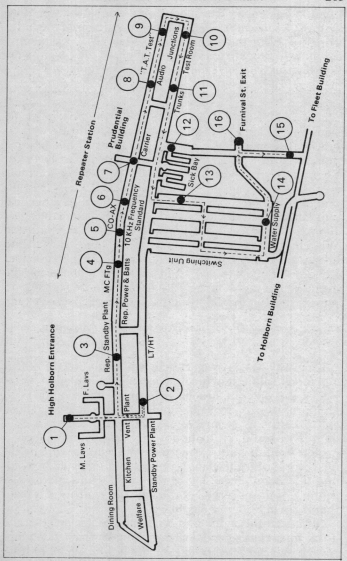

London Passenger Transport Board during the war. The first, of 18 December 1942, probably legitimized the hasty works of 1940; the second, of 24 May 1943, was almost certainly to prepare for sheltering more of the government than then had citadels against the V2 rocket threat of 1944.[33]

Fig. 27b A view of the ventilation plant at Kingsway – roughly at point 14 in 27a.

Kingsway has its own artesian well, and reserves of fuel and food to allow it to function in complete isolation for six weeks. It is entered through an inconspicuous door in High Holborn: its size – to walk round it all takes at least an hour and a half – its cleanliness, order and quietness are an impressive testimony to the government's determination to protect itself. It is also extraordinary to think that this bright busy world of technicians lay almost unsuspected beneath one of London's busiest streets for more than a quarter of a century. If the government can hide this from us, it is plain that it can hide almost anything.

If we bear this in mind, it is not hard to imagine that the government has a good deal more tunnel which it does not reveal. We can attempt to estimate how much more from

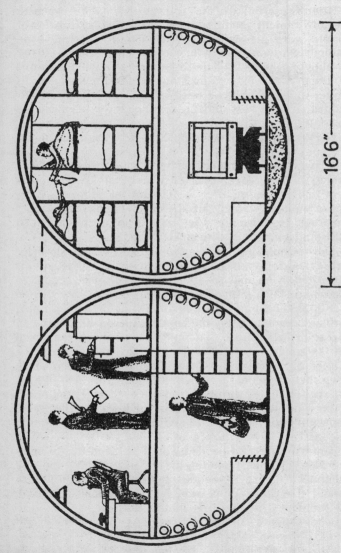

16'6"

Fig. 28 The government's shelter tunnel under London might look like this.

O'Brien's description of the arrangements made to evacuate the government to the west in 1940. Two categories of people were planned for: 'seat of Government – the Cabinet, Parliament, and the most essential officials to the number of some 16 000', and another less essential group of 44 000.[34] If this first group alone seems a great many to shelter underground, we must remember O'Brien's complaint that in 1944 'Citadel accommodation was available for [only] 8500'.

The first mention of the complete system was by Chapman Pincher in the *Daily Express*[35] in 1959. Reporting then on a *new* government citadel being built out in the country (see below), he said: 'It replaces ten miles of reinforced tunnels built under London after the last war at enormous cost. These tunnels, which are below Whitehall, Leicester Square,[36] Holborn and Victoria are not deep enough to withstand a near miss with an H-bomb.'

The 'ten miles' (16 km) may be journalistic enthusiasm, or a true description of the enlargement in 1951. The latter is suggested by an analysis of the amount of space needed to accommodate a seat of government of the size O'Brien mentions. The minimum area for civil-defence operational staffs recommended by the Home Office is 40 square feet (3·7 sq m) per head.[37] Sixteen thousand people then need 640 000 square feet (60 000 sq m). A reasonable design for a shelter for this many, if we bear in mind the precedent of the deep shelters, would be a pair of tunnels 16½ feet (4·5 m) internal diameter with two decks in each bore, the upper giving working or sleeping space, the lower runs for cable and ventilation. It would be handy to have a goods railway in one, and a walkway in another.

The working area needed would be given by 7·6 miles (12·3 km) of tunnel (counting the upper deck only), and if we reckon that eight people could sleep in a 7 foot (2·1 m) run of tunnel, that calls for an extra 2·6 miles (4·2 km). The total, 10·2 miles (16·4 km), is almost suspiciously close to Pincher's figure, though the actual geographical extent would only be 5 miles (8 km).

One can make a guess at the alignment of these extensions

by plotting the locations of government and public buildings served by telephone exchanges near the deep tubes (see page 209). Immediately one notices a striking concentration along the two known tunnels. It seems not unreasonable to suppose that where we find dense alignments of these buildings with no known deep tube beneath, they stand over extensions to the tunnel system, dug either in the late 1940s or the early 1950s. Two such alignments suggest themselves. One runs from *St Pauls* in an arc southwesterly towards *Waterloo*. If there is a tunnel here, it is probably quite old, for it passes under the Central Electricity Generating Board's national grid-control centre[38] at Bankside, an outpost of the Ministry of Defence, the Ministry of Transport, several HMSO buildings – including the Parliamentary press – and the new *Rampart* trunk exchange. It is not hard to imagine a short connection from *Waterloo* to rejoin the tunnel somewhere under Whitehall.

The other striking alignment of buildings runs down Victoria Street, or just to the north. Here are representatives of several departments, notably the Foreign Office's Communications and Electronic Security Department, the headquarters of London Transport, Scotland Yard, the Board of Trade and Westminster City Hall. This tunnel would join the proto-Victoria Line at Victoria (if such a thing ever existed).

The known and suggested tunnel is then a bit more than 5 miles (8 km) long, and I would imagine that it is double, as suggested above, and that the proto-Victoria Line is – or was – merely a cable duct. On the other hand, one can imagine that it was in fact a proper tunnel. The total length would then be nearer 10 miles (16 km).

We can estimate the cost of such a scheme by reference to the deep shelters, which in the end cost £750 000 a mile (£470 000 per km) run of single tube at 1943 prices. An extra 7 miles (11 km), fitted up with communications and air filtration as a seat of government, can hardly have cost less than £9–£18 million ten years later. This is 10–11 per cent of the admitted expenditure on civil defence during the years 1951–5.

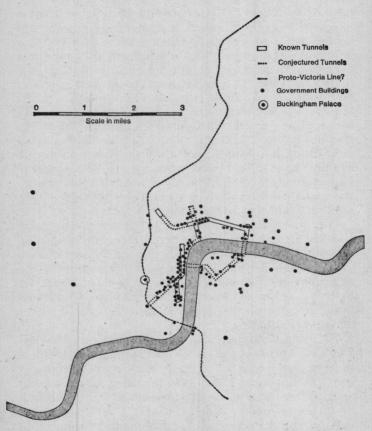

Fig. 29 The dots show the positions of selected government buildings in central London.

These exits must emerge in buildings owned or controlled by the government; as we have seen, the tunnel under Whitehall was connected to many buildings there. But where there are no government buildings, one would

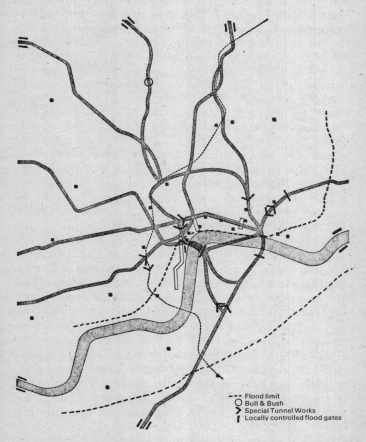

Fig. 30 Locations of quick-acting and slow, locally-controlled doors in the deep tubes. The quick-acting doors are known as 'Special Tunnel Works' and are controlled from BULL AND BUSH.

imagine the constructors might be in something of a quandary. At one time I thought that there might be connections between the secret tunnel system and the deep tubes: however, I am assured by some friends who know the tube system well that this is not so. The only mysterious feature of the London Transport tunnels is a system of doors against flood – and presumably blast – which are hidden in the running tunnels and are closed hydraulically on command from a protected room 110 feet (33 m) below ground at the unfinished *Bull and Bush* station between *Hampstead* and *Golders Green*. This control room is entered through a small building whose attempt to simulate an electricity substation is somewhat marred by the conspicuous air intake on its roof. There are 20 of these quick-acting automatic gates known as 'Special Tunnel Works', whose particular feature is that they will open and shut as a train passes through them, suggesting that they are involved in some scheme which envisages trains running during a button-down period – these trains, perhaps, being for the transport of officials and members of the government only. There are 22 other gates which have to be operated locally and whose closure is permanent during the emergency. When they are shut, a signal shows at *Bull and Bush*. Broadly speaking these gates surround the part of London which is likely to be flooded if the Thames overflows. There are some oddities: *Charing Cross* has flood gates on all lines, suggesting that there is some hope of keeping the platforms dry, even though one would expect it to flood first of all since it is so close to the river wall. And there is an odd set of gates 1000 ft (300 m) east of *Liverpool St* on the Central Line: two back to back about 20 ft (6 m) apart, apparently protecting a cross passage between the running tunnels from which lead two more passages: one to the underground sidings east of *Liverpool St*, while the other disappears – on the drawings at least – into dotted lines. (LTE drawing DS 51820, dated 20.4.72.)

One thousand feet (300 m) east of the *Liverpool St* underground platforms puts one roughly below the junction of Bethnal Green Road and Shoreditch High Street. There is nothing spectacular to be seen on the surface: a large telephone exchange lies on the east side of the road, with an extensive basement and one exhaust for an emergency diesel running up the back of the building. Opposite there is a row of derelict houses, one of which has had its ground floor front faced in glass bricks, and has anonymous mahogany doors very like those at *Down St*. But this may be a meaningless coincidence. However, this cross passage underground, so expensively protected against flooding, may be one of the few connections between the deep tubes and the secret system.

The effect of all the gates together would be that trains could run on the Central Line, through the special gates east of *Liverpool St*, as far as *Bethnal Green*. Further progress eastward would be stopped by ordinary floodgates there to prevent flooding from the Lee valley. Trains could run on the Piccadilly Line through the special gates at *Russell Sq* and *Green Park*.

Trains on the Bakerloo Line would be stopped from the north by gates north of *Charing Cross*, and south of the river by gates at *Waterloo*. In effect, the line would be cut in two. The Victoria Line, presumably designed with flooding in mind, so that there are built-in barriers at stations to prevent surface water entering the tunnels, is blocked only by a special gate at *Green Park*.

The Northern Line, north of the river, is blocked by floodgates at *Charing X* and *Bank*, south of the river at *Waterloo* and *London Bridge*, and has special gates, presumably sited south of the deepest inundations, at *Kennington*.

Present usefulness of the tunnels

This account of the London tunnel system has been criticized[39] on two grounds: first, that in a real emergency the government would operate from the national and regional seats of government out in the country; and second, that in a period of lesser trouble it would defend its premises in London with tanks and sandbags – as it has in Northern Ireland, without having to go underground.

However, we do not have to explain why the tunnels exist – they were built in reaction to nuclear threats during and just after the Second World War. We have to explain why they are still in use, and apparently added to from time to

time. Supposing that there were a revolution on the boil,
reason to fear a coup d'état, possibly aided by air strikes with
conventional weapons and paratroops landed by foreign
powers. It might be necessary in the end for the government
to retire to the country, but it would doubtless want to
be able to keep a presence in London, for even in these
sophisticated times possession of the emblems of power –
Buckingham Palace, Westminster, Downing Street – might
be crucial in keeping public opinion behind the regime. But,
at the same time, life in these buildings might be too
dangerous for more than purely ceremonial appearances.
Hence it would be a sensible option to keep the tunnels in
good repair and to maintain and even extend the communications facilities already underground. Just as the Post
Office finds it economic to excavate deep cable tunnels,
because although more expensive initially than ducts below
the roads they make for cheaper maintenance of the cables
once installed, the extra cost of building a trunk exchange
underground in central London (remembering that the site
is almost free) is probably not all that extravagant. Thus
there is the Defence Message Switching centre under
Trafalgar Square.[40] There is also the Mercury trunk unit
under the Post Office Tower, Q-Whitehall, an inter-
exchange switching centre for the civil service dial-in
Whitehall telephone system in the Horseferry Rotundas
which is now part of the foundations of the new government
offices between Monck Street and Marsham Street, and, it is
said, a new telecommunications centre being built under St
Pauls under cover of the work on the new Jubilee Line. (But
there may have been one there since 1940.) And there is said
to be an unopened extension to the Bakerloo Line as far as
Camberwell. And in a time of lesser aggro the fact that in
Northern Ireland the government sits it out on the surface
does not mean it would not welcome tunnels there if it had
them. Furthermore, one must remember that non-vital but
sensitive records and activities can be evacuated from
Belfast; for all but the inner core of government there is no
retreat from London.

Fortress architecture

Animated by the IRA, the Grosvenor Square riots in 1968 and the generally rising level of confrontation between the forces of the state and those of the citizenry, contemporary public architecture is beginning to show some fortress-like trends. The most obvious feature, to be seen for instance at Mondial House, the new internal exchange in the City, the Guards barracks in Knightsbridge and the American Embassy, is a moat to make access through windows difficult and to keep car-bombs at a distance, together with the recessed first couple of floors above ground level (the American Embassy is recessed all the way up). A recent article on fortress architecture[41] suggests that steel-supporting members should be clad in concrete so that two explosive attacks are necessary – one to strip the cladding, the second to cut the steel. Some radio masts are supported at a single point: this should be shrouded to prevent observation and design of an effective charge. Hollow spaces where slow-burning mining charges can be placed should be avoided at low levels in new buildings – or, indeed, old ones. In some military buildings gun slits are built into the outer walls and lower storeys: at the Guards barracks, the high perimeter wall is broken up with slots from top to bottom that appear, at first, to be a pleasant architectural device, but on closer examination seem designed to allow those inside to cover the outward approaches with small arms. On the Kensington Gore side the slots are arranged to enfilade the wall and cover approaches up and down the street; on the park side they face straight out. The barracks at Kensington Gore is said to stand above a large Army headquarters under Hyde Park and the Museums. It is interesting that the tall block of flats for married soldiers in this complex also provides a well-defended high site for HF, VHF and, if necessary, microwave aerials.

A much more blatant example of protective architecture was to be seen at Leconfield House, MI5's former office in Curzon Street. One hears that the service kept its card index of suspects there, together with all its elaborate case documentation. Those interested in espionage would no

Fig. 31 Machine-gun ports at Leconfield House, Curzon Street, formerly an office of MI5.

doubt have liked to destroy or capture this material: to prevent such an attempt, mounted perhaps as a spill-over from a political demonstration at the near-by American Embassy, the prudent civil servants had installed double steel shutters, steel doors pleasantly grained to resemble wood, and at first-floor level, machine-gun ports commanding approaches up and down Curzon Street. It was vacated in January 1978 and the files transferred to Curzon Street House.

It is not surprising that other preparations have been made elsewhere. But the London tunnels would still be useful as fall-out shelters and against chemical or biological attacks and, more particularly, as a strong and handy refuge for the government in time of severe civil disturbances. We return to this point later. One supposes that in the 1950s the peacetime government was rearranged: the buildings over the tunnel contained all the people needed for the 'black move', so that in a moment of national or international crisis they could easily slip downstairs to safety.

The mystery of the air-conditioned buildings

It is odd that many of the new air-conditioned office blocks built in London since 1960 stand on the suggested tunnel alignment (see Figure 29).

It was only when considering the nature of these buildings that the ideas offered in this chapter began to form in my mind. The coincidence of prolonged strikes, at both the Barbican and Horseferry Road sites, suggested some connection between the two places. I wondered whether both strikes could serve the interests of a third party – say, for want of a better bogy, Russia. If that were true, then both sites must have some national importance. This was easy enough to see at Horseferry Road – the buildings were to be, and are now, government offices, and they stand physically on the Rotundas. Was the Barbican, then, ostensibly an ordinary business development, also something important? Perhaps the two places were joined by a tunnel. The deep shelters at *St Pauls* and *Chancery Lane* gave one leg, but there is no publicly known deep tube near the Rotundas. To fill the gap I guessed at a deep tunnel under Whitehall, and so deduced (whether rightly or wrongly) the existence of the Post Office cable tunnel some months before I found Harbottle's map.

The general structure of the thing soon became clear in much the form of Figure 32.

Then I embarked on the attempt to get some information out of the London telephone sectors, found the wartime history of the tubes, and finally plotted out the positions of the main government and service buildings. But as the existence of the tunnel became more certain in my mind, so the importance of the air-conditioned buildings dwindled. I had at first thought that they were intended as a citadel so that the seat of government could ride out the threat or execution of chemical or biological (CB) attack, for, say, up to several months – far longer than it could last in its tunnels. The accommodation in the offices shown in Figure 32, at a reasonable allowance of space, would be about enough for 16 000 people.[42]

But there are two apparently insuperable objections. The

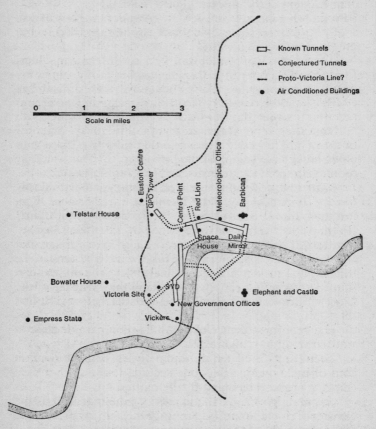

Fig. 32 It is very odd that, of the 16 sites of major office blocks built in London during the early 1960s, no less than twelve lie on or near the suggested network of secret government shelters.

first is that if an enemy, by threat of a CB attack, frightened the seat of government into its glass-walled citadel, then one air-burst H-bomb – perhaps fired by some other evilly-disposed nation – would kill the lot by flying glass. The other objection is more serious. A building with air filtration to guard against CB warfare is not just an air-conditioned building with trimmings, but a completely different animal. Size, structure, filters, ventilating plant, must all be purpose-designed. As a test case, we may consider the new New Scotland Yard building. I was assured by the Chief Engineer of the Metropolitan Police, in 1968, that there was no filtration against war gases or pathogens at all. Yet if the citadel theory were right, one would expect protection here almost above all.

If one could accept the theory, it would explain a number of other puzzling points. For one thing, many of these big office blocks came into existence because of some odd bit of luck in the planning stage. Reading Marriott's *The Property Boom*, one often gets the impression that a hidden hand was helping the developers of these monsters. For instance, the design of Centre Point, at Tottenham Court Road, was never submitted as it should have been, to the Fine Arts Commission, who might have held it up for years. Of the Euston Centre (where MI5 is said to have offices on the visibly curtained fourteenth floor), Marriott writes, 'throughout the LCC were extremely cooperative with Joe Levy [the developer]. It was like having a fourth partner in the consortium.'[43] It feels as if in the true Home Office style of secrecy, compromise and indirectness, these developers were induced by nudges and tweaks and sudden slight collapses in the wall of officialdom to put up more or less the kind of building the government wanted on sites that had been chosen long in advance.

Above all, it would explain the biggest mystery of them all: why Centre Point, 385 feet (120 m) high, with 302 000 square feet (27 180 sq m) of floor space, has now stood empty for ten years. It would explain why the original owner, Harry Hyams, got the site from the GLC for the ludicrously low ground rent of £18 500 a year over a fixed term of 150 years. On this interpretation one would assume that the building was being kept empty as an immediately available CB shelter for the hub of government and that, as well as cheap ground rent, Hyams was being paid a heavy but secret subsidy to keep it empty.

(On revising this passage in 1977, I was rather tempted to strike it out. But, on the other hand, there certainly is something slightly odd about Centre Point, although having looked more closely at its history in the meantime, it is less odd than it had seemed. A political figure of Camden Council, who interests himself in Hyams and Centre Point, tells me that he has asked the technical officers of the council about the possibility of Centre Point being connected with the secret tunnel system, and says that none of these people dismiss the possibility out of hand. 'There is no evidence against it,' he says, although the sceptical reader may decide that there is equally little evidence for it.)

Flight from London

There is a persistent rumour that there is a tunnel running from Buckingham Palace to the outskirts of London, so that the Queen and her associates can flee, unhampered by disorder on the surface, from the threat of nuclear attack or revolution. Some versions of the story have the western end of this tunnel at London Airport, so that she may fly, if necessary, straight to Canada. If one looks logically at the government's protection problem, there is a good case to be made out for the existence of some such deep-level tube leading to the outskirts. There was not much point in digging shelters for the 16 000 people who make up the 'seat of government' under the centre of the city, if after the attack the exits are blocked by miles of rubble and fall-out-contaminated ground. The existing deep tubes would probably not be satisfactory, since their many station entrances would admit blast and fall-out, and they might well be crowded with refugees and shelterers. For the same reason, any deep escape route for the government would have to be kept secret if it were to be any use on the day. Since one of London's more pressing transport needs was for a long time a deep-level tube serving the airport, it would be interesting to know whether this rumour has any better foundation than collective paranoia.

A more obvious escape route from central London is offered by the Broad Walk in Kensington Gardens. This

Fig. 33 In 1954 elm trees lining the Broad Walk in Kensington Gardens were summarily felled, leaving a clear strip 25 yards (22·9 m) wide on each side of the path. It seems likely that this was intended as an emergency airstrip for the post-attack evacuation of Queen and government from London. (Photos: TIMES NEWSPAPERS LTD).

wide strip of tarmac is 1000 yards (900 m) long and clear of well-grown trees for 25 yards (22·5 m) or so on each side. It is significant that the elms which used to line it were summarily felled in 1954 – one of the years of maximum civil-defence effort – as being infected with elm disease, although a local protest group said that only 4 per cent were sick. The Walk seems then to have been widened to its present generous expanse. Saplings were planted to replace the elms, and are now quite substantial little trees – about 9 inches (22 cm) in diameter. But in an emergency it would be the work of a few hours to cut them down and clear them, and they would, if felled by blast, present no obstacle. The huge old trees they replaced would have blocked the strip for days if they had been blown down. This seems to be the only place in the middle of the capital from which fixed-wing aircraft could operate. It is large enough, for instance, for the take-off of a Hawker-Siddeley 748 twin-engined transport, which can carry 52 people for 500 miles (800 km).

Government citadels outside London
Sokolovsky rightly says:[44]

> Reliable communications ensuring control of the country as a whole during the war cannot be considered new and different from a peacetime communications system . . . Important communications centres should be set up in underground quarters, protected from nuclear explosions. Their locations should form a net-work allowing us to obtain communications in case any one centre was put out of commission.

To unravel the network of civil-defence installations outside London, described in general terms in Chapter 1, we again rely on precedent and communications to guide us. In this case the latter is the more powerful tool.

As before, countryside civil-defence communications are buried in the civilian network, and we have to dissect them out. The first necessity is a fairly detailed map of the British trunk-telephone work. This is not, as far as the author knows, published by the GPO. Certainly it is not in the two most recently published atlases – the Oxford *Atlas of Britain*, or the Reader's Digest *Complete Atlas of the British Isles* – although the latter has a small and extremely schematized version. Fortunately we can construct a rough but adequate map from other sources. The starting point is the London STD book, *Dialling Instructions and Call Charges*[45] distributed free to every telephone user. This lists every telephone exchange in the British Isles that can be dialled. It is functionally divided into three sections: the London Directory Area,[46] already referred to; the London Toll Area[47] from about 10 to 20 miles (16–32 km) from Oxford Circus; and the rest of the country.[48] In recent years, the last two sections have been amalgamated. This last section contains some 5000 exchange names and the code numbers necessary to dial them.

Although much trunk routing is done by decoding these groups entire to produce routing instructions which, of course, will differ radically from exchange to exchange – the routing instructions to get from a particular London exchange to Cambridge might be 'fifteenth wire from the left', while from Cambridge to London it might be 'third on the right' – they originally consisted of three functional parts: 'O', which connected the subscriber to trunk apparatus, a three-figure group which specified a switching centre, for example *Fyvie* is 651, and a one- or two-figure group which connected that switching centre to a particular dependent exchange – in the case of *Avonbridge* it is 86 from Fyvie. This last used always to be built into the mechanics of the switching centres, so that if one were on the Fyvie exchange and wanted a number on Avonbridge, one simply

---

Fig. 34 An attempt to construct a map of the GPO's national trunk cable network, which contains, buried within itself, the civil-defence communications system. Undersea cables to our allies are: 1 to Denmark; 2 to Germany; 3, 4 to Holland; 5, 6 to Belgium; 7 to France; 8 to France via Jersey; 9 to France via Guernsey; 10 to Australia via South Africa, plus many pre-war cables to America; 11 TAT 3 to Newfoundland; 12 TAT 1 to America; 13 Cantat to Canada; 14 Scotice to Canada via Iceland and Greenland; 15 BLACK DOG to Norway; 16 to Sweden. 'O' is Oswestry, the Emergency Control Centre.

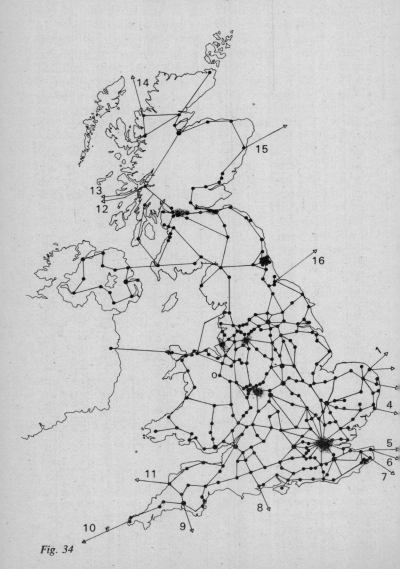

Fig. 34

dialled 86 and then the number. The usefulness of this organization from our point of view is that we can establish a hierarchy of STD numbers which corresponds to a physical reality on the ground: those exchanges with only the first two elements are switching centres, and the rest, with longer numbers, depend from them like clusters of grapes. (In practice all the switching centres have three-figure codes, but so also do some neighbouring charging areas.)

A little more help can be gleaned from the GPO's annual Report and Accounts, which, since 1961, has given brief details of works in progress. Under the heading 'Trunk and Junction Plant, Cable Routes' we find bare entries: 'Banbury–Birmingham, Basildon–Cambridge', etc. By collating these, and plotting them on a map, we get about 10 per cent of the system, and by boldly joining up the dots of the switching centres, we can make some progress towards a rough map of the whole.

But, unfortunately, it will be very rough. The GPO is understandably coy about publishing exact cable maps and they take great care to duplicate and triplicate important routes – to guard against natural disasters as well as sabotage. The sketch map opposite shows the London–Birmingham cables, reconstructed from a variety of sources, and a proposed cabling scheme of 1950 for East Anglia. An attempt to transfer this sketch to road maps will demonstrate that, although in the simplicity of Snowdonia deduction of the actual run is not too hard, in more populous parts the number of choices open to the route planner is so large that one can do little more than make a schematic map. Even so, such a map gives us some help, so long as the scale is kept small.

There are two types of cable and three methods of signalling. For distances of 15 miles (24 km) or less, a pair of wires suffices. Over longer ranges it is necessary to use 'carrier' radio frequencies running along a pair for each half of the conversation. The four wires employed make up a 'quad' which can carry perhaps a couple of dozen conversations. For very long distances, coaxial cable is used: a thin-walled tube, about half an inch (12 mm) in diameter, with a wire down the centre. This guides a high-frequency radio signal that can carry 600–900 telephone conversations. Coaxial cable is used to link zones. Coaxial carrier and audio are used between groups, depending on the distance and the traffic density, while audio alone is used from groups to their dependent exchanges – which have, of course, to be within 15 miles (24 km).[49]

An actual piece of trunk cable usually contains some of all these. Thus the TV cable from London to Wenvoe, laid in 1951, had two coaxial cables – tubes 0·37 inch (19 mm) in diameter with a central wire – for TV, four tubes the same size for telephony, which could carry a total of 1200 two-way conversations, and 374 audio pairs for short trunks and junctions.

Trunk calls are routed through transit centres, between which the long-haul trunk cables run. We are interested in the physical run of the long-haul trunk routes because buried in that system is the civil defence system. In the reorganization of the late 1950s, when the Post Office laid some 750 miles (1200 km) of extra trunk cable, it is reasonable to assume that they took pains to run the new cable as near as possible to hidden military and civil-defence sites, or alternatively, put new sites as close as possible to existing cables.

The implication of this is that where possible, the Post Office is likely to use the same physical run to connect dependent exchanges back to their switching centres themselves. So, it is fairly obvious that the main trunk route in North Wales runs around the coast. But, since this passes an airfield at Lanbedr and might be cut by a strike there, it is not surprising to see traces of another run over the hills to Colwyn Bay via Blaenau Ffestiniog.

This process applied to the whole country, choosing runs which avoid targets, produces the map shown at Figure 34.

There is a Post Office Defence Network Emergency Manual Switching System (Fall-Out Protected) (PODN EMSS FOP) with between 20 and 50 centres including Bristol, Cambridge, Reading, London (two) and elsewhere. I was shown Cardiff's installation which consisted of little more than a patch-board and a stock of breeze blocks to make a small fall-out shelter for a couple of operators. It is evidently intended as a supplement to the DCN, for use only in centres that have not been damaged by blast.

Another useful source of information can be derived by considering the broadcasting system. In either war or revolution, it would be an essential tool of government. It was of great importance during the General Strike, and gave the government an enormous advantage by enabling the Prime Minister and prestigious figures like the Archbishop of Canterbury to speak directly to the people. It was considered vital during the Blitz. It is the basic tool of control during fall-out, and will be the only way the national, regional and sub-regional seats of government can keep in touch with their subjects during emergency conditions. In the case of war, the BBC estimates that some 10 million out of a total of 25 million transistor radios will survive a counter-city strike. In revolution, control of the air waves would be a major objective of both sides. To make use of this important channel, preparations have been made to ensure the continuity of broadcasting under difficulties. The BBC's arrangements are naturally very interesting, and equally naturally not revealed. But, again, we can make some deductions from published material.

Because radio waves, at most of the frequencies used for broadcasting, do not carry very far (this is done deliberately so that national broadcasting systems do not interfere with each other), it is necessary to have a number of transmitters up and down the country to give an even coverage. The transmitters are often in remote places, so it is necessary to provide some means of getting programme material, which is usually generated in the big cities, out to the appropriate broadcasting station. This is done by the GPO who link the two with telephone cable.

As before, we would expect the BBC's emergency network to be embedded in its peacetime arrangements. We can specify in advance the three things we are looking for. The first is transmitters on the medium or long wave rather than VHF because these frequencies penetrate underground to fall-out shelters, and so do not need rooftop aerials for good reception, and because they can be picked up on every transistor radio (only 60 per cent can receive VHF). To confirm this view, London flood warnings are still broadcast on medium wave. The second is a system which is basically regional so that our masters can say different things to different parts of the country. It is very likely that in the wake of a nuclear attack or an attempted revolt some areas would be damaged and others not, some would be disaffected and others not; there might be a surplus of food in one for distribution which would only aggravate the people in the neighbouring hungry region if they knew about it. News management will obviously be most important, so we are looking for a system which is fundamentally regional with transmitters capable of being combined into a national network. Finally, it will also happen that the government needs to speak to the whole nation, and this perhaps at a moment of great difficulty when sophisticated networks are out of order.

It is likely that the Wartime Broadcasting System (WTBS) is made up out of medium-wave transmitters, plus the Droitwich long-wave transmitter which can speak to the whole country. This would be arranged so that each region would have its own broadcasting system, which could also transmit a national programme. After a nuclear attack broadcasting would be limited to essential information transmitted at set times, in order to save electricity at transmitters, and batteries in receivers. The transmitters would tend to be those of higher power, sited away from likely targets.

Having identified the transmitters, we must contrive to get programmes to them from the national, regional and sub-regional seats of government. Although in principle, broadcast-quality sound can be transmitted over any two telephone channels (one alone has not enough bandwidth), in practice the Post Office provides the BBC with dedicated channels to distribute programme material from cities out to transmitter sites. It is likely again that the civil-defence network is buried in these. Imposing the BBC's organizational diagrams for the medium-wave chain on the GPO network, we have the chart below (Figure 35).

In late 1978 the BBC changed many of its transmitters in conformity with a general reorganization of wavelengths throughout Europe. In fact, only a few very old transmitters were physically altered or moved; most of the rest just had their frequencies changed. One might expect that the main shape of the WTBS is still much as shown.

The microwave system

A conspicuous feature of modern Britain is the Post Office's system of microwave towers. The best known is the one which rises some 650 feet (198 m) above Tottenham Court Road in London, but there are 150 others throughout the country. It has long been suspected by those interested in civil defence that there must be some connection between these structures and the S-RCs, though precisely how they were related was difficult to determine. Some S-RCs are close to towers, others are miles away. When the first edition of this book was published, I had not enough information to offer a map of the microwave system: some work done since then has made it possible to draw most of this, and to suggest how the two systems may fit together.

First it is necessary to look at the basic principles of a microwave network. In principle it offers facilities for sending telephone conversations numbered in the thousands by (to use the proper technical name) super-high-frequency (SHF) radio beams which follow line-of-sight paths between relay towers. Each microwave station consists of a tower, a set of directional aerials – paraboloid dishes or horns – which collect the signals from the next tower down the line and channel them to radio receivers in a building at the base of the tower. These signals are then either sent to their user by landline, or amplified and retransmitted through an identical set of aerials. The Post Office typically erects massive towers with lavish accommodation and ample stand-by power equipment. The average cost per tower for microwave routes mentioned in the Post Office Report and Accounts, 1961–70, is about £100 000.

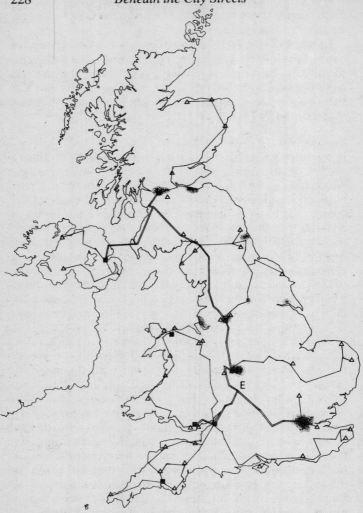

Fig. 35 The G P O distributes radio-programme material for the B B C by landline. This map shows the result of superimposing an organizational chart of the Home Service on the G P O trunk network. This too is a guide to the civil-defence communications network. The squares are studio centres, the triangles transmitters. 'E' is the B B C's emergency control at Evesham.

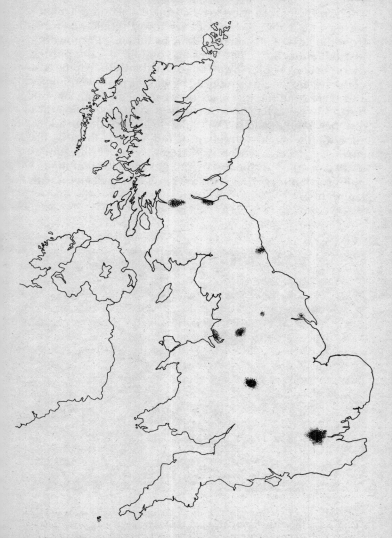

Fig. 36 The G P O microwave system.

The principal criterion to be satisfied in planning a micro-wave route is that the top of each tower should be visible from the next. This could be done by building low towers – just tall enough to clear trees and buildings – and putting them perhaps 5 miles (8 km) apart. Evidently the capital cost of the system would be reduced by making the towers higher and increasing the distances between them. On a smooth Earth a tower H feet high can be seen from ground level at a distance D miles where $D = \sqrt{2H}$. (This includes an allow-ance for the slight refraction of radio waves towards the earth's surface.) A beam which grazes the earth D miles away can go on to the top of another tower H feet high D miles further on still. So two towers H feet high give a path length of $2D$.

Fig. 37a Model of the first design for microwave towers in the Backbone chain, circa 1955. Notice the perspex screening around the aerial galleries, presumably to conceal the direction of shoot, and blastproof accommoda-tion in the lower part.

Fig. 37b A typical GPO microwave tower as actually built. The horn aerials direct narrow beams of radio waves at the next towers along the chain about 25 miles (40 km) away. This tower, at Kelvedon Hatch is 325 feet (99 m) high, and built of steel. It would be very resistant to H-bomb blast.

At first sight, since the higher the tower, the greater the range, it would seem sensible to build it as high as possible. But there are several limiting factors. The first is that distance is proportional to the square root of height: a tower 200 feet (60 m) high carries 20 miles (32 km); an extra 800 feet (240 m), giving 1000 feet (300 m) in all, gives only another 25 miles (40 km). On the other hand, the cost of building increases with the square of the height. It follows that while the cost in tower building of covering a given distance increases with the fourth power of the inter-tower distance used, and the cost in equipment is roughly proportional to the *number* of towers, there must be a point of balance, beyond which increased height and reduced number of towers gives no saving. In addition, the higher a tower is, the more flexible it becomes and the stronger the winds its top is exposed to, with more likelihood of gales flexing the aerials so much that the beam completely misses the next tower. All these considerations combine to produce, in Britain, a maximum tower height of about 350 feet (107 m) with an average path length of 23 miles (37 km). (These are only rough figures.) The London and Birmingham towers are exceptionally stiff concrete structures and can therefore be 650 and 500 feet (198 and 152 m) high respectively. Path lengths vary in practice between 12 and 50 miles (19 and 80 km).

Planning a microwave route is done by first selecting suitably spaced hilltops from the map, and then by plotting the height of the ground along the proposed route on graph paper (see Figure 34), which is designed to exaggerate vertical separations while allowing for the curve of the earth. It is not sufficient that the beam should just clear the earth at every point; allowance must be made for trees and buildings, and some extra above that, to prevent the direct and reflected rays arriving out of phase with each other at the far end.[50]

The purpose of the microwave system
The first of the present chain of towers in this country seem to have been built from 1950 on as part of air-defence prepara-

tions against attack by Russian aircraft carrying atom bombs. Its purpose was to transmit data and in some cases radar pictures from remote sites to central air-defence control-rooms, so that RAF's fighter commanders could deploy their forces to the best advantage against high-speed attackers. It was necessary to carry the radar displays by microwave, since cable had not the capacity to do the job effectively.[51] The construction of heavily protected microwave-linked radar stations (one is to be seen on Bolt Head) and fighter control rooms (one beneath the present microwave tower on the Wenallt above Cardiff) went on through the fifties at vast expense and in great secrecy.[52]

From 1953 onwards the system was extended to guarantee the communications of central government during an attack. The GPO planned a chain of concrete towers (see Figure 39) code-named *Backbone*, which linked the three major cities, as well as having connections with the air-defence chain. The Backbone repeater stations were to have been massive concrete blocks, with the aerials enclosed in perspex so that their directions of shoot would have been hard to discover (see Figure 37a).

In the 1960s, corresponding to the second spasm of civil-defence spending (see Figure 16), the entire air-defence system was reorganized to take advantage of higher-powered radars and to cope with supersonic aircraft, both as attackers and interceptors. The number of early-warning stations was reduced. Coverage of the North Sea, as Britain's back-up of NATO's screen against the East,

---

Fig. 38 Ground contours between Stokenchurch and Bagshot GPO towers. The form of lattice used exaggerates heights while allowing for the curve of the earth and refraction towards the ground of radio beams. The numbers refer to: 1, Stokenchurch Tower; 2, RAF Medmenham (whose functions as HQ of the Defence Communications Network have been transferred to RAF Rudloe Manor); 3, Bagshot Tower. The effective spread of the microwave beam from the direct line varies between 5° and 1° according to frequency: the height of the two towers – 350 feet (106 m), 342 feet (104 m) – seems chosen to restrict illumination of the ground to a small area at Warren Row. The dotted line shows a technically acceptable path using much lower and cheaper towers.

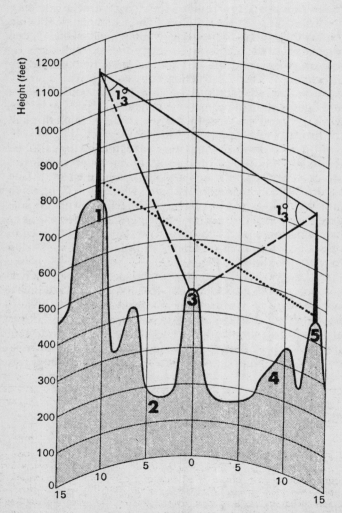

Fig. 38

Distance (miles)

6 65
65
50
29

Fig. 39 The GPO 'Backbone' system as planned in 1955. The system of towers shown here represents a relatively simple and straightforward approach to the problem of guaranteeing government communications between major cities. The logical route out of London, direct to Stokenchurch, suggests that once bypasses had been provided for Birmingham and Manchester, the system was not intended to serve many hidden sites.

is maintained by long-range warning stations at Saxa Vord in Shetland, Buchan near Peterhead, Boulmer near Alnwick in the Borders, at Staxton Wold near Scarborough, Patrington near Hull, and at Neatishead near Norwich. (The spacing of 100 miles – 160 km – between these agrees with that between long-range sets in the American SAGE system.[53] It seems that the present GPO microwave system exists, at least in part, to serve these sites. The route to Staxton Wold, for instance, has a greater information-handling capacity than that between London and Birmingham.

With the reorganization of air defence in the early 1960s, the GPO system was also rebuilt. The original, simple Backbone chain was modified to take in numbers of dispersed sites in the country. Generally speaking, much larger and more permanent towers were built alongside the older, smaller towers. In the centre of London the 500 foot (150 m) concrete tower replaced a 50 foot (15 m) lattice one perched on the roof of Museum telephone exchange – which is odd, since the new works to the same outlying towers as the old. Then, although the GPO says in its publicity material for the Tottenham Court Road tower that it creates thousands of new telephone channels to other cities without the expense of digging new cable duct and laying new cable, it seems that its present contribution of some 6000 channels, and ultimately – it is claimed – 150 000 channels – is hardly worth its £8 million cost when compared with the existing cable capacity out of London of 13 000 channels, and even less so when one considers that the GPO is already installing a 100 000 telephone-channel cable between London and Birmingham. As an alternative, the Post Office claims that the microwave system is necessary to distribute colour television, but again it appears that this is merely an incidental convenience.

A third oddity concerns the construction of the towers. We have already noticed that the London tower is much higher than it need be. In order to achieve this height while keeping the swing of aerials within a limit of one third of a degree of arc, its designers claim that it had to be made of

concrete.[54] This may be true of the exceptionally high
structures in London and Birmingham, but other concrete
towers in the system are nothing like as tall (*Stokenchurch*,
Charwelton, *Cannock Chase*, *Sutton Common*, *Heaton
Park*, *Morborne*, *Wootton under Edge*, *Bristol*) and one,
Tinshill, to the north-west of Leeds, is less than 100 feet
(30 m) high. On the other hand, many of the lattice towers
are 300 feet (90 m) high and more. So the choice of concrete
cannot be on the grounds of stiffness.

The final peculiarity of the system is the way it wanders
about, particularly in its efforts to get out of London. To get
to Birmingham, on the main telephone route of the nation,
the beam goes from *Tottenham Court Road* in a 12-mile
(19 km) hop to a small tower at *Harrow Weald* very close to
R A F *Bentley Priory*, the Second World War fighter control
centre for London and today H Q of No. 11 (Fighter) Group.
Then it swings north to a repeater at *Zouches Farm*,
Dunstable – which it could have reached direct – and so
onward to *Charwelton* near Daventry. To get to Bristol and
Southampton, the route leaves London to the south-west to
a repeater at *Bagshot*. There it divides: the Bristol beam
swings sharply north to a second repeater at *Stokenchurch* –
whence again it could have gone direct – and on to Wantage,
with a smaller beam going to *Charwelton* again. Another
odd spot is north of Leeds where two towers – *Tinshill* and
Hunter Stones – stand only five miles apart. Duncan
Campbell has suggested[55] that the unusual density of
microwave channels here is to serve an American satellite
terminal at Menwith Hill which may relay intercepted
telephone conversations to the National Security Council in
the U S A.

Logically a microwave system for inter-city telephone
traffic would consist of low, simple towers erected on the
shortest routes between the six largest cities. But of the fifty-
odd GPO towers I have discovered, only two are in
the centres of big cities, and only four more near any
others (Southampton, Bristol, Manchester, Edinburgh).
The heaviest communication capacity is often in the most
remote countryside. Partly this is because cities tend to be

built in river valleys which are low and therefore unsuitable
for microwaves. But there is still a rather rural feel about this
system.

Granted that the system handles colour television, some
inter-city telephony, and serves the early-warning radar
sites, there are still things about it that need explanation. The key to the riddle seems to lie in the Bagshot–
Stokenchurch link. On drawing the beam path on a 1-inch
map, one is immediately struck by the fact that it goes within
50 yards (45 m) or so of the celebrated S-R C at *Warren Row*.
When one plots ground heights along the route, and makes
allowance in the diagram for beams which spread 0·5° from
the direct path between tower tops, it becomes apparent that
the hill in which Warren Row is burrowed is the only spot
on the entire 22 mile (35 km) route which is illuminated by
the beams at all. This means that if one placed a dish aerial
there connected to suitable radio equipment, one would
immediately be in contact with every other point in the
country served by the microwave system.

In the first two editions of *Beneath the City Streets*, I got
rather carried away by this discovery and 'found' a great
many secret sites on microwave beams, using, as my friend
and critic Duncan Campbell pointed out, a circular argument to show that they were secret because they were on the
beam, and that the beam was placed as it was in order to pass
over them. The first rapture of this discovery having abated,
it is indubitably true that some microwave beams do pass
within yards of a few secret sites, and that in order that they
should, the routes seem to have been quite contorted.
For example, there are the hardened telephone exchanges
at Cambridge, Tunbridge Wells and Whiteknights Park,
Reading, built in the 1950s to route through trunk
traffic round London and presumably to replace London
altogether if it should be taken out by nuclear attack.
There is the S-RC at Warren Row, another at Preston.
The Prime Minister's country residence at Chequers is
on a possible beam from Stokenchurch to Zouches Farm.
All these sites and some others lie within 100 yards
(90 m) of the line between towers, and are therefore close

enough to the beam to be covered by the beam spread of about 0·5°. The chance of a site picked at random in the central area of Britain – taking it to be a rectangle roughly 100 miles (160 km) from east to west, from London to Bristol, and 250 miles (400 km) long, up as far as the Border – falling on these narrow corridors is about 250:1. One can hardly think it happened by accident. Yet it is hard to divine what the purpose might be. It is true that if a site is illuminated by a microwave beam it can be furnished quite easily with a large number of telephone or telex channels by putting a simple aerial to face one of the towers and mixing out the appropriate groups and sub-groups. But one-way communication is not much use. If the intermediate site is to be able to transmit as well it must use another frequency to that travelling in the same direction between the towers, or else it will cause interference at the far receiver. Another frequency means installing extra receivers at one of the towers and if one has to do that, the intermediate site could have been anywhere within sight of the tower rather than precisely on the beam. In fact one can argue that it is a positive nuisance having the intermediate site in the beam because if it uses the existing frequencies on the beam, it cuts out half the links; if it uses other frequencies they may degrade service by shining straight into the aerials used by the first service – a situation which is generally considered undesirable. Perhaps someone will find the explanation one day . . .

Even so, it is possible that the microwave system has been built not only to provide broad bank links between its obvious terminals – which are not all accounted for by any means, but also to serve, in some way which has not yet been understood outside the Post Office, a set of secret sites in between towers. Evidently this is perfectly possible to do, for, in general, in flat country, one can take secret sites in pairs, draw a line through each pair, and put towers on the intersections. This would make the ostensible routes rather meandering – as in fact we see them, particularly leaving London, and near Leeds. But it must be admitted that the acid test of the original theory: discovering

secret sites which one did not already know about by
following microwave beams, has not so far been very
successful, in spite of the efforts of quite a number of people.

An odd sidelight on the Post Office's problems is offered
by the planning inquiry into the tower at Cannock Chase.
They asked for permission to build at one of three sites which
lie on a line bearing 127°/307°. Unless this alignment is
fortuitous, it suggests that it was important for the tower to
line up with at least two other places.

The Post Office explanation of the microwave system is
well put in their expert witness's statement at the planning
inquiry into the siting of the tower at Wootton under Edge,
Gloucestershire, in 1962:

> The Post Office is responsible for ensuring that in the
> event of attack on this country adequate communications
> for the administration of the country are available up to
> the time of attack and as far as possible to assist in the
> restoration of damage afterwards. This means that com-
> munication services must be provided in advance, routed
> in diverse ways, for the operational needs of the Fighting
> Services and of Civil Defence and for the dissemination of
> essential information.

He went on to explain that the telephone network was
vulnerable because its cables ran along main roads, and
because its switching centres tended to be in large towns
and cities that might well be attacked. The answer was to
supplement the cable system with microwave radio.

Like most statements of the Post Office, this needs some
glossing to reveal its full meaning. In the few minutes *before*
a nuclear attack by bombers or rockets the radio stations,
and their towers, would indeed be vital because they
would be carrying the information and orders necessary
to co-ordinate air defence. Immediately *after* the attack,
though, when 'normal landline communications might be
destroyed', it is likely that the microwave stations would
have suffered even more. *Effects of Nuclear Weapons*
suggests[56] that radio aerials are some 40 times as vulnerable
as buried cable. But the towers themselves would stand very

much closer nuclear bursts. The concrete sort are especially resistant: at Nagasaki, concrete factory chimneys failed only at the 15 p.s.i. (1 kg/sq cm) line, and were quite undamaged at 6 p.s.i. (0·4 kg/sq cm). This would imply that they would resist a 5-MT burst at 4 miles (6·4 km), making them only some ten times more vulnerable than buried cable. During the fall-out phase, then, buried landlines would be the main communication medium. But after the fall-out phase was over, and aerials could be replaced or readjusted on the surviving towers (few of which are near targets anyway), these aerials would again present an attractive vehicle for communication.

If it were resisting a revolution, the government would be anxious to protect its communications against interference. The cable network is very vulnerable to sabotage, since every 200 or 300 yards (180–270 m) along its thousands of miles there is a manhole and the possibility of damage. It is evidently impossible to guard all of these even in a theatre of war (see, for instance, the sabotage of German cable communications in northern France just before D-Day).[57]

But, in contrast, the microwave system offers great capacity with high security. As against 300 or so manhole covers on the London to Birmingham cable, traffic can go by a total of four towers, all of which can easily be guarded. The two terminal towers stand directly over the underground accommodations they serve, so it would be hard to interfere there. The vulnerable aerials are several hundred feet up in the air, and so, also out of reach. The two concrete towers in the country are equally forbidding and would be extremely difficult to demolish even if saboteurs could get control of them. Furthermore the ostensibly peaceful system can be prepared long before trouble arises to serve all sorts of places the government does not wish to advertise. On the day when they are to be used, it would only be necessary to take readily available television outside broadcast equipment to the prepared sites in order to provide some thousands of telephone channels.

Although microwave communication is more private and secure than cable, and far more than lower-frequency radio,

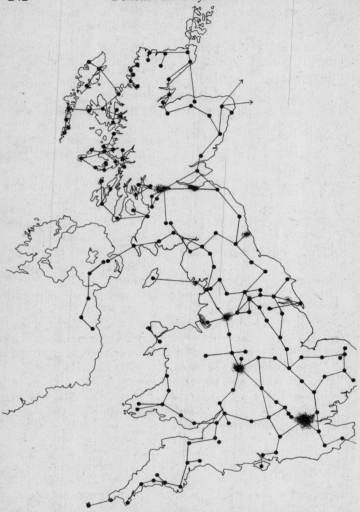

*Fig. 40 Main G P O microwave system. The chain of concrete towers gives
a sabotage-proof link between the major cities, and is evidently intended to
safeguard government communications during a time of civil disturbance.
The rest of the system serves radar and a variety of other sites.*

which is almost indecently public, it is still not ideal from these points of view. Anyone with the appropriate equipment on a microwave beam can receive signals, can jam legitimate communications or replace them with his own stronger signals. As an example of this last, some technological pranksters inserted short films into television services in England and France around Christmas 1976 by swamping the legitimate signal in the microwave distribution path to remote transmitters with their own. The safeguard is that for reception and decoding of the many thousands of telephone and telex signals that may be carried on a microwave beam, bulky and expensive equipment is needed. If the government were fighting a war or containing a revolution, it would not be difficult, by daily helicopter patrols of the microwave routes, to be sure that none such was in place. However, in peacetime, things are not so easy for the home team, and it is fairly certain that embassies in London, as in many other capitals, are used as stations from which to monitor transmissions. This may explain another oddity in the British system.

The best current technology can offer is laser communication by glass fibre: a medium that has huge capacity and is practically untappable. However, it must be laid in cable ducts and is therefore vulnerable to sabotage.

Over much of the country there are no fewer than four independent microwave systems. As well as the Post Office, the Gas and Electricity Boards have an elaborate network, so has the Civil Air Traffic Control Organization, as does the American Air Force. Often the towers of all four stand within 10 miles (16 km), and could just as well – and much less expensively – have been a single tower. But they may have been separated in order to multiply the chances of survival of enough towers to make up one workable system after attack.

There are two more long-range military radio systems. The first employs tropospheric scatter: a technique that relies on reflection and refraction of radio signals in the 400 MHz and 900 MHz bands from inhomogeneities at the top of the troposphere. This lies about 11 miles (18 km) above the equator and 3½ miles (6 km) over the poles. These inhomogeneities scatter radio signals forward as well as reflecting them backwards, so communication can be obtained over ranges of 400 to 1000 miles (650 to 1600 km). Very high powers are needed and very directive aerials. Those used are normally pairs of vertical dishes some 60 feet (18 m) in diameter.

The second system uses very low-frequency (VLF) radio, in the range 10–16 kHz. These frequencies have the useful property that they are long enough to bend round the earth's curve. This means that long distance communication does not rely, as with high frequencies (HF) on reflection from the ionosphere, and so is less upset by nuclear bursts in the atmosphere. VLF waves also penetrate the sea to a depth of 30 feet (9 m) or so, which means that Polaris submarines can receive their orders without breaking surface to expose an aerial. The drawback to VLF is that it needs huge aerials at the transmitter. However, its great reliability makes it useful for command of missile submarines and for relaying air defence reports. There are three stations in Britain: *Rugby*, *Criggion* (Shropshire), and *Anthorn* near Carlisle. *Rugby* serves the Royal Navy's Polaris submarines – possibly backed up by the others; *Criggion* was built during the war to provide Churchill and Roosevelt with a radio telephone link. Although scrambled, the Germans were able to read it with little difficulty;[58] *Anthorn* relays reports from Fylingdales ballistic missile radar back to the American air defence HQ at Cheyenne Mountain, Colorado.

NOTES

1. Unlike the last two chapters, this one owes nothing to official information given to me personally.

2. Sir Stanley Angwin, *Journal of the Institution of Electrical Engineers*, vol. 94, no. III, p. 7.

3. *Eleventh Report from the Select Committee on the Estimates*, Session 1962–3, *The Home Office*, HMSO, 1963, Q 1088, 89.

4. *The Times*, 17 September 1963. We can estimate a cost for these 400 miles (640 km) by taking an average of costs of trunk cabling projects

mentioned in the GPO's *Report and Accounts* for 1963. A sample of eight gives an average cost per mile of about £10 000 (£6250 per km). On this basis, the relaying would have cost £4 million, which is not incompatible with the £1·4 million the Home Office spent on civil-defence line communications in the one year 1962–3.

5. Thomas Jones, *Whitehall Diary*, vol. 1, Oxford, 1969, p. 7.
6. Alan A. Jackson and Desmond F. Croome, *Rails through the Clay*, London, 1962, p. 162.
7. Jackson and Croome, p. 108.
8. R. M. Titmuss, *Problems of Social Policy* (*History of the Second World War, United Kingdom Civil Series*), London, 1950, p. 343.
9. Jackson and Croome, p. 108.
10. T. H. O'Brien, *Civil Defence* (*History of the Second World War, United Kingdom Civil Series*), London, 1955, p. 531.
11. Margaret Gowing, *Britain and Atomic Energy, 1939–1945*, London, 1964, p. 000 and Appendix I.
12. See Jackson and Croome, pp. 301ff for the basic accounts of these matters.
13. W. Churchill, *The Second World War: The Commonwealth Alone*, London, 1964, vol. 4, p. 50. The entrance to this shelter is still visible.
14. Churchill, p. 43.
15. C. M. Kohan, *Works and Building* (*History of the Second World War, United Kingdom Civil Series*), London, 1952, p. 386.
16. This shelter is now an extremely interesting museum, preserved as it was on the last day of war. It can be visited on application to the Cabinet Office. See also *Sunday Times Magazine*, 16 May 1965.
17. O'Brien, p. 532.
18. E. G. Stewart, *Historical Index of Gasworks, 1806–1957*, North Thames Gas Board.
19. O'Brien, p. 532.
20. Churchill, p. 49.
21. cf. Major-General R. F. H. Nalder, *History of British Army Signals in the Second World War*, London, 1953, p. 219.
22. T. G. Turley, 'Cabling problems in subways and tunnels', paper read before the Institute of Post Office Electrical Engineers, 4 June 1945.
23. W. F. Boryer, *Post Office Engineers' Journal*, vol. 39, p. 146.
24. R. H. Harbottle, *Provision of Line Communications for the Fighting Services During the War*, London, 1946.
25. *The Times*, 5 January 1967.
26. Jackson and Croome, p. 301.
27. Kohan, p. 386.
28. H. Bishop, 'The war-time activities of the Engineering Division of the BBC', *Journal of the Institution of Electrical Engineers*, 1946, p. 169.
29. Bishop, p. 169.
30. John R. Day, *The Story of the Victoria Line*, London, 1969, p. 3.
31. Kohan, *Works and Building*.
32. 8 September 1951.

33. Post Office Works Act, 1959, s.4(2)(8).

34. O'Brien, p. 325.

35. 28 December 1959.

36. Interestingly, O'Brien (p. 531) mentions *Leicester Square* as having been suggested for a deep shelter, but rejected because it was an interchange station. This may be another piece of admission by indirection.

37. cf. Home Office Civil Defence Circular 1/1967.

38. During my researches into civil defence in 1967, I was refused access to this place by the C E G B.

39. See *Undercurrents*, no. 9.

40. Anarchists Anonymous, *The Other Underground*, discussed in *Undercurrents*, no. 9, pp. 5–6.

41. Untraced article by Michael Calvert.

42. See Oliver Marriott. *The Property Boom*, London, 1967, for floor areas of the major buildings.

43. Marriott, p. 161.

44. Sokolovsky, p. 332.

45. The version used was that for London, 1968.

46. *Dialling Instructions*, pp. 6, 7.

47. *Dialling Instructions*, p. 5.

48. *Dialling Instructions*, pp. 8–37.

49. Gibson, who gives a general account of the British STD system.

50. This allowance for the 'first fresnel zone' is about 100 feet (30 m) for a 2 GHz beam 20 miles (32 km) out from the transmitter.

51. cf. James Martin, *Telecommunications and the Computer*, New Jersey, 1969, pp. 72–7.

52. *Financial Times*, 1 June 1961.

53. cf. Martin.

54. Creasey *et al.*, *Proceedings of the Institution of Civil Engineers*, vol. 30, January 1965, p. 33.

55. *New Statesman*, 9 February 1979.

56. *Effects of Nuclear Weapons*, pp. 191, 255. The comparison is calculated on the basis of the areas of lethal circles.

57. M. R. D. Foot, *S O E in France*, H M S O, 1966.

58. David Kahn, *The Codebreakers*, New York, 1969.

8 Secret sites

The emphasis of the argument, both so far in this book, and in the author's mind over the last ten years, has been on civil defence. This is perhaps because of the strangeness of hidden civilian fortresses, because of the rumpus caused by *Spies for Peace* in 1963 and because of the perennial debate: whether civil servants should be protected against nuclear attack while the rest of us fry in the open. (My own feeling, which I hope has been made clear, is that protection for central government makes it not worth an attacker's while to frighten us into attempting a revolution which we could not carry through. Thus, paradoxically, protection for *Them* is also protection for *us*.) But of course, from the point of view of government, the civilian control system is not of the first importance. The main security of any government is in its armed forces. It must, at all costs, preserve the means to issue orders to them and to receive information from them. It seems that in war, the command of British forces is exercised from the bunker of HQ UK Land Forces (which lives in peacetime at Wilton, near Salisbury). This might also be the site of the National Seat of Government (NSG). In case it is attacked and destroyed, command is exercised by the HQs of the Home Defence Regions, which are spread out across the country, also in bunkers. These military Regional HQs also house the Home Office's Regional staffs, which similarly form an alternative civilian government. Below this level the civil and military organizations divide, each having its own accommodations and communications. The next element in the civil chain is the sub-Regional Control, the s-RC as we shall call it.

One can make a rough estimate of how many sites there

might be. The s-RCI was shown had room for 400 people. The 'black move' of 1940 was to include 16 000 people, for whom 40 such accommodations would be necessary. Allowing that the 20 or so needed for the Home Office control system will be extra to this plus the nine military districts, and that bureaucracies have a natural tendency to expand, we are looking for something like 100 sites of this size, or perhaps 50 bigger ones. One would imagine that on tactical grounds alone there could hardly be fewer.

Below the military network, linked together by its own television system so that commanders can pore over maps together, although separated by some hundreds of miles, which doubtless continues into NATO, there comes the system of civilian control. Two things make one think that this is of considerably lower status; the way the Home Office tends to move into protected accommodation the military has grown out of, and the general irrelevance of civilians to modern warfare. The main problem they pose is of preventing them interfering disadvantageously: in many senses, in a modern war, the populace must be regarded as being as dangerous as the enemy, though happily less equipped to do harm. This view of the people as a possible military menace merges, of course, into the counter-revolutionary philosophy in which they *are*, or may become, the enemy.

It is quite impossible to identify all these hidden sites since some of them at least have absolutely no visible clues at all. For example, I was told of an experience a man had had when he was doing his national service as a second lieutenant in the Signal Corps. With three other young officers he was taken one day in a covered lorry about half an hour from Catterick. They went up into the hills to the west, where there are ranges, and pulled up outside a farmhouse. There was nothing at all unusual about it from the outside; inside there was no furniture, but a lot of military policemen. They were taken to a lift which went down about 100 feet (30 m). There, he says, were four or five floors of a communications centre. If that is true of Catterick, then one would expect there to be something much the same at Blandford Forum in

Dorset, the other Signals depot. But although I have looked, I have found nothing.

Many other sites are modestly conspicuous to those who live locally, but very difficult to find in a systematic manner. For instance, when one raises the subject of war-rooms with locals in the Dorchester area (which I happen to know quite well) they immediately mention two sites – one on the east side of Portland, a long way underground, which was ex-cavated by blasting, and is entered through a hut in a field; and a curious and very solid concrete building set in an old quarry not far from Weymouth. Yet a stranger would prob-ably find it very difficut to discover these, and there are probably several other similar sites in that part of the world, serving the naval dockyard and the underwater weapons research establishment at Portland. Judge how difficult it must be, then, to find them all.

When I was researching an article on civil defence in 1967, I had an interesting conversation with a senior civil servant on how one made an installation secret that had employed perhaps 500 men, taken a couple of years to build, caused great disruption in an otherwise peaceful piece of country. His reply was: 'It is amazing how quickly people forget if you don't make a fuss. When you've finished, you just put the grass back, put up a neat cattle fence round the site, an ordinary farm gate – no Official Secrets Act notices or electric fences – and leave it alone. Go back in a couple of years and people will say: "Under *what* meadow?" '

The starting point for any inquiry into these questions must be the discovery by Spies for Peace in 1963 of 13 sites, then called regional seats of government (RSGs) at: Catterick, York, Nottingham, Preston, Edinburgh, Dover, Armagh, Cambridge, Warren Row, Kingsbridge, Brecon, Kidderminster, Kelvedon Hatch. (All of these places fall on the cable routes of Figure 40.)

O'Brien gives the locations of wartime RSGs, which were then just offices in large towns. All but two – *Edinburgh* and *Nottingham* – have moved, and even they have moved a short way into available underground accommodation. *Edinburgh* is at Barnton Quarry, *Nottingham* has probably

moved to the RAF's wartime Group HQ at Watnal. A
charming rumour puts *Cambridge* a few miles north of the
city in a surface hemispherical metal dome, camouflaged to
blend with the surrounding terrain. There is a massive
concrete block in the grounds of government offices in
Brooklands Avenue, Cambridge. But it may well protect a
trunk-telephone exchange, designed, with others at
Reading (Whiteknights Park) and Tunbridge Wells, to
lessen the peacetime load on London, and in war to replace
the capital as a communication centre altogether. It seems
that site 41 is at *Bawburgh* outside Norwich. *Warren Row* is
an 'underground factory' near Reading said to have moved
to Guildford in 1977. *Brecon* is presumably in the grounds of
one of the army camps there – perhaps Dering Lines where
there is an airstrip.* *Armagh* is said to have been tunnelled into a hill during the late 1950s. Policy seems to have
been to adapt existing structures whenever possible. This
description by Ian Hay of what almost certainly has
become the home of *Dover* will doubtless stand for others
as well:[1]

> Today [1946], if you gaze upwards at the face of the cliff
> overhanging that harbour, you may observe, about mid-
> way between the top and bottom, what looks like a railed
> terrace, from which a few uniformed figures are looking at
> you or across the straits to the opposite coast. Let us
> project ourselves into space and join them there . . .
> Within the high cliff overlooking Dover Harbour a
> complete communications centre [has] been constructed,
> capable of serving as a GHQ to an entire Expeditionary
> Force. A certain amount of accommodation was available
> already, in the underground galleries driven through the
> chalk nearly a century and a half ago to house French
> prisoners of war. These now had to be produced, as it
> were, to infinity; Canadian sappers were entrusted with
> the job, and a great job they made of it. Toiling like coral
> insects, they excavated space for three large Operations
> Rooms, one for each arm of the Services and all adjoining,

---

* Defence Lands Committee Report, HMSO, London, 1971–3, p. 324.

for this was essentially a matter entailing Combined Operations of the closest kind. In addition they provided sleeping quarters, kitchens, canteens, and hospital accommodation for the staff of highly trained specialists concerned, not forgetting their ancillary Wrens, ATS and Waafs. The post office installed the usual highly sensitized nervous system, and the secret citadel was completed – ready, if need be, to be employed as GHQ for the British Liberation Army on D-Day – had the invasion been launched from this area.

(In fact it was not. Two other citadels had been constructed; one under Wentworth Golf Course and the other, which was actually used, under Southwick Fort, Portsmouth.)

Another helpful pointer is the slight correlation between known secret sites and motorways. This brings to mind the experience of the Allied efforts against the Germans in the Low Countries in 1940. Then, the hordes of refugees so jammed the roads that defence was impossible. The network of motorways that now covers Britain and Europe would have an obvious military function, as providing fast, easily policed routes for deploying troops and armour. It is highly significant that in France the job of keeping the motorways clear of refugees in time of war is confided to the tough CRS, while in Belgium it is the responsibility of the national, paramilitary gendarmerie. In Britain, too, movement across country on the ordinary roads after a nuclear attack or serious civil disturbance would be very difficult. We can expect that the motorway system would be cleared of civilian traffic. In fact, Spies for Peace claim to have found a document to this effect in *Kelvedon Hatch* in 1963, which ordered the police to clear civilians off the dual carriageway A13, a main road into London from the east, which passes within a couple of miles of the s-RC near Brentwood. Three American Army supply bases are all within a few minutes of the M5, running between Bristol and Birmingham.

Whenever possible, the Home Office likes to move into other people's vacated bunkers when establishing its controls. A helpful starting point is therefore a list of protected underground accommodation that has been vacated at one time or another by higher priority users, usually the RAF or Army. An interesting, but not wholly accurate account of RAF systems since the war is John R. Bushby's *Air Defence of Great Britain* (Ian Allan, 1973), from which one can extract a number of sites that might suit. The Defence Lands Committee Report (HMSO, 1973) is also useful, though far from comprehensive.

Very briefly, the story of the RAF's early warning system is this: before and during the war, detection of attackers was by the huge Chain Home Radar stations whose towers are still to be seen at Dover, Stoke Holy Cross, Stenigot, etc. The radar buildings were above ground, and the centres to which they reported relatively unprotected – the London Centre, for instance, was in a flimsy hut at the edge of Biggin Hill airfield.

After the war the system was refined, and by 1946 the Sector Operations rooms were at *Dirleton* (mis-spelt by Bushby as Divelton), on the disused airfield at *East Fortune*, East Lothian; *Patrington*, where there is now a radar; *Neatishead*, which is one of the Sector Operations Centres in the present system; *Trimley Heath*; *Felixstowe*; *Wartling*, Eastbourne; *Longley Lane*, Preston – now an s-RC.

In 1951–5 there was another revamping against Russian nuclear bombers, and radar sites were fully hardened. They included *Buchan*, *Boulmer*, *Bempton* on Flamborough Head, *Neatishead*, *Trimmingham* on the Norfolk coast, *Bawdsey*, *Wartling*, *Ventnor* and *Sopley* near Bournemouth. The first two are still radars. *Bempton* is shown in the Defence Lands Committee Report as being for disposal – which could be to the Home Office. *Bawdsey* is still a 'radar communications station'.[2] *Neatishead* is a Sector Operations Centre. *Trimmingham*, I am told by a correspondent, has been sold out of the government service – it does not appear in the Defence Lands Committee Report. *Wartling* was, in 1966, being bandied about in rather a public way between the RAF and the Home Office,[3] but is now a wreck, with all underground accommodation filled in. *Sopley* has suffered the same fate. *Ventnor* is still a radar. It seems that there was also a radar site at *Bolt Head* which Bushby does not mention, so there may have been others yet which one knows nothing of.

The Sector Operations Centres to go with these radars were *Barnton Quarry*, Edinburgh; *Shipton*, north of York; *Bawborough*, west of Norwich; *Kelvedon Hatch, Box* and *Longley Lane*, Preston.

In 1955 the first high-powered centimetric radars arrived from America. These made really accurate position finding easy, and eliminated the need for editing reports from several radars in the Sector Operations centres. Fighter control is now done from the radar sites with threat analysis and assignment of defence forces done centrally at West Drayton and Bentley Priory.[4]

The Linesman air defence system, now scrapped, had three elements: the Master Radars – now the SOCs; a set of independent stand-by radars and manual controls, called SLEWCs; and civil ATC radars.[5] The SLEWCs are not

Fig. 41a In the early 1950s revamp of the radar system, controls were built underground, with their entrances disguised by innocent-looking cottages built to a standard design. This one is at Anstruther, Fife, executed in granite. The one in Fig. 41b is at Truleogh, Sussex. (*Photos:* DUNCAN CAMPBELL)

mentioned anywhere else: they may be radar sites like
Patrington and others one comes across inland – simple,
relatively unprotected sites – or they may also have separate
underground control centres which might now be available
for s-RCs.

Anyway, eliminating all the sites that are known either to
have a defence function, or to be out of government hands,

Fig. 41b.

or are known s-RCs, we have Trimley Heath and Bempton.
Both are possible s-RCs. In addition one might suggest
Wentworth Golf Course; Southwick Castle is probably
too near a target – Portsmouth Dockyard), and on a larger
scale, Carlisle. Although it is fairly near two targets,
Anthorn VLF radio transmitter and Chapelcross nuclear
power station, each about 12 miles (19 km) away, it otherwise seems ideal for the site of a control. It is isolated and has
its own local radio station. As part of its preparations for the
Second World War, the RAF built a vast underground
bomb store at Llanberis near Snowdon, Wales. This
might well have been abandoned for its original purpose as
being too far from operational bomber fields, and is used
now as s-RC for the sub-region. There is an emergency
communications centre under the central telephone
exchange in Wharf Street at Leicester, but it is unlikely to be
an s-RC because of the city's target status. This is connected by a tunnel with the East Midlands International
Exchange, *Cardinal*. Ford Widley, Portsmouth, which
is owned by the Corporation, has a civil defence control
in the underground galleries, and a radio mast which
seems similar to those at Kelvedon Hatch and Warren Row.
It is, though, more likely to be the Portsmouth city control
than an s-RC.

Characteristics of s-RCs
We can try to draw up a list of criteria for s-RCs:

    (i) Trunk communications must be readily available: at
least 100 lines (the staff of an s-RC is 400) in two
directions. This implies a site on or near a trunk
route, so as to avoid laying expensive and, in peacetime, unproductive cable.

    (ii) Broadcast lines must be available.

    (iii) The land on which the s-RC stands must belong
to the government and be likely to remain in its
possession, so that access and ventilation – if it is
underground – shall not be interfered with. This
suggests sites either in large, active establishments,
either military or civil – *Catterick*, *Cambridge* – or

sites that are unlikely to be altered or used for anything else – e.g. castles, as at *York* or *Dover*.

(iv) It should be away from a major target city, or a counter-force target.

(v) But it should be near a small town so that maintenance staff are readily available, and hotel accommodation can be found for people taking part in exercises.

(vi) It should be inside its sub-region.

(vii) It should be above flood level.

Bringing all the available information together produces the table shown on page 257.

In an emergency, secure communications abroad would be essential. There are several methods available: undersea cable; radio, either short-wave, VLF, tropospheric scatter or forward scatter; microwave; radio via satellites.

Cable presents no particular problems. Most of the cables to Britain are shown on Figure 34. They provide multiple links with America, the other nations of the Commonwealth and our European allies. But cables can be cut by enemy action, which can hardly be prevented. Radio is also necessary. The BBC has short-wave and LF stations at Skelton, Wooferton, Daventry, Crowborough, Droitwich and Rampisham, which provide European and worldwide coverage. The GPO has VLF transmitters at Rugby and Criggion, and there is the BMEWS VLF transmitter at Anthorn.

The Foreign Office has a chain of radio stations across southern England with several clustered near Milton Keynes. Their headquarters are at Hanslope Park, and there is a training centre at Poundon Hill.

Receivers are easier to replace after an attack, but the BBC's overseas monitoring service at Caversham near Reading would be hard to improvise:[6]

The job of the Monitoring Service is to provide speedy and accurate reports of significant news and comment from foreign broadcasting stations in all parts of the world. It is a national service, supplying information not

Region	Regional military commands	Sub-region	Counties	s-R C sites*
North	NE District, York	11	Cleveland, Durham, Northumberland, Tyne & Wear	*Catterick/Shipton/Bempton*
Yorks.	NE District, York	21	Humberside, Yorks.	*Watnal/Fiskerton*
East Midlands	RAF Cranwell	31	Derby, Lincs., Notts.	
		32	Leics., Northants.	
East	E District, Colchester	41	Cambs., Norfolk, Suffolk	*Bawburgh/Cambridge*
		42	Beds., Essex, Herts.	*Kelvedon Hatch*
Greater London	London District, Horse Guards	51	Greater London	Masham Street
South East	SE District, Aldershot	61	Kent, Surrey, East and West Sussex	*Dover Castle/Deepdene Ho.*, Dorking, Guildford
South West	SW District, Taunton	62	Berks., Bucks., Hants., I.o.W., Oxon.	Winchester?/Reading?††
		71	Avon, Dorset, Glos., Somerset, Wilts.	Corsham, Bulbarrow Hill
		72	Cornwall, Devon	*Hope Cove, Bolt Head*
Wales	Wales, Brecon	81	Clwyd, Gwynedd	Llanberis
		82	Dyfed, Glamorgan, Gwent, Powys	*Brecon*
West Midlands	W Midland, Shrewsbury	91	West Midlands, Staffs., Warwicks.	*Kidderminster*
		92	Hereford & Worcs., Salop	Langley Lane, Preston
North West	NW District, Preston	101	Cumbria, Lancs.	Southport
		102	Cheshire, Manchester, Merseyside	*Barnton Quarry*
Scotland	Scotland, Edinburgh		Scotland, Central, North Zone, West Zone, East Zone	Anstruther Prestwick Kirknewton

*Italics indicate positive identification by Spies for Peace.

††s-R C 62 used to be *Warren Row*, the target of the famous Aldermaston March of 1963. However, when I visited it in June, 1978 with a camera crew from the BBC's *Tonight* programme, it was empty and abandoned to the amours of local youth. Fire extinguishers were still in place, and their annual record of inspections showed that the site had not been in use since 1970, although care and maintenance work had clearly been carried out until only a few months before our visit. Rumour has it that s-R C 62, with the telephone exchange that used to be at Whiteknights Park, Reading, is now in the basement of an office block in the region.

only to the BBC itself, but also to government departments, the Press and other bodies connected with international affairs. It works in close collaboration with its United States counterpart under an exchange agreement which gives virtually world-wide coverage . . . One of the main tasks of the Monitoring Service is reporting major events, official statements, comments and propaganda from Communist countries.

One can imagine that Caversham Park would be an indispensable ear to the world during the possible negotiations of a nuclear war, and doubtless its staff are provided with alternative and hardened accommodation.

Fig. 42 An American HF and VHF direction-finding station of standard type. This one is at Torii Base, Okinawa, Japan, but there are similar installations in Britain at RAF Chicksands and USN Edzell. (Photo: OWEN WILKES.)

The BBC monitors broadcasting; the more onerous and important task of monitoring long-distance military, diplomatic and commercial radio traffic, is carried out by the Composite Signals Organisation, whose headquarters and decoding centre is at Government Communications Headquarters, Cheltenham. Abroad, radio monitoring is carried out by military units – mainly elements of the

Royal Signals Corps – in Northern Ireland, Germany, Cyprus and Botswana. These 'Radio' units – as the Signal Corps calls them – have a training school at Loughborough.

The extreme importance of this branch of intelligence work in modern war is only now beginning to emerge. In fact, some proponents go so far as to say that the Second World War was won for democracy by the allies' superior signals intelligence. See, for instance, *Bodyguard of Lies* by A. Cave Brown, and *The Ultra Secret* by F. W. Winterbotham.

The GPO has transmitting stations at Leafield and Dorchester and a receiving station at Ongar Street. There is also a worldwide shipping service operated by a HF transmitter from Portishead near Bristol, and a receiver which appears to be at Burnham to the west of London.

Microwave communications abroad are only available to Europe via Dover. One can imagine that, if enough towers survive the initial bombardment, the system will be kept busy.

Tropospheric scatter systems offer 70 or so voice channels over distances of 500 miles (800 km) with good reliability. Royal Signals stations in the *Ace High* chain are at Coldblow Lane, Stenigot, Brizlee Wood, Mormond Hill and Shetland. They link NATO in Europe with Norway and the Faroes, but since the aerials are 60-foot (18 m) diameter dishes perched on edge, they are very vulnerable to blast.

The USAF operates another chain, apparently on a lower frequency with longer hops. The two obvious sites are near Martlesham Heath, Essex, and at the BMEWS station Fylingdales. The chain probably originates in Europe and carries on to the USA via Iceland, Greenland and Canada.

Satellite communications are the easiest. Although elaborate terminals like the GPO's three dishes at Goonhilly are necessary for multichannel or television working, a modest number of telex channels can be provided by equipment small enough to be towed behind a Land Rover. There are half a dozen or so fixed dishes in the UK working to satellites. The drawback seems to be that satellite communications, being broadcast over huge areas, are inherently insecure, and can easily be jammed, since they rebroadcast any signal they receive. And since the ground aerials for all these communication links and indeed the satellites themselves are extremely vulnerable to the blast of rocket-borne nuclear weapons, it is hard to see what rational purpose they will serve in the Third World War.

The national seat of government

If precautions were made to provide and protect a secret seat of government in London, how much more so must they have been made in the provinces. The first we hear of an alternative to London is in Churchill:[7]

> Elaborate plans had been made to move the seat of government from London. Complete branches of many departments had already been moved to Harrogate, Bath, Cheltenham, and elsewhere. Accommodation had been requisitioned over a wide area, providing for all Ministers and important functionaries in the event of the occupation of London.

But by October 1940 he had decided 'not to be beaten out of London', and therefore released the accommodation reserved in the west of England for the military.

O'Brien's references have already been cited; he merely adds that the complete move would have involved 60 000 people. Various national treasures were housed in the Manod slate quarry, near Blaenau Ffestiniog, North Wales: the Crown Jewels, the Rubens ceiling from the Banqueting Hall in Whitehall, the bronze screen and stalls from the Henry VII Chapel in Westminster Abbey, and several important paintings from the National Gallery, were kept in temperature-controlled buildings within the hillside.[8] The site is still (1975) in the possession of the government but it may have a different role in the next war, since Chapman Pincher wrote in 1959 that the new national seat of government was being 'equipped to house the nation's art treasures in the event of emergency'. This is confirmed by the abandoning of the quarry at Bradford-on-Avon where the British Museum's treasures were hidden during the war.

Naturally, a dispersal to hotels and boarding houses, such as we are told about for the 1940 plans, would have been of little use even under high-explosive bombardment. We may be sure that some western equivalent of 'Paddock' existed, which could accommodate at least a few hundred people. If it did not exist then, the H-bomb makes it essential. The next public reference is Chapman Pincher's in 1959. He said that 'a chain of underground fortresses from which the government could control Britain and mount a counter-offensive in the event of an H-bomb attack, is being built outside London . . . The new forts, which have already cost £10 million, have been excavated so deep in the rock that they could wishstand anything but a direct hit', and, in a splendid piece of jingoism: 'The H-forts will be linked with the pits housing the Blue Streak retaliatory rockets.'

At first sight, the national seat of government could be anywhere but, on the grounds of common sense, we can set a few limits:

- (i) Bearing in mind the speed with which international crises can blow up in the missile age, the NSG needs to be at the most within two hours' journey from London, and well served by road and rail.
- (ii) Since it would hardly be possible to evacuate 16 000 people from London in two hours, the NSG must be provided with an almost complete alternative staff. This implies a site in or near quite a large town.
- (iii) Away from possible targets.
- (iv) An excavation in rock would be desirable.
- (v) Since the NSG's communication needs will be massive, the criteria we developed for the s-RCs will apply with even more force.
- (vi) Broadcasting will be even more important, and a site not too far from the one BBC transmitter – at Droitwich – capable of reaching the whole nation would seem to be indicated.
- (vii) Since the major air battle will presumably be fought

over the North Sea, a site as far to the west as is
consistent with the other limits would be desirable.

(viii) Bearing in mind the traditionalism of civil-defence
thinking, it is likely that Second World War sites
have a better than even chance of being used again.

These thoughts immediately direct one's attention to the
Bath–Cheltenham axis. The first real rock – the limestone of
the Cotswolds – to be found on going west or west by north
from London is here. There appears to be a major trunk and
radio landline artery running along the west side of the
escarpment. Bath is served by an excellent railway line from
London, and Cheltenham is not hard to reach. The normal
journey times by rail are 1¾ and 2¼ hours respectively. The
second condition above seems particularly well satisfied by
Cheltenham with its large population of retired service
officers. Such people, with a knowledge of official procedures, a proved sense of responsibility, lots of spare time
and a pension at stake, would make an excellent reserve staff
for the NSG.

Closer examination is equally encouraging. At Cheltenham
there are two government office sites. One at Oakley backs
into the limestone escarpment which offers 600 feet (180 m)
cover in a mile and a half (2 km). A sign at the entrance says
that it is the 'Government Communication Head Quarters'
(GCHQ), the Foreign Office's signals department, and
apparently one of the few elements of that organization
not housed in London. During the last war the Foreign
Office's 'Department of Communication', which employed
7000 people at Bletchley Park, Buckinghamshire, was
responsible for breaking the codes of our enemies and
allies.[9] GCHQ is lavishly equipped with computers: three
Univac 1180s, two IBM 360s, two ICL 1900s, three
CDC 6600s and many smaller machines. Today it plays the
same part in Britain as the National Security Agency does in
America, producing about 85 per cent of the secret intelligence available to the government. No doubt it would
be a vital part of the national seat of government in war, and
since its computers are essential for codebreaking, one
would expect that it has protected accommodation where it

is, and a duly equipped alternative site not many miles away.

Going south towards Bath, nothing in particular strikes the attention until the GPO microwave tower at *Wootton under Edge*. It has one pair of horns working via a repeater, at Sparsholt Firs above Wantage, to the *Stokenchurch* tower near High Wycombe, a single horn to the south-east which appears to work with a horn on a tower at RAF *Rudloe Manor*, and a pair to Bristol. Going south again, there is a railway tunnel at Old Sodbury, but if anything is buried in it, nothing shows on the surface. Farther south, past the RAF base at Colerne, with its warnings of 'a restricted place within the meaning of the Official Secrets Act' (indicating a site of no great importance) and to the village of Hawthorn which stands over the London–Bath railway tunnel at Box.

Hawthorn is of considerable interest. It is one of the few places mentioned by Kohan[10] in his list of the GPO's wartime capital works programme. Immediately under the entry for the *Holborn* exchange (tunnel scheme) he notes: 'Hawthorn (Corsham) Post Office and Telephone Exchange . . . £15 000'. The sparseness of the list and the urgency of the times force one to conclude that the items mentioned in it were of vital national importance. And, as we have seen at *Holborn* and *Paddock*, what was of vital importance then tends to be so now. Another entry, Hendon Ring Main Exchange . . . £90 000, seems to have concealed spending on *Paddock*.

Box was a Fighter Command Group Headquarters and may now be an alternative computer centre for Britain's air defences. The post office at Hawthorn stands literally across the road from the main entrance of RAF *Rudloe Manor* (since the manor itself is some distance to the north this seems to be another example of an installation moving from dispersed Second World War accommodation into something more solidly appropriate to the nuclear age) and its microwave tower. This is now the headquarters of the Defence Communications Network. Also, just inside the entrance there is an air shaft for the railway tunnel below, with a 7 foot (2 m) concrete lid to guard against high-

explosive bombs. This testifies to the importance of something below during the last war, for the air shafts to the
Chipping Sodbury tunnel a few miles to the north have no
such protection. There is an extraordinary collection of
army and naval establishments in the village, with even the
WRVS represented, all overshadowed by enormous spoil
heaps from the worked-out stone quarries below.

There is a most interesting installation at Neston, a village
a mile to the south, where there is Britain's sold
H-bombproof security deposit. Owned by Wansdyke
Security Limited, it is accommodated 100 feet (30 m) below
ground in a Bath stone quarry called Goblin's Pit. Most
important British companies keep microfilmed copies of
their essential records there: a more useful and important
collection of archives for the government of a devastated
Britain bent on recovery it would be hard to imagine.

In fact Corsham seems to be the site of the largest of the
four underground factories built by Beaverbrook in 1940.
Intended to accommodate 50 per cent of Bristol Aircraft's
engine production, it took three years to build and cost a
total of £12 million. It had a floor area of 2 million square
feet (18 000 sq m) divided into many small chambers, but at
its peak output employed only 8000 men – as against a
theoretical maximum of 50 000 – and produced no more
than 42 engines a month.[11] Remembering that in 1940
Beaverbrook was in charge of providing protected accommodation for the government in London, and that by 1943
the V2-German-atom-bomb scare was at its height, one
might explain the discrepancy between expenditure and
achievement at Corsham by supposing that it also contained
a final emergency seat of government. That could be true
today, for the caves at Corsham could house the 16 000
people of the 1944 'black moves' three times over and more.
It seems likely that there is at least a military headquarters at
Corsham. In this context the spur from the microwave
system to RAF Rudloe Manor at Hawthorn, near Bath, is of
great interest. One of the RAF's three Fighter Command
Group headquarters was near by during the war, and extensive accommodation is available under a 200 foot (60 m) rock

cover. Linesman, the British air-defence system, depends – unlike the American SAGE or European NADGE systems – on one computer site alone. Although, unbelievably, this is said to be above ground at West Drayton[12] where it would be wrecked by the blast from a single 1-MT weapon bursting on London Airport a mile and a half away, it is hard to accept that no better protected alternative exists, and it may well be here, tucked safely behind the potential aerial combat zone over the North Sea and northern Europe. If the installations were at the level of the railway, they would have some 200 feet (60 m) of rock cover. Twenty-two 1-MT missiles would be needed to hit a small installation in such a position, though of course it would have no protection against a 25-MT bomb accurately delivered by aircraft. Large quantities of military stores were kept in the caves, but in 1975 they had been moved to a new site in Wales and large areas were offered for sale to the public. But since *Rudloe Manor* remains, this may still be a good site for the national seat of government.

One can discern a few other likely sites. There is one pocket of solid rock on Salisbury Plain, out of which came Salisbury Cathedral, at Chilmark. The quarries are now occupied by an RAF bomb store. The exhibition of radiation-warning signs on some of the gates makes one suspect that nuclear weapons may also be kept here. A natural place to hide sensitive military installations would be in the huge complex of ranges on Salisbury Plain, and the nearby microbiological ranges at Porton, east of Salisbury. (There is an odd HF aerial there, visible from the road.) This area is the only large piece of land in Britain which is, for practical purposes, out of sight of civilians. Other range areas, such as Lulworth, Castlemartin, or Dartmoor, are usually open to walkers at weekends. The recent Report of the Committee on Crown Lands, which dealt in the main with military ranges, reads oddly when it comes to the western of the three Salisbury Plain ranges.[13] In almost every other case, the Committee was at pains to recommend reduced military use, and increased public access. In this one case the reverse is true. They even suggest that the annual church service at the ruined village of Imber be stopped. It may well be that the ostensible motives for this apparent secrecy are the real ones: to give the army the fullest use of rather scarce and essential range areas. But it might also serve to screen other matters.

It is significant that when the GPO moved out of the hardened telephone exchange at Whiteknights Park, Reading, in 1978 (it seems to have moved into a new site in Reading, together with s-RC62 which had been at Warren Row), a number of circuit manuals were left behind. One is said to show the other exchanges on the civil-defence network served by Whiteknights Park. Two of these are 'Warminster One' and 'Warminster Two'. According to General Shelford Bidwell's *The Third World War*, operations would be directed by HQ UK Land Forces, which has its peacetime habitation at Wilton, several miles from Warminster. It would not be hard to visualize two bunkers, one for the military and one for the politicians, under the Imber ranges, and with them, a convincing reason to exclude the public.

Farther from London there are three promising areas. The Forest of Dean is persistently rumoured to be the site of a massive excavation intended to protect those of the nation's administrative and scientific élite who are not needed for the national seat of government. It lies on the suggested civil-defence cable route into South Wales, and has many disused coal mines. But to set against this, one has to note that the mines are all said locally to be filled in, flooded and abandoned, and that there are none of the conspicuous signs present, as at Corsham, that any of them have been converted to another use. Across the Severn Estuary, and about 15 miles (24 km) southwest of Corsham, there is another almost abandoned coalfield at Radstock, and 5 miles (8 km) on to the southwest, the Mendips with their natural caverns offer a sanctuary. The suggested civil-defence cable bends round the south end of the Mendips at Shepton Mallet, where there is also a military prison. One can imagine that in the hectic pre-war months it might have been necessary to improvise a stronghold for the most essential core of the state – the Royal Family, the Cabinet, the service chiefs. Since the obvious sites nearer London that we know about were already occupied by other agencies, and Corsham was not ready until 1943, the Mendip caves seem an obvious choice. Although, again, a cursory inspection of the hills round Shepton Mallet reveals nothing more odd than a deserted railway tunnel converted to a test bed for aero-engines by Rolls-Royce, that does not mean there is nothing there.

There is one concrete hint from the history of the war years that the Royal Family were provided, before Corsham was completed, with the nation's best available protection.

In 1939 two nuclear scientists escaped from France and came to Britain, bringing with them the world's entire supply of heavy water. At first the 26 cans containing 185 kilograms of the precious substance were lodged at Wormwood Scrubs prison, but then 'gradually transferred to a fortress at the other end of the social scale: they were put in the charge of the Librarian of Windsor Castle'. In France it had been housed in a specially built air-raid shelter; Gowing, a historian of the United Kingdom atomic-energy programme, continues: 'After its many and varied adventures the heavy water now seemed safer than it had ever been since it was made.'[14] At that time no one had any clear idea how an atomic bomb would work. Heavy water seemed to be an essential ingredient, with the role of controlling the atomic reaction. So whichever country possessed the world's then minute stock of this material might have a vital lead. Since the heavy water, with its then unknown implications in nuclear war, was perhaps the nation's most valuable single package, it is not unreasonable to suppose that it was kept in the nation's best protected spot. This supposition is reinforced by the thought that His Majesty's Librarian would be responsible for protecting the Royal Family's enormously valuable art collection, and so is likely to have had at his disposal protected storage at least as good as Bradford-on-Avon or Blaenau Ffestiniog (reading Temple Richard's account[15] of the works at Blaenau one gets the distinct impression that the National Gallery found itself

right at the back of the queue for a very scarce commodity).
What was good enough for the world's supply of heavy water
was doubtless good enough for the person of the monarch
and his closest advisers. In itself this tells us nothing about
the location of the store, except that 'Windsor' suggests
somewhere to the west of London. It is worth noticing that
the railway line that passes Windsor goes directly through
Box Tunnel, and also – before the track was taken up – to
Shepton Mallet. Another possible site might be the quarry
at Warren Row, which afterwards became the home of
s-RC 62. This was also used during the war to store British
Museum treasures.

If Britain were to be properly prepared to fight a nuclear
war, it would be necessary to protect the seats of government
against the largest weapons the enemy could bring to bear.
At the moment this means a 100-MT warhead, which
excavates a crater 2500 feet (750 m) in radius in rock. So
5000 feet (1500 m) of cover is required horizontally, and
3300 feet (1000 m) vertically. There is no great difficulty in
digging a vertical shaft to this depth in rock, but the
chambers below are apt to be hot and to require constant
pumping to prevent flooding. It is perhaps better to stay
above the water table by burrowing horizontally into
a mountain – which also makes access easier – as the
Americans have done at Colorado Springs. The SAGE
operations centre there is under 800 feet (240 m) of rock.

There are not a great many sites in England and Wales
where the required cover is available in hard rock, without
digging excessively long tunnels. On Dartmoor the steepest
rise is at Amicombe Hill, giving 1700 feet (520 m) in three
miles (4·8 km), which is scarcely enough. Snowdon gives
3000 feet (910 m) in three miles (4·8 km) from several
directions, and there may be disused mineral works there
that could be exploited. There may be more at Llanberis
than a disused bomb store. Skiddaw in the Lake District
would do, and the Cheviots give 2000 feet (600 m) of cover.
There are innumerable sites in the Highlands, particularly
around Balmoral, but they are correspondingly difficult to
get to. I have no evidence that any of these rather extreme

solutions has been adopted. But, if they have not, one wonders what Britain is doing in the nuclear game at all.

This analysis of the criteria for the NSG is as it appeared in the first two editions, and was – obviously – arrived at by arguing by analogy with the s-RCs. But I am getting increasingly sceptical about the whole idea. Given the power and accuracy of modern strategic weapons (the American cruise missile can deliver a warhead to within 20 *feet* – 6 m – at a range of 2000 miles – 3200 km) it seems foolish to concentrate the nation's government in one place which can no longer be made secret enough to guarantee non-attack, nor strong enough to survive a strike.

Furthermore, if there were a fullblown NSG, one would expect to have heard about it by now.

The Americans have given up on the whole idea – there used to be a vast underground site in the Appalachians – and now send the President and his staff aloft in a specially fitted Boeing 747, which can fly indefinitely over the USA, almost invulnerable to missile attack.

We seem not to be able to afford this lavish solution – nor is British air space large enough or remote enough from enemy intruders for this to be attractive. But there are other ways. The best defence against a nuclear weapon is, as an Army handbook succinctly puts it, 'not to be there when it goes off'. This happy situation cannot be guaranteed for any particular person, but the chances of survival of a group are very much increased by spreading its components about the countryside. The guess that the Cabinet-rank Commissioners in their RSGs form a dispersed national government may be all the truth, and not just an alternative to the NSG.

After a nuclear war, or to cope with a serious revolution, the government might prefer to operate on the surface but in a remote, easily defended area. It might be that the lavish provision of airfields and microwave routes in the Hebrides has this partly in mind, for, given electronic communications and air transport, this would be a highly practical and defensible area to set up shop. With some hundred habitable islands to choose from, it would be hard for an enemy to discover where the government was; while modest air and naval forces would give good protection against attack. Apart from the weather and the midges, the beauty of the surroundings might perhaps compensate for the end of civilization as we know it.

NOTES

1. Ian Hay, *The Post Office Went to War*, London, 1946, p. 79.
2. Bushby, p. 66.
3. Bushby, p. 270.
4. *Evening Standard*, 22 November 1966.
5. *Janes' Weapon Systems 1971–72*, p. 173.
6. *BBC Handbook*, HMSO, 1969, p. 114.
7. Churchill, p. 48.
8. H. Temple Richards, *Some Special Storages, the Civil Engineer in War*, Symposium, vol. 3, London, 1948.
9. David Kahn, *The Codebreakers*, p. 448, New York, 1969. Donald McLachlan cunningly calls it 'station X' in his *Room 39*, London, 1968.
10. Kohan.
11. W. Hornby, *Factories and Plant* (*History of the Second World War, United Kingdom Civil Series*), London, 1958, p. 208. The three other major schemes were: the aircraft factory in the Central Line (p. 106), a machine-gun factory in a natural cavern in the Midlands, and a purpose-built tunnel near Coventry to house bombed-out factories, which was intended to have an area of 250 000 square feet (22 500 sq m), but ended up with considerably less.
12. Rex Malik, *The Observer*, 13 October 1968.
13. *Report of the Defence Lands Committee 1971–73*, HMSO, London, 1973, pp. 291–302.
14. Gowing, pp. 50, 51.
15. p. 237, note 79. It is true that the Royal collection of Holbein portraits was kept at Blaenau Ffestiniog, where they were photographed in 1943 for an edition produced in 1945 by the Phaidon Press. But they may have been moved to a store of lower security importance simply because they were to be photographed by, as it turned out, a German émigré who fought against us in 1914.

9   *The impact of latent nuclear war on democracy*

This book was researched simply to satisfy my own curiosity. I had written an article on civil defence in 1967 for the *Sunday Times* magazine, but I found after it was finished that it raised far more questions in my mind than it settled. Hence most of the work reported here.

Looking back over it, I sometimes feel that parts of it represent rather a wasted effort. It is, after all, ridiculous to spend months guessing and scavenging about in old journals to unravel what one's own government is doing. It is even more ridiculous, because there are people working every day within a couple of miles of where I write this, who know the whole true story of what I have stumblingly tried to deduce.

But, since they are unlikely to tell us what they know, the odd study of, as one might call it, 'counter-government research' is perhaps worth while. A second opinion on the value of what is done on our behalf, particularly in the crucial areas of national policy we have touched on, is surely worth while. If I have not effectively provided it, then someone better qualified may be stimulated to improve on my work.

But as they stand, these results prompt some reflections, which I put down here in no particular order.

The balance of terror
In the ten years since the first edition of this book was published, the accuracies and powers of the American and Russian missiles have increased, and brought a counter-force strike against land-based silos within the foreseeable future. However, it is a very great matter to make missile launchers mobile and so restore the advantage of the

defence (see page   ). It is a matter of easy arithmetic to show that, as far as one can see, the nuclear aggressor will bring down a heavy blow on his undefended cities and industries. So, as long as they are important, we can expect the Third World War to be postponed.

But, brooding as I have been over these figures for some time now, it seems that what is *really* happening in the nuclear business is very different from what is ostensibly happening. One's attention is so concentrated on the effect of strategic weapons on the enemy, when they are eventually used, that one forgets the continuing effect on the people who own them. It is as if the nuclear governments were in tacit conspiracy to overawe each other's people. When Russia rattles her rockets, the USAF, or USN responds, but the real, ultimate effect is to increase the American war machine's hold over the American people. Each side's possession of strategic weapons is an invaluable bogy in the woodshed for the other.

As part of this process, it seems that the effects of nuclear weapons have been considerably exaggerated. An H-bomb has not quite the all-destroying properties that most people assume. I was surprised when I saw the figures; and depending on whether or not he too is surprised, the reader may be willing to believe that the H-bomb has been oversold, and perhaps deliberately oversold, as a weapon of current politics. Given enough H-bombs, it is true, a vast amount of damage can be done, but there are definite constraints on this damage; there are limits to the number that can be killed. This is perhaps not a thought that our rulers care to emphasize.

One can detect quite a degree of subtlety in this political process. Counter-city war, as we have seen, does not appear to be a promising way of using nuclear weapons. It is not one that the Russians are interested in, yet the American defence establishment is preoccupied with it almost to the exclusion of all else. This makes little sense in military terms, but a great deal as a propaganda tactic. By attributing counter-city aspirations to the Russians, the American government brings the H-bomb into every citizen's bedroom. Instead of war being a relatively remote business involving professionals, it is now aimed at *us* – the taxpayers. It is a device which enables a government to hold its *own* citizens hostage in peacetime, to involve their hopes and fears more directly in the arms business than any modern government has managed before. In this view opposing governments who threaten, or are said to threaten, counter-city strikes against each other's populations are like bandits selling protection. They must work in pairs or the threat evaporates and the citizenry refuses to pay up. As evidence of their success, we may note that American spending on defence was in 1962 some 50 times higher than it had been in 1935.

Doubtless no nuclear government is any more anxious to go to nuclear war than its citizens. But that is not the point. By invoking the spectre of counter-city war, the government can get larger taxes for military spending than they otherwise could, they can spend them in secret with little or no informed public interference, and by spending these huge sums it obtains vast amounts of influence, jobs for supporters, power and, to put it crudely, *fun*. It is obviously more amusing to be the commander-in-chief of the world's most powerful military forces than simply to carry out the civilian functions of government – settling trade disputes and opening hospitals and so on, all under the critical eye of the taxpayer. The military life is still the most enjoyable for the *homme moyen sensuel*, possibly even more so since war has gone out of fashion. One has only to remember the pitiful state of the military between the wars in America and Britain to realize that Russia's H-bomb is money in the bank to them now.

It is difficult otherwise to explain (or at least, I find it so) the size of America's nuclear forces. At the moment she can send some 3200 land- and sea-based missiles against Russia. That is about 100 times as many as are needed to give a realistic deterrent threat, but, given the present size of Russia's missile forces (which is of course determined partly in response to America's), about a fiftieth of the size necessary to achieve a first strike ability. In fact, the number of missiles America has seems to satisfy no immediately

obvious strategic criterion. In my view, it is more credible to
see it as an index of the racket the American people would
stand.

It is odd how in this blackmail operation pacifists work
directly with the military. For instance, my conclusions in
Chapter 8 that it is not impossible that Britain might survive
a nuclear war, and that in some ways it might have some
beneficial effects, were received with horror by the more
liberal, anti-war critics. They take the position that nuclear
war is so frightful it is heresy even to suggest that it may not
be the end of all things. Mr Sartori wrote in *Nature*
(8 January 1971): 'Fostering such complacency can only
make the public more receptive to the idea that initiation of a
nuclear war by the West is a rational possibility to be enter-
tained under some circumstances.'

It is conceivable that *some* circumstances might arise in
which it would be better to fight a nuclear war, suffer
30 million dead and lose £50 thousand millions of capital
stock. It is difficult to imagine what they might be to make
such a sacrifice worth while, but surely it is irrational to
suppress the information, to remove the option – however
remote – from the calculus of political possibilities.

But in any case, my aim in presenting these calculations is
not to make nuclear war more likely, but to refute those who
believe that it is the ultimate catastrophe. For, if we believe
that, there is no way to resist the military, the weapons
manufacturers, the politicians who say to us, 'Pay yet more
taxes for defence, or the ultimate disaster will fall on you.'
We have to be able to reply: 'You can't fool us. We have
some idea of the chances that there will be a nuclear war, we
know roughly what sort of damage it will and won't do if it
happens, and we are willing to pay only so much, to devote
only so much attention from the serious business of living to
guarding against it.'

Every time a liberal, humane person says nuclear war is so
frightful it must not even be discussed, the military smile,
because to the ordinary taxpayer the only alternative is more
spending on defence.

A politically more subtle use of nuclear blackmail is seen

in Switzerland, a country that is famous for having one of the most perfect civil-defence systems in the world. One suspects that universal conscription outside the home, the ever-present cellar beneath it, the constant small reminders that in this world it is unwise to trust too much to anyone's good will, must be worth a fortune to the longheaded elder Swiss in disciplining their spawn. For it is always a problem for the older generation to instil into the restless minds of youth that life is a serious business whose main task is to maintain the prestige and incomes of those elderly persons who might otherwise seem to have no useful role to perform. Civil defence is probably not the least useful weapon in their armoury.

An insight into the workings of the trick is given by the Swiss civil-defence handbook, a chunky 300 pages, sent free to every household by the federal ministry of justice and police. It starts well enough with the usual sort of civil-defence advice. But interspersed with this homely material is matter of another sort; home truths that tend to make us Britons turn pink and twiddle our toes:

> Experience teaches us that every state is menaced both from within and without, and survives only because of a hard determination to exist . . .
> . . . The love people bear for their country is founded on the harmony of man's first welcome from the world . . .
> One cannot ask citizens to defend their country if they do not think it worth defending. The first problem of national defence is a moral one. This book appeals to the values of life. It tries to teach how they may be defended.

It has a definite air of Germanic fervour – which is not surprising, since more than two-thirds of the country speaks German, and thinks quite differently from the remaining French and Italian speakers. (Interestingly, it was the German part which insisted on Swiss neutrality during the last war; the French section was rather taken with Hitler.) Even so, for the official publication of a European government, this is a heady document. Connoisseurs of paranoia will hail it as a masterpiece, for it brings vividly home to the citizen every threat to a modern state, from gamma radiation to the insidious catalogue of *traîtrise, défaitisme et pacifisme, propaganda et déclaration d'amour*.

Interspersed with wholesome pages on binding a broken tibia – which can arise from a simple skiing accident, let alone the machinations of the 'new order' in the East, which seems to have the authors badly rattled – or how to stock the emergency larder, there are little nuggets to worry about. 'Press, radio, television can sap our firmness. Be vigilant!' They give examples of the sort of remark which might sap the good Swiss:

> It is tempting to fall back on historical determinism. Civilizations are born, develop, die, just like men. Our western world is old. We should abandon it to the young peoples whose future is coming . . .

and

> We are entering an era of Venus [says an American psychiatrist]. We should abandon virile games and take up more feminine pursuits – art, society, refined culture.

There is a depressing and realistic preview of the Third World War. Long before it begins we must be alert and learn to keep our mouths shut. Spies are interested in everything – railway timetables, the telephone number and habits of this or that civil servant. Railway uniforms are found hidden among grasses near a main line. A watch is kept and three spies are caught. Children at play find a wireless set buried in a wood. Alas, they bring it home and spoil a promising lead. Four spies are sentenced to death, and their appeals are refused by the Federal Assembly.

'The beds are cold this winter. But we hold on.'

The city is attacked, is flattened. Every street becomes a battlefield, every ruin a fortress. (The owner is of course entitled to compensation for property requisitioned by the armed forces. He should be careful to get a receipt from Divisional HQ.) A thoughtful two pages on the laws of war as they affect civilians with a drawing of some who did not pay attention tied to stakes before a firing squad.

A chapter on the Resistance. 'All those who participate in the Resistance risk their lives. This is not a game, it is a pitiless war.'

But why should an enemy waste time and effort in crushing little Switzerland when he can achieve the same results by guile? Note the fictional adventures of the wicked Party of Social Progress, the PPS. An agent of a foreign power reports: 'We have placed at its head MJ, an intelligent and active man, devoured by ambition and much in need of cash. The bourgeois parties offered him slender hopes.'

A sample of the PPS's sinister wares is a wall poster:

'Why spend these millions on the military?
We could build homes
Pay for holidays
Raise pensions
Reduce the hours of work
Reduce our taxes.
YES to a better future!'

Here is the organization table of a revolutionary movement, its HQ abroad, its front in the homeland, its secret cells, its sleeping members, unsuspected by even their best friends among the gullible Swiss. Agents of the enemy unleash a terrible scandal about the finances of the Federal Council (happy the land where such scandals are only the work of enemies). The weaker citizens dispute among themselves, the stronger stand firm in their confidence! We must be constantly on our guard against calumnies on our chiefs and authorities. Absolutely.

Altogether this handbook is a work of passion and breadth which sits uneasily beside the bland nothings of our own civil service. From one point of view one can detect self-interest; from another plain barminess. But perhaps there speaks British insular complacency. After all, the Hungarian revolution and its disquieting sequels happened as far from the Swiss border as North Wales is from London. France and Italy nip Switzerland pretty close: both might have communist governments in five years or less. Not to mention the PLO raging round central Europe, seeking whom it may devour. But the possibility that he might be right never made a Calvinist tone down his rebukes. The National Director of civil defence, Hans Maurenthaler, asked about the curious absence of civil defence among the nuclear powers, comments:

> . . . we live in a world of tension, of brutality and of blackmail, that is everything but peaceful and reassuring. The best proofs of this are:
> Disarmament conferences; non-aggression pacts; non-proliferation treaties . . .
> To misunderstand this menace, to want to minimize it or even steadily to deny it while knowing that it exists amounts to evidence of laxity, foolishness or even depravity.

If the superpowers had not obligingly invented the H-bomb, the Swiss government would have had to invent something equally threatening.

So, simply because the H-bomb has not yet been used in anger, does not mean that it has not had a profound effect on the modern world. Without it we might have learnt to live more in amity. Or, of course, we might have torn each other apart with the weapons that were quite effective enough in the Second World War.

When might it be used? In spite of the Soviet military's obvious determination to fight and survive a nuclear war, it is difficult to believe that such a course would be in the broader interests of the civilian leaders of Russia.

I am coming to believe that there is a much more serious threat to the technological way of life than the H-bomb. It is the transistor. Over the last two or three hundred years in the West we have followed a course of development that coupled increasingly powerful machines to small pieces of human brain to produce increasingly vast quantities of goods. The airliner, the ship, the typewriter, the lathe, the sewing machine, all employ a small part of the operator's intelligence, and with it multiply his or her productivity a thousandfold.

As long as each machine needed a brain, it was profitable

to make more brains and with them more profits. Industrial populations grew in all the advanced countries, and political systems became more liberal simply to get their cooperation. (You cannot safely put a bulldozer in the hands of an aggrieved slave.)

But now we are beginning to find that we do not need the brains – at least not in the huge droves that we have them. Little by little, like a calm tide creeping over flat sand, with a finger of water here, a rush of foam there, artificial intelligence is dispossessing hundreds of thousands and soon millions of workers. Because 'the computer' is seen only in large installations doing book-keeping, where it puts few out of work, this tendency goes on unnoticed. But in every job economics forces economies on management. Little gadgets here and there get rid of workers piecemeal. And so far the real thrust of artificial intelligence has not yet begun. In journalism, for instance, it is now quite unnecessary to have printers. Journalists can type straight onto a small computer that edits their work, checks spellings and punctuation, arranges it in columns, sets it in type and makes up the newspaper page. Any job that can be specified, say, a thousand rules, can now be automated by equipment that costs £200 or so. The microprocessor, which now costs in itself perhaps £20, is the heart of a computer. It has not begun to be applied: over the next 10 to 15 years millions will be installed in industry, distribution, commerce. Machinery, which has almost denuded the land, will now denude cities.

Politically, this will split the population into two sharply divided groups: those who have intelligence or complicated manual skills that cannot be imitated by computers, and those – a much larger group, who have not. In strict economic terms, the second group will not be worth employing. They can do nothing that cannot be done cheaper by machinery. They cannot contribute their own intelligence, because the machines will have enough of their own. The working population will be reduced to a relatively small core of technicians, artists, scientists, managers, surrounded by a large, unemployed, dissatisfied and expensive mob. I would even argue that this process is much further advanced than it seems, and the political subterfuges necessary to keep it concealed, are responsible for the economic malaise of the western nations and their galloping inflation. This is not surprising: if one has to pay several million people who are in fact useless, as if they were not, this is bound to throw a strain on the economy and arouse the resentment of those who are useful, but who cannot be paid what they deserve for fear of arousing the envy of the others.

If the unemployed can be kept down to a million or so in a country like Britain, the political problem they present can be contained by paying a generous dole, and by lavish social services – even though they are beginning to crumble under the strain. The real total of unemployed is much larger, but they are hidden in business. What happens when automation advances further and the sham can no longer be kept up? A recent report from the Manpower Commission said that Britain's 90 largest firms planned to get rid of a third of their workers when current technological improvements were brought into use. To cope with millions of unemployed and unemployable people needs – in terms of crude power – greatly improved police and security services. It demands that factories and computers should be put out of cities, preferably where they are inaccessible to the mob or the saboteur. It suggests that the unemployed should be concentrated in small spaces where they can be controlled, de-educated, penned up.

And, seen from the right point of view, this is just what is happening. All over the West, police and security forces have been growing apace. Civil defence, active in Russia, being revived in America and many other countries, puts useful national industrial assets out in the country, underground. The useless masses gravitate to decaying cities like New York: one can foresee a time when the rest of America will put barbed wire across the bridges and throw enough supplies over them to keep the mob quiet.

Unless some drastic alteration occurs in economic and political thought, the developed nations are going to be faced in the next thirty years with the fact that the majority of their citizens are a dangerous, useless burden. One can see that when civil defence has moved everything useful out of the cities, there might be strong temptation on governments to solve the problem by nuclear war: the technological élite against the masses. Doubtless, to salve consciences, it would be dressed up as a war between superpowers. But it would not be surprising if the only survivors were just those who found the dead masses the most oppressive. In short, America and Russia, Britain and France, India and China, Egypt and Israel might agree to take in each other's dirty washing.

So one might guess that when Russian industry is as auto-mated as America's, then we may look for action. Happily it lags some way behind; and because it spends so much effort preparing for war – which is very labour-intensive – it is likely to lag further behind. Crudely speaking, the longer the Russians prepare for war, the longer we can expect peace.

Appendix A

This article appeared originally in the *New Scientist*, 13 July 1978.

Can a secret be SECRET if it isn't actually secret?

The story begins, in part, a long time ago when Philip Agee 'defected' from the Central Intelligence Agency (CIA) and published his *CIA Diary*, exposing some of the inner workings of 'the company'. Later another American journalist, Mark Hosenball, with others, exposed CIA employees hidden in US Embassy staffs around the world. The CIA said that one such man working out of the US Embassy in Athens lost his life as a result, but it seems that he had been exposed some years before by the East Germans.

Hosenball also revealed some details of the US National Security Agency's (NSA) worldwide electronic eavesdropping network. It is now well known that electronic intelligence gathering produces more than three-quarters of all military and diplomatic intelligence for the developed nations, but there is still great reluctance to publish the details. It is important to understand why this is so because it has a bearing on what is to come. Of course, as the details are still secret, one can only hazard guesses, but it seems that the beginning of the story goes back to the late 1930s and the now famous Enigma coding machine, used by the German High Command during the Second World War for their most secret radio messages. Enigma was imitated by the British at Bletchley Park, and its Japanese equivalent by the Americans. With the aid of this high-level intelligence, so the tale now runs, the war was won.

As the lay public now understands matters, penetration of the Enigma codes was the most closely guarded secret of the war. After the war, the Americans would have been happy to publish what had been done, but the British (according to Anthony Cave Brown, *Bodyguard of Lies*, W. H. Allen) refused. The reason was simple: around the world, armies and foreign offices, ignorant of the vulnerability of ciphers produced by machines of the Enigma type, used them for their most secret signals – which could be read with relative ease by the UK and US. (There may, of course, be some more obscure reason. But this is convincing enough.)

Presumably, by the middle 1970s the imposture became threadbare, for several actors in the Enigma drama have now told their stories. But there is still sensitivity about electronic and signal intelligence gathering. This too is understandable, for electronic intelligence (ELINT) and signals intelligence (SIGINT) produce the best possible evidence of the enemy's capabilities, intentions, hopes and fears. Information does not have to filter through possibly untrustworthy spies, taking weeks on the way; it comes direct at the speed of light from the enemy's own hand. The German Army used to say: 'All radio traffic is high treason' – not that this helped in the long run. But electronic intelligence gathering is a retiring trade. It is helped if the enemy forgets that you are listening and becomes careless. It needs fields for aerial farms, quiet to concentrate, frequent cups of tea, no radio jamming, no commando attacks on the perimeter fence. Naturally, governments do not want attention drawn to it. Proper military protection of all Britain's SIGINT sites would need several battalions of infantry.

Two journalists trod on the tail of this dozing dragon in 1976 when Duncan Campbell – a frequent contributor to *New Scientist*, but then working for *Time Out*, a left-wing London-based weekly – wrote, aided by Hosenball, an article exposing some of the workings of Britain's signal intelligence organization, the equivalent of NSA in purpose if not size. It seems that as a result of this article, Hosenball was deported in 1977, even though, at his appeal, he and Campbell tried to show that the information they used was available in newspaper clippings and telephone books.

Stimulated by the Hosenball–Campbell article, an ex-corporal of the British Army's Royal Signals, John Berry, made a statement to the Agee Hosenball Defence Committee. This found its way to *Time Out*, which sent one of its reporters, Crispin Aubrey, with Duncan Campbell, to interview him. The three were arrested immediately after the interview by Special Branch officers and charged under Section 2 of the Official Secrets Act, which prohibits the passing on of any information by employees of the Crown, or its knowing reception by third parties. This, though unfortunate, was perhaps to be expected. But having arrested Campbell, the police used their right of search under the Official Secrets Act. In his flat they found the fruit of many years' research into the infra-structure of defence and government. As I understand the matter, it had been culled from sources open to the public. As a result, Campbell was also charged under Section 1 of the Act which prohibits the 'collection' of material 'contrary to the safety and interests of the state' which 'might be directly or indirectly useful to an enemy.'

At the committal proceedings in 1977, the Crown argued that, although in detail the information which Campbell had collected was openly published and item by item not classified, when put together and used as the basis for deductions about systems of defence, the result was a 'dangerous interest' contrary to the Act. This was where I became an unwilling actor, or at least a scene shifter, in the piece. Back in 1963, to spice up the marches on Aldermaston, which were losing zest, some members of CND, who were to call themselves 'Spies for Peace', discovered the famous Regional Seat of Government, RSG6, at Warren Row, near Reading. They revealed to an astonished world that the government had, in complete secrecy since the Second World War, constructed an elaborate chain of fall-out-proof citadels throughout the country from which Britain would be ruled in the unhappy event of nuclear attack. The government made great efforts to find the culprits, but no prosecutions were brought.

In 1967 Peter Watkins made a film for the BBC called *The War Game* which showed, rather too realistically for many stomachs, just what nuclear war would feel like for the unwilling civilian participant. A famous scene portrayed a police firing squad executing looters in a British city. The *Sunday Times Magazine* asked me to find out how far Watkins's nightmare scenario corresponded with government planning. After a little prodding, the Home Office revealed a good deal more of its secret civil defence system. Even after the article had been published, I remained interested in the subject, and tried to answer questions the Home Office had raised in my mind, but had not answered. After a good deal of research, using openly published material and what had already been given me by the Home Office, I wrote the first edition of *Beneath the City Streets* (Allen Lane, 1969; Penguin, 1970). Before publication, the manuscript was sent to James Callaghan, then Home Secretary, and returned without comment. Although it was pointed out to both me and the publisher that this was in no way an endorsement of the book, we felt that if it contained any dangerous material the government had had ample time to object, and that we could go ahead without endangering national security.

I have often been asked why, after so much fuss had been made about 'Spies for Peace' in 1963, there was no objection to my book four years later, which in some respects went a good deal further. I think the answer is that in 1963 the government was in the middle of the huge and urgent task of moving its war infrastructure from under and around the major cities, where it had been buried against the Russian atom bomb of 1953, out to the country where it might be safe against the Russian H-bomb of 1961. Angry public debate about the ethics of sheltering the top brass while the rest of us fried in the fall-out might delay this essential work. But by 1967 it was mostly done. The Home Office even took a series of whole-page advertisements in national papers to boast of its achievements. Although civil defence is an emotive subject, the reality is banal enough, and it seems to me that some intelligent people at the Home Office calculated that my book was accurate and unsensational enough to allay paranoia among the public at large without being penetrating enough to help the Russians. One must always remember that while security is seen from the outside to veil exciting secrets, from inside government it is often an expensive and demoralizing nuisance (see Margaret Gowing, *Independence and Deterrence*, vol. 2, Macmillan). If my book made it possible to relax some security in this area, then it was perhaps all to the good.

So matters stood. The book stimulated a certain amount of interest in a small circle. With the help of Campbell and many others, I desultorily accumulated more material. In the mid-1970s Penguin went through a severe financial crisis and dropped about a third of the books it published. *Beneath the City Streets* was one title which it let go out of print as not being worth the capital locked up in it. This was a disappointing decision but not an unreasonable one. By 1976 the book had become almost unobtainable, and I received many letters and phone calls asking where it might be had. This is annoying for a self-employed writer who sees himself losing revenue, so I decided to produce a second edition. A publisher – Hutchinson's – was found, and matters went ahead.

But, by the time we were ready to go to press, Aubrey, Berry and Campbell (ABC) had been arrested. Hutchinson's became understandably nervous about their position, so we sent the manuscript of the revised book to the Secretary of the D Notice Committee. The D Notice system is a method of voluntary security which should, ideally, protect the outskirts of the Official

Secrets Act. The Defence Press and Broadcasting Committee is a group of civil servants and editors. It issues 'D Notices' on general or particular topics which are dangerous to security, and the theory is that the press will voluntarily follow its guidance. The day-to-day work of the committee is carried out by its Secretary, a senior retired military officer with experience in intelligence. He is readily accessible and will usually advise one over the telephone whether publication of a piece is likely to be damaging to national security. He is in informal contact with senior serving military officers and civil servants, and is therefore well placed to effect liaison between Whitehall and the press. However, the system has been working less well than it might.

The Secretary, Rear Admiral K. H. Farnhill, replied that though he could not say that a new edition of a book eight years old would contravene any D Notices, he had to point out that some parts might be useful to terrorists, and he would ask that we consider whether publication was advisable in the national interest. Hutchinson's too had a sharp financial crisis and handed the manuscript back. It would be easy to be bitter, but one must remember that publishers exist to make a profit and that a book like this, although of great interest to the author and aficionados of the subject, is a marginal affair in publishing terms, not worth the odium of an Official Secrets Act prosecution.

I then decided to publish the book myself to make sure that it came out. An advertisement for subscriptions in *New Scientist* produced a most encouraging response. At the same time, not wishing to help terrorists, I resubmitted those pages of the manuscript that contain new information to the D Notice Committee in an effort to discover which parts I should remove. After a lengthy gestation, Admiral Farnhill's opinion was this time rather different. Campbell and Aubrey had been committed on a Section 1 charge. Newspaper reports of the Crown's case seem to have been the first signals he had had that there might be a new standard of security to be observed. He advised me that in his view the new edition raised questions of the application of Official Secrets Act 'on which I am neither authorized nor competent to express an official opinion'. It was not just details of information which were in doubt, but the context, associations and deductions from them. Admiral Farnhill advised me to look to the outcome of the ABC trial, but, as I replied, because part of the evidence against these people is secret, their acquittal or conviction would provide no guidance as to how one should behave in a different case. He went on to say that the book now did contravene certain D Notices (which four months before it had not) and referred me to 28 pages of manuscript (some 8000 words) which contained offensive matter. It seemed to me, and also to a third publisher, Granada, who was now interested in issuing the book, that this was unnecessarily vague. But Farnhill said he could go no further in telling me what to take out. To make matters worse, several people reminded me that compliance with D Notices was no guarantee against prosecution under Section 1 of the Official Secrets Act.

It would again be easy to criticize Admiral Farnhill and the D Notice system as being obstructive, but I believe that would be unjust. I have found him personally sympathetic to my problems and those of the press generally, and as anxious as anyone to discover clear guidelines. The difficulty, it seems to me, lies deeper within the establishment. I wrote letters to the Home Secretary, the Minister of Defence, the Attorney General, and the Commissioner of Police, pointing out that as Section 1 of the Official Secrets Act is phrased, and has been interpreted in the courts, almost anything can be an offence, and that the only way one can be sure of not offending is to be told so by the Crown. I was anxious not to compromise the security of the state, so would they please help?

The Commissioner replied that 'It is not part of the duties of the Commissioner of Police to judge in advance whether the publication of any material would be a criminal offence.' The Home Secretary did not reply, and the Minister of Defence, through a minion, asked to see the manuscript – which now made its third journey in six months to the MoD Main Building.

After a two-month delay, the Second Permanent Under Secretary replied that he could not suggest specific amendments. 'The fact is that the new material which you have researched is in a category, Defence Communications, where for security reasons neither the Defence Secretary nor any other Ministers can confirm or deny its accuracy or give any measure of clearance for its publication. But there is no doubt that information of this sort would be of great assistance to any enemy.' A month later the Attorney General wrote endorsing this opinion and the D Notice Committee's second letter.

In short, they would not tell me what to take out because that would be telling me secrets. When I replied that I already knew the secrets or I would not have put them in, and asked whether they would prefer the lesser evil of telling me what I knew already, or the greater one of me telling the world, they replied that they at least did not propose to give any secrets away and that was that. My argument that everything I had learned was in easily accessible public sources and that surely the government would not have so carelessly exposed itself, was met with shrugged shoulders. The argument that if I were to be found guilty of *collecting* information contrary to Section 1 of the Official Secrets Act, then the Minister of Defence or the Home Secretary or the Postmaster General must previously have been guilty of *publishing* it (which seems worse) and thus be contrary to Section 1, was met with equal indifference. When I asked if, after I had done my best to prune my manuscript in accordance with these somewhat unsatisfactory guidelines, they would reconsider it, the answer was yes. When I pointed out that given enough time or luck this process would reveal exactly what ought to be cut out, they said yes it would, and when I said let's not waste time; tell me now, they said no.

In several private conversations with MoD and Special Branch people I have been asked: 'Why do you want to do our enemy's work for them?' When I say, surely nothing I can do could match the resources of a professional military intelligence organization, they say you would be surprised. Well, I would be. I am.

So I, and many other people, particularly in the technical press, are left in a difficult position. We find that while apparently trivial facts about defence systems litter the landscape, we may put ourselves in jeopardy of 14 years' imprisonment if we put two and two together. To take the argument of the Crown in the ABC committal hearings to its logical conclusion, if the Prime Minister assures the nation today that no one will get more than a 10 per cent pay rise, and tomorrow gives the Bottle-washers 30 per cent, you may bring yourself within Section 1 by printing the two facts side by side. We are forced to be our own censors when we do not know what is secret (because it is secret) and we cannot easily guess what not to print because it all seems so obvious.

By threatening prosecution for unauthorized disclosure of what journalists know already, while refusing to say what may or may not be said, the government in effect makes it dangerous to write anything that is not a handout from a Ministry. Of course, matters have not come to that pass in many areas of journalism. But the history of the vaguely worded Official Secrets Act – deliberately drafted that way, according to Cave Brown, to give the greatest possible protection to what is now MI6 – has always been an alarming one. Assurances are often given by the government that it will be responsibly and restrictively interpreted. And then everyone is surprised by major extensions of its application.

This is the perplexing position as it appears from outside Whitehall. In order to resolve it, so that I can get my book published and think about something else, I have been trying to understand how it looks from inside. Within the Establishment there is one major fact which we, outside, overlook: Britain is at war. The Third World War is under way, and is being fought by the Third World against the developed countries. Some of the battlegrounds are airliners, airports, shopping centres and high streets; its targets are politicians, police, military leaders – and citizens at large. Unfortunately, war has not been declared, and there are no hard and fast frontiers. There are many sympathizers with the enemy in our own country, both conscious and unconscious. They are, to put it bluntly, traitors. If they cannot be brought within the Treachery Act, then the Official Secrets Act will have to do. Once you are at war, peacetime standards have to go. If it were not for the unfortunate fact that the present Prime Minister failed to stop my book nine years ago, there would be no question of my republishing a word of it. There is no need to give any aid or comfort to the enemy, and, as I have several times been admonished, 'Your own common sense should tell you what not to print.'

The trouble is that we civilians have been brought up on Russia as an enemy. We have constantly been told of the cunning and duplicity of the KGB. Back in 1969, it is true, I – and anyone else who made deductions from published facts – could tell them nothing. They knew it all already. Now the enemy is less sophisticated and more fluid. You do not know what he knows. You could rely on the KGB not to blow up Colonel B because we could deal the same way with their Colonel V. But you cannot make the same assumption about the Scarlet Fraction. They do not have a Colonel B, they have never – until now – heard of ours, and they have no means of finding out who he is unless we tell them. If they do, they may well go and waste the poor man. Hence then the inevitable conclusion – on the inside looking out – that anyone who mentions his name is a traitor, and on the outside looking in that the government has taken leave of its senses.

So the answer to the question at the head of this piece: 'Can a Secret be SECRET if it isn't actually secret?' is 'Yes please!'

The papers of captured terrorists show that their intelligence – in the military sense – is often ludicrously primitive. Of course, because their aim is usually political in their kidnappings, assassinations and blowings up, it matters more that the target should have some symbolic importance. And it is not hard to achieve that. But still, given better intelligence, there is no doubt that terrorists could do a lot of real damage to a country which is organized against nuclear war rather than banditry.

A new enemy imposes a new kind of censorship which varies according to the audience and the journalist's ability to deduce. As one policeman succinctly put it, 'A stupid right-wing writer can be allowed to go further than a clever left-wing one.' That something has already been published is no guide in applying it, because terrorists do not usually have competent research organizations, or access to specialized libraries. So censorship must vary with the audience of the medium in question. The *Annals of Embryology* may make more daring leaps than *Freaks Weekly* because its audience is less likely to express its political tensions with gelignite.

But however sensible this recipe may be in military terms, it raises acute difficulties in practice. Basically, information sells books and papers. You cannot have a free market place for information, and hope to impose tariffs on its sales according to the political colour of its sellers and purchasers. There are, of course, already wide differences in the giving of information. No doubt the lobby correspondent of *The Times* is told many things the *Morning Star* never hears. But that is quite different from trying to stop people finding out by themselves.

A similar sort of confusion arose at the beginning of the Second World War. From the military standpoint there is no sense in publishing *anything* that might be helpful to an enemy. From the political standpoint, it is often necessary that you should. So there were fierce dramas in 1940 when, for instance, the censor cut reports out of the daily papers that the Luftwaffe had bombed London the night before. The press thought this absurd. The R A F thought there might be some doubt in the Germans' minds where they had been and what effect they had obtained, and that it was treasonable to remove it. Today, for instance, it is certainly helpful to terrorists to know where London is. There are plenty of sane people at MoD who would, if they could, remove the capital from the maps, arguing that it is better a few civilians get lost than one bomber gets to his target. From the political standpoint you have to tell some of the people some of the truth some of the time, and a compromise was worked out in 1940: a revival of the old D Notice system of voluntary censorship which took the press a little way into the government's confidence and relied on good sense to keep information from a clearly recognizable enemy whom nobody wanted to help anyway.

After the war the enemy became less credible and the D Notice system gradually fell into desuetude. The left-wing press found the whole thing rather absurd and took to publishing the D Notices, guides to secrets which need protecting, themselves. The establishment gave up faith in the system and has now, as we see, fallen back on the bludgeon of the Official Secrets Act. This leaves both sides in difficulties. The press's problem should be clear enough by now; on the other side, because censorship is now an *ex post facto* matter for the courts, no one in government can say in advance what ought or ought not to be printed.

What compounds this problem is that although one expects government to speak with a single voice, this is not what happens in practice. (A cynic would say that to this we owe such freedoms as we have.) To create an offence against Section 1 of the Act there have to be two ingredients: information useful to an enemy, which is collected or published 'contrary to the interests and safety of the state'. To go back to the example of London, it is certainly 'useful to an enemy' to know where it is, or even that it exists, but it is (presumably) in the interests of the state that this information should be published, if only to *bona fide* tourists. Now, it seems that it is for the Minister of Defence to say that the information is likely to be useful to an enemy, but it is for the Attorney General to say that its publication is contrary to the interests of the State. So, in my case, having said that parts of my manuscript might help an enemy, the Minister of Defence would not go further and decide whether publication would be a good or bad thing. Which is what one wants to know.

That difficult question is for the Attorney General. No one can dispute his decision in court; conversely, no one can anticipate it beforehand. He will have to balance the old, old arguments in favour of freedom of speech against the realities of national security. In the short term, most governments would like to stop journalists publishing anything that has not been authorized. In the long run, it does not answer, and in its heart the British Civil Service knows this better than any other in the world.

On a more practical plane, I have suggested to the Attorney that if he does not tell me what to take out now, and in consequence I make a mistake and publish something dangerous and he decides to prosecute me, he will have to put in evidence exactly the information which he now refuses to part with. But in the meantime the book may have been printed and widely distributed. It seems slightly perverse. Furthermore, if I then profit by his belated cooperation to remove the offending material and republish the book, it would be possible for anyone who could be bothered, to compare editions 2 and 3 to see what had so agitated the government. If the Attorney tried to prevent me publishing edition 3, it would have to be on the grounds that it did *not* contain secrets.

Finally, if it comes to the worst, it would be hard to convince an impartial observer that there is anything very dangerous in the book. If there were, something effective would have been done about it long ago. The plain fact is that you cannot have effective censorship without some degree of trust – in telling people what not to print you give away some secrets.

What we lack in Britain is some central, intelligent organ that will balance the military disadvantages of publication against political and social gains. Without it we cannot have effective security or indeed anything but confusion. At present this delicate process has to be performed in the conflict between caution and daring in the minds of writers and publishers, and that in almost complete ignorance of the real issues. There must be a better way.

Appendix B

The Section 1 charges against Campbell were dropped by the Crown in September. The day after this cheering news, I sent the following letter to the Minister of Defence:

Dear Mr Mulley,

In view of the abandonment by the Crown of the 'collection' charge against Duncan Campbell under S1 of the Official Secrets Act, I am planning to go ahead with the publication of my book *Beneath the City Streets*.

I am sincere in not wishing to include material which might damage national security, but at the same time I am reluctant to remove material which may legitimately be published and which would interest my subscribers (several of whom, ironically, are MoD Establishments). Since you are reluctant to specify what you want removed, I shall have to guess as best I can. I propose to remove:

(i) a map of those parts of the microwave system which seem to serve the air defence organization. In the text I propose to say that the microwave system plays a part in transmitting radar data to operational headquarters, without being specific about sites;

(ii) and to reduce the article about SIGINT which I sent to Admiral Farnhill to a couple of pages which deal with the matter in general terms, again without mentioning specific sites.

These proposals are not made in the hope that you will give me some guarantee against prosecution – that possibility seems to have been well explored – but to eliminate the possible harm that my book might do.

Yours sincerely

Peter Laurie

Answer came there none.

297

Index

Index

301

MODERN SOCIETY – NOW AVAILABLE IN GRANADA PAPERBACKS

Peter Becker
Tribe to Township   60p ☐

Nicholas Deakin
Colour, Citizenship & British Society   £1.00 ☐

J W B Douglas
The Home and the School   95p ☐

Dr Christopher Evans
Cults of Unreason   75p ☐

John Howard Griffin
Black Like Me   95p ☐

Margaret Mead
Culture and Commitment   75p ☐

Marion Meade
Bitching   60p ☐

Tony Parker
The Twisting Lane   75p ☐

Desmond Morris
Man Watching   £4.95 ☐
The Naked Ape   95p ☐
Intimate Behaviour   95p ☐
The Human Zoo   95p ☐

HISTORY – NOW AVAILABLE IN GRANADA PAPERBACKS

Ronald Auguet
The Roman Games   £1.00 ☐

Peter Becker
Path of Blood   50p ☐
Rule of Fear   40p ☐

N Branson & M Heinemann
Britain in the 1930s   £1.25 ☐

Angus Calder
The People's War   £1.50 ☐

Frederick Engels
The Condition of the Working Class in England   £1.25 ☐

Christopher Farman
The General Strike   £1.00 ☐

Michael Grant
Cleopatra   £1.25 ☐
Julius Caesar   £1.25 ☐

Brian Inglis
Poverty and the Industrial Revolution   £1.25 ☐

Joyce Marlow
The Tolpuddle Martyrs   £1.25 ☐

Conor Cruise O'Brien
States of Ireland   £1.75 ☐

Thomas Packenham
The Year of Liberty   £1.75 ☐

Christopher Sinclair-Stevenson
Inglorious Rebellion   £1.25 ☐

Robert Crisp
The Outlanders   £1.00 ☐

TRUE CRIME – NOW AVAILABLE IN PANTHER BOOKS

Ludovic Kennedy

A Presumption of Innocence	£1.25	☐
10 Rillington Place	95p	☐

Stephen Knight

Jack the Ripper: The Final Solution	£1.25	☐

Peter Maas

The Valachi Papers	95p	☐

John Pearson

The Profession of Violence	95p	☐

Ed Sanders

The Family	95p	☐

Vincent Teresa

My Life in the Mafia	95p	☐

Colin Wilson

Order of Assassins	95p	☐
The Killer	60p	☐

Leslie Waller

Hide in Plain Sight	£1.25	☐

THE WORLD'S GREATEST NOVELISTS
NOW AVAILABLE IN PANTHER BOOKS

Alberto Moravia

Bitter Honeymoon	75p	☐
Mother Love	60p	☐
The Wayward Wife	60p	☐
Conjugal Love	50p	☐
The Fetish	75p	☐
Roman Tales	50p	☐
Time of Indifference	60p	☐
The Two of Us	50p	☐
The Lie	75p	☐
The Empty Canvas	£1.50	☐

Gore Vidal

Washington D.C.	95p	☐
Burr	£1.95	☐
1876	£1.00	☐
A Thirsty Evil	75p	☐
The Judgment of Paris	95p	☐
The City and the Pillar	80p	☐
Julian	95p	☐
Two Sisters	75p	☐
Myron	60p	☐
Myra Breckinridge	75p	☐
Messiah	75p	☐
Williwaw	60p	☐
On Our Own Now (Collected Essays 1952–1972)	£1.50	☐
Kalki	£1.25	☐

THE BEST IN BIOGRAPHY FROM PANTHER BOOKS

Dirk Bogarde
A Postillion Struck by Lightning   £1.25 ☐

Elizabeth Longford
Winston Churchill   £1.25 ☐
Wellington: Pillar of State   £1.25 ☐
Wellington: The Years of the Sword   £1.25 ☐

Jasper Ridley
Lord Palmerston   £1.50 ☐

Han Suyin
The Morning Deluge (*Volume I*)   £1.75 ☐
The Morning Deluge (*Volume II*)   £1.25 ☐
Wind in the Tower   £1.75 ☐
The Crippled Tree   95p ☐
A Mortal Flower   £1.50 ☐
Birdless Summer   £1.25 ☐

Roger Manvel & Heinrich Frankel
Hitler: The Man and the Myth   £1.25 ☐

Kim Philby
My Silent War   95p ☐

Dusko Popov
Spy/Counter Spy   75p ☐

Garson Kanin
Hollywood   95p ☐

THE WORLD'S GREATEST NOVELISTS
NOW AVAILABLE IN PANTHER BOOKS

Peter Ustinov

The Frontiers of the Sea	95p ☐
The Loser	95p ☐
Add a Dash of Pity	95p ☐
Krumnagel	95p ☐

Han Suyin

. . . And the Rain My Drink	£1.25 ☐
Destination Chungking	£1.25 ☐
A Many-Splendoured Thing	£1.25 ☐
Cast But One Shadow	60p ☐
The Four Faces	£1.25 ☐
The Mountain is Young	95p ☐

Autobiography

The Crippled Tree	95p ☐
A Mortal Flower	£1.50 ☐
Birdless Summer	£1.25 ☐

Biography

The Morning Deluge (*Volume I*)	£1.25 ☐
The Morning Deluge (*Volume II*)	£1.25 ☐
Wind in the Tower	£1.75 ☐

All these books are available at your local bookshop or newsagent, or can be ordered direct from the publisher. Just tick the titles you want and fill in the form below.

Name ....

Address ....

....

Write to Panther Cash Sales, PO Box 11, Falmouth, Cornwall TR10 9EN.

Please enclose remittance to the value of the cover price plus:

UK: 25p for the first book plus 10p per copy for each additional book ordered to a maximum charge of £1.05.

BFPO and EIRE: 25p for the first book plus 10p per copy for the next 8 books, thereafter 5p per book.

OVERSEAS: 40p for the first book and 12p for each additional book.
Granada Publishing reserve the right to show new retail prices on covers, which may differ from those previously advertised in the text or elsewhere.